PERSONALITY DISORDERS

Personality disorders

Paul M. G. Emmelkamp and
Jan Henk Kamphuis
Faculty of Social and Behavioral Sciences,
University of Amsterdam

Psychology Press
Taylor & Francis Group

HOVE AND NEW YORK

BP53

First published 2007
by Psychology Press
27 Church Road, Hove, East Sussex BN3 2FA

Simultaneously published in the USA and Canada
by Psychology Press
270 Madison Avenue, New York, NY 10016

Psychology Press is an imprint of the Taylor and Francis Group, an informa business

Copyright © 2007 Psychology Press

Typeset in Palatino by Garfield Morgan, Mumbles, Swansea
Printed and bound in Great Britain by TJ International, Padstow, Cornwall
Cover design by Jim Wilkie
Cover image: "Portrait of the Dancer Aleksandr Sakharov" by Alexej Jawlensky
© DACS, London 2007, Städtische Galerie im Lenbachhaus, Munich

British Library Cataloguing in Publication Data
A catalogue record for this book is available from the British Library

Library of Congress Cataloging in Publication Data
Emmelkamp, Paul M. G., 1949–
    Personality disorders / Paul M.G. Emmelkamp and Jan Henk Kamphuis.
        p. ; cm. – (Clinical psychology, a modular course)
    Includes bibliographical references and index.
    ISBN-13: 978-0-415-38518-3 (hardback)
    ISBN-10: 0-415-38518-0 (hardback)
    ISBN-13: 978-0-415-38519-0 (pbk.)
    ISBN-10: 0-415-38519-9 (pbk.)
    1. Personality disorders. I. Kamphuis, Jan Henk. II. Title. III. Series.
    [DNLM: 1. Personality Disorders–diagnosis. 2. Personality Disorders–therapy.
WM 190 E54p 2007]
    RC554.E55 2007
    616.85'81–dc22
                                                                      2007002655

ISBN: 978-0-415-38518-3 (hbk)
ISBN: 978-0-415-38519-0 (pbk)

8/2/10

To: Ellen, Esther, Julie, and Lotte

To: Minke and Thomas

Contents

Series preface

Clinical Psychology: A Modular Course was designed to overcome the problems faced by the traditional textbook in conveying what psychological disorders are really like. All the books in the series, written by leading scholars and practitioners in the field, can be read as standalone text, but they will also integrate with the other modules to form a comprehensive resource in clinical psychology. Students of psychology, medicine, nursing, and social work, as well as busy practitioners in many professions, often need an accessible but thorough introduction to how people experience anxiety, depression, addiction, or other disorders, how common they are, and who is most likely to suffer from them, as well as up-to-date research evidence on the causes and available treatments. The series will appeal to those who want to go deeper into the subject than the traditional textbook will allow, and base their examination answers, research projects, assignments, or practical decisions on a clearer and more rounded appreciation of the clinical and research evidence.

Chris R. Brewin

Other titles in this series:

Depression
Constance Hammen

Stress and Trauma
Patricia A. Resick

Childhood Disorders
Philip C. Kendall

Schizophrenia
Max Birchwood and Chris Jackson

Addictions
Maree Teesson, Louise Degenhardt and Wayne Hall

Anxiety
S. Rachman

Eating and Weight Disorders
Carlos M. Grilo

Acknowledgements

We wish to thank several people and institutions for helping to bring this book together. First we wish to thank the patients with whom we have worked over the years. Further we would like to acknowledge discussions with a number of colleagues, especially Ank Benner, Clive Robins, Auke Tellegen, Irma Timmerman, Carol van Velzen, and Roel Verheul, who helped to shape our ideas about personality and personality disorders. We alone remain, of course, fully responsible for the ideas expressed in this volume. Finally, we express our profound gratitude to the staff of the Netherlands Institute for the Advanced Study in the humanities and social sciences (NIAS) in Wassenaar, who helped to gather much of the material discussed in this book, when Paul Emmelkamp was a fellow at the NIAS.

Description of personality disorders 1

Personality disorder patients demonstrate to mental health professional the limits of their expertise, yet no group of emotional disorders is more often encountered in psychiatric practice. Those with personality disorders crowd the rosters of clinic dropouts, treatment failures and referrals to other agencies ...

(Vaillant & Perry, 1980, p. 1562)

Clinical picture

What are personality disorders? Personality refers to individual differences in usual tendencies to think, feel, and behave in certain ways. For example, people reliably differ in their preferences and tendencies to seek social stimulation and excitement, in emotional vulnerability and expressiveness, in orderliness, etc. – all part of normal personality variation. Abnormal personality or personality pathology refers to maladaptive traits that are overly rigid and/or extreme. Constellations of such pathologically amplified personality traits may constitute formal personality disorders (Strack & Lorr, 1997). A formal personality disorder then, can be defined as a chronic psychiatric disorder with onset in adolescence continuing into adulthood, characterized by pathological personality traits that lead to a disruption in the development and maintenance of mutual interpersonal relationships, to an extent that this in turn leads to prolonged subjective distress of self and/or others.

Presumably, a core distinguishing feature of personality disorders versus clinical syndromes is the degree to which the level of functioning represents a change from baseline. In clinical syndromes such as depression or panic disorder, people find their lives disrupted; they can no longer function as they used to because of fear of panic (e.g., panic disorder), or unusual lack of interest and energy (e.g., depression). In clinical syndromes, the experiences and behaviours are perceived as ego-dystonic, i.e., not typical for the person. The disorder is something they "have", much like the flu or a broken leg. It is thought of as a mental disease, with symptoms. Personality disorders, on the other hand, concern how people have matured into adult personalities, and the building blocks are often referred to as traits. Associated problems do not typically fall into circumscribed, specific categories. Rather, these problems involve personal identity and dissatisfaction and dysfunction in interpersonal relationships. It is about difficulties related to how people typically experience and respond to themselves, others, and the world around them: i.e., ego-syntonic pathology. The hallmark of personality disorders is disturbed relationships, both in personal and professional life. In short, (one or more) personality disorder may be involved when your personality gets you persistently and pervasively into trouble, especially in the spheres of (intimate) relationships and work.

Although thinking about personality and its pathology is quite old (e.g., see Millon & Davis, 1995), it was not always a welcome topic in psychiatry. Personality disorder patients were alternatively referred to as patients with "relationship difficulties", or "patients who are difficult to place", or sometimes even the "difficult patient". They were not known as the psychiatrist's favourite patients (see Tyrer, 2001). Moreover, personality disorder diagnoses have been frequently abused. The patient who did not improve, the patient who was "difficult", the patient who "did not want to do better", all ran the risk of receiving a personality disorder, to a large extent on the basis of lack of progress in treatment and therapist frustration. Some (e.g., Lewis & Appleby, 1988) have argued that the diagnosis should be discarded altogether, as it leads to prejudices and suboptimal treatment decisions for those involved.

The predominant psychiatric classificatory system, the American Psychiatric Association's Diagnostic and Statistical Manual of Mental Disorders (DSM), defines personality disorder in its current fourth edition (DSM-IV-TR; APA, 2000, p. 685) as "an enduring pattern of inner experience and behaviour that deviates markedly from the expectations of the individual's culture". This pattern is manifested in two (or more) of the following areas: (1) cognition, (2) affectivity, (3) interpersonal functioning, and (4) impulse control (criterion A). The enduring pattern is inflexible and pervasive across a broad range of personal and social situations (criterion B), and leads to clinically significant distress or impairment in social, occupational, or other important areas of functioning (criterion C). The pattern is stable and of long duration, and its onset can be traced back at least to adolescence or early adulthood (criterion D); it is not better accounted for as a manifestation or consequence of another mental disorder (criterion E), nor due to the direct physiological effects of a substance or a general medical condition (criterion F). DSM's counterpart, the World Health Organization's International Classification of Diseases (ICD-10; WHO, 1992, Section F60), states that a specific personality disorder is "a severe disturbance in the characterological constitution and behavioural tendencies of the individual, usually involving several areas of the personality, and nearly always associated with considerable personal and social disruption", and provides similar specific criteria.

Common features of the classificatory systems are the insistence on a longstanding, pervasive, and persistent pattern of experience and behaviour that is different from cultural expectation and problematic in terms of personal suffering and/or impairment in functioning; and the stipulation that this pattern can not be better or more parsimoniously explained by clinical or medical syndromes, or by the physiological effects of substances. Both systems recognize that it may be necessary to develop specific sets of criteria with regard to social norms, rules, and obligations for different cultures. In the remainder of this book the DSM-IV categorization will be used, but notable differences with ICD-10 will be commented on. Keywords in these definitions are *enduring*, *pervasive*, *distress*, and *impairment*. Hence, these definitions rule out transient periods of abnormal functioning, or conditions secondary to another, Axis-I disorder. For example, patients with panic disorder may become quite avoidant of social situations as well as dependent on others for their daily functioning. Such avoidance and dependence should not be confused with premorbid characterological manifestations. Likewise, the antisocial behaviours of severely addicted individuals should not be confused with premorbid personality functioning. Moreover, personality disorders must be of early onset and manifest themselves across contexts and persons; it is important that an enduring pattern of disturbed relationships is evident, not merely conflicts with one or two different persons or circumscribed avoidance of one situation (e.g., public speaking).

Functional impairment and distress

Both the ICD-10 and DSM-IV-TR definitions of personality disorder include a reference to functional impairment. One important distinction between ICD-10 and DSM-IV-TR is that the presence of subjective distress and presence of social malfunctioning are combined in ICD but separated in DSM. Accordingly, a person can qualify for a personality disorder in DSM due to subjective distress but without exhibiting pervasive social malfunctioning; in ICD-10 this person would not meet formal diagnostic criteria.

What are the consequences of having a personality disorder for a person's life? Evidence suggests that individuals with personality disorders are at substantially elevated risk for a wide range of adverse outcomes (Johnson, First, et al., 2005; Skodol et al., 2002; Zanarini, Frankenburg, Hennen, Reich, & Silk, 2005) (see Chapter 3). Empirical studies on functional impairment typically compare the psychosocial functioning of personality disorder patients to either patients without personality disorder or to patients with specific Axis-I disorders. Generally, individuals with personality disorder are significantly more likely to have a variety of relationship difficulties, including separation and divorce, and to have problematic work histories, including unemployment, frequent job changes, and periods of disability. Patients with personality disorder are also more likely to exhibit physical aggression towards others or self (e.g., suicide attempts); these findings may in large part be ascribed to the so-called "dramatic" personality disorder patients (see the next section).

DSM-IV classification

With the adoption of a multi-axial system of diagnosis for mental disorders in DSM-III (APA, 1980), the presence or absence of personality disorders has received separate, mandatory attention in addition to the "usually more florid" Axis-I psychopathology. The consequences for clinical practice and diagnostic thinking have been enormous: personality pathology should now be integrated in any comprehensive diagnostic assessment of every patient. The research community has also jumped to this opportunity, and two traditionally separate strands of literature, i.e., that of abnormal personality and normal personality, have since increasingly joined efforts. On the other hand, much of the literature has been on dissatisfaction with the current construct validity of personality disorders, and has primarily focused on two personality disorders (PDs) in particular (borderline PD and antisocial PD), leaving the empirical data on the other eight personality disorders still quite scarce (Blashfield & Intoccia, 2000).

In its current edition, the DSM distinguishes 10 discrete personality disorders, a personality disorder not otherwise specified category, and two provisional diagnoses. The personality disorders are combined into three clusters labelled A, B, and C. Cluster A, the "odd" cluster, includes paranoid personality disorder, schizoid personality disorder, and schizotypal personality disorder. Cluster B, the "dramatic" cluster, consists of four personality disorders, including antisocial personality disorder, borderline personality disorder, histrionic personality disorder, and narcissistic personality disorder. Finally, Cluster C, the "anxious" cluster, includes avoidant personality disorder, dependent personality disorder, and obsessive-compulsive personality disorder. Specific criteria sets have been developed for both of the provisional personality disorder diagnoses (i.e., depressive PD and negativistic PD). Future research will show whether or not these diagnoses are well conceived and warrant inclusion.

Phenomenology of the personality disorders

Next, we will present prototypical descriptions of the 10 personality disorders, each followed by a brief clinically illustrative vignette. It is important to recognize that these descriptions are somewhat unrealistic and contrived, as most patients do not meet all criteria for one particular disorder, but instead manifest personality pathology that is a combination or mix of the various personality disorders identified in the DSM-IV. This state of affairs more than likely points to imperfections in the current conceptualization of the structure of personality disorders, which will be more thoroughly discussed in Chapter 2.

Cluster A

Cluster A consists of the paranoid, schizoid, and schizotypal personality disorders. The cluster has been referred to as the "odd" or "eccentric" cluster, presumably because these adjectives capture some of the unique qualities of the comprising personality disorders, perhaps because of the symptomatic overlap with psychotic disorders, as will be discussed in the next sections. Each DSM-IV personality disorder consists of an essential feature and a set of specific, operationalized diagnostic criteria.

Paranoid personality disorder. In essence, all seven criteria of DSM-IV's paranoid personality disorder are alternative variations of profound mistrust and suspiciousness regarding the motives of other persons. These patients are hypervigilant to hidden meanings and threats, but in a contentious, hostile way. In interacting with such personalities, one might sense the tendency to "watch one's words", which in turn of course fosters the mistrust of the paranoid personality disorder. Paranoid personality disorder individuals tend to be secretive and hypersensitive to insults, which they will not "forgive and forget". Four (or more) out of the seven criteria need to be met to satisfy the formal diagnosis.

DIAGNOSTIC CRITERIA FOR 301.0 PARANOID PERSONALITY DISORDER

A. A pervasive distrust and suspiciousness of others such that their motives are interpreted as malevolent, beginning by early adulthood and present in a variety of contexts, as indicated by *four (or more)* of the following:

   (1) suspects, without sufficient basis, that others are exploiting, harming, or deceiving him or her
   (2) is preoccupied with unjustified doubts about the loyalty or trustworthiness of friends and associates
   (3) is reluctant to confide in others because of unwarranted fear that the information will be used maliciously against him or her
   (4) reads hidden demeaning or threatening meanings into benign remarks or events
   (5) persistently bears grudges, i.e., is unforgiving of insults, injuries, or slights
   (6) perceives attacks on his or her character or reputation that are not apparent to others and is quick to react angrily or to counterattack
   (7) has recurrent suspicions, without justification, regarding fidelity of spouse or sexual partner.

B. Does not occur exclusively during the course of Schizophrenia, a Mood Disorder With Psychotic Features, or another Psychotic Disorder and is not due to the direct physiological effects of a general medical condition.

Note: If criteria are met prior to the onset of Schizophrenia, add "Premorbid", e.g., "Paranoid Personality Disorder (Premorbid)".
Source: Reprinted with permission of APA.

Arnold, a 45-year-old contractor, presents for treatment after his girlfriend left him. He is feeling angry and depressed, and suspects that, although his ex vehemently denies it, she is seeing someone else. In fact, this has been the cause of most of their troubles, him insisting that she was looking at other men, and showing interest. Looking back, Arnold has had similar problems with both his ex-wives; he finds people cannot be trusted, "so you have to treat them strictly and check them". In his work, he is a ruthless negotiator, who keeps his cards close to his chest. Several deals have gone sour because the other party was not willing or able to meet all his demands, or felt that Arnold was not forthcoming with them. As he grew older, Arnold has lost many friends who "disappointed" him, typically because their loyalty to him was less than perfect. In therapy, he has difficulty opening up because he believes the therapist may privately think very different things than he in fact says and is just showing a professional front.

Schizoid personality disorder. Patients with schizoid PD tend to lead a withdrawn, isolated life. They are quietly distant, and prefer to be on their own, with minimal needs for relatedness. Typically, schizoid PD patients tend to be somewhat low in energy and their emotional life is rather flat and unexcitable. Usually, they have few close interpersonal relationships if any, and they are emotionally detached in social situations; they are indifferent to criticism or praise. It is extremely rare for schizoid PD patients to seek treatment for these characteristic behaviours. If they report for treatment, it is because they have developed other Axis-I disorders. Some research suggests genetic continuity of schizoid PD with schizophrenia, which is not surprising as its diagnostic criteria are phenomenologically similar to the negative symptoms of schizophrenia. Indeed, persons with schizoid PD resemble individuals who have prodromal or residual schizophrenia, but an important difference is that the schizoid PD does not include the psychotic-like positive symptoms of schizophrenia. Four (or more) out of the seven criteria need to be met to satisfy the formal diagnosis.

DIAGNOSTIC CRITERIA FOR 301.20 SCHIZOID PERSONALITY DISORDER

A. A pervasive pattern of detachment from social relationships and a restricted range of expression of emotions in interpersonal settings, beginning by early adulthood and present in a variety of contexts, as indicated by *four (or more)* of the following:

    (1) neither desires nor enjoys close relationships, including being part of a family
    (2) almost always chooses solitary activities
    (3) has little, if any, interest in having sexual experiences with another person
    (4) takes pleasure in few, if any, activities
    (5) lacks close friends or confidants other than first-degree relatives
    (6) appears indifferent to the praise or criticism of others
    (7) shows emotional coldness, detachment, or flattened affectivity.

B. Does not occur exclusively during the course of Schizophrenia, a Mood Disorder With Psychotic Features, another Psychotic Disorder, or a Pervasive Developmental Disorder and is not due to the direct physiological effects of a general medical condition.

Note: If criteria are met prior to the onset of Schizophrenia, add "Premorbid", e.g., "Schizoid Personality Disorder (Premorbid)".
Source: Reprinted with permission of APA.

Jim, a 27-year-old male, is working as a forester. He does not find it necessary or desirable to connect much with other people. In talking to him, one is struck by the flat, unresponsive quality of his account. Jim likes to be on his own, has no close friends, and sees no problems with this. As such, he has schizoid features, but does not meet the DSM criteria for schizoid PD, as no distress or (arguably) impairment is evident from his presentation. However, behavioural features of the disorder are clearly present.

Schizotypal personality disorder. What is most striking about schizotypal PD is the peculiarity and eccentricity in thought and behaviour. Persons with schizotypal PD often hold unusual, sometimes "magical", idiosyncratic beliefs. What has no meaning to most persons may have very special meaning to the schizotypal PD individual. Such meaning may be akin to mild ideas of reference, for example believing that the clouds have taken on a configuration that has personal relevance, but they may also be more like "sixth sense" private experiences. Taken together, the DSM-IV criteria impress as a rather heterogeneous set of mildly psychotic phenomena, and indeed ICD-10 considers schizotypal PD a psychotic syndrome rather than a personality disorder. Five (or more) out of the nine criteria need to be met to satisfy the formal diagnosis.

DIAGNOSTIC CRITERIA FOR 301.22 SCHIZOTYPAL PERSONALITY DISORDER

A. A pervasive pattern of social and interpersonal deficits marked by acute discomfort with, and reduced capacity for, close relationships as well as by cognitive or perceptual distortions and eccentricities of behaviour, beginning by early adulthood and present in a variety of contexts, as indicated by *five (or more)* of the following:

   (1) ideas of reference (excluding delusions of reference)
   (2) odd beliefs or magical thinking that influences behaviour and is inconsistent with subcultural norms (e.g., superstitiousness, belief in clairvoyance, telepathy, or "sixth sense"; in children and adolescents, bizarre fantasies or preoccupations)
   (3) unusual perceptual experiences, including bodily illusions
   (4) odd thinking and speech (e.g., vague, circumstantial, metaphorical, overelaborate, or stereotyped)
   (5) suspiciousness or paranoid ideation
   (6) inappropriate or constricted affect
   (7) behaviour or appearance that is odd, eccentric, or peculiar
   (8) lack of close friends or confidants other than first-degree relatives
   (9) excessive social anxiety that does not diminish with familiarity and tends to be associated with paranoid fears rather than negative judgements about self.

continues

Gail, a 45-year-old librarian, presented for treatment because she felt depressed that her relationships were "somehow never working out". She was an attractive woman, somewhat unusual looking in her Indian flowing dress with large African earrings and sandals. Gail was an artistic person, with, among other things, apparent talents in sculpture. Her main interests included astrology, Reiki, and journalling. She found she had a particular facility for becoming involved in sensory experiences, including mind-altering drugs, alternative movies, and nature. Her leisure time consisted mainly of walking on her own and "talking with trees". Such experiences made her feel somewhat distant from her colleagues, working in the university library. She experienced anxiety when meeting people, even with colleagues, whom she had known for years, because "people could not be trusted". She had never had a female friend. Her social contacts were limited to men, although she found it difficult to trust these men, and while looking for a "soulmate", she usually found men who were just out "for a trip with her".

Cluster B

Cluster B consists of the antisocial, borderline, histrionic, and narcissistic personality disorders. The cluster has been referred to as the "dramatic" or "emotional" cluster, which indeed reflects a prominent feature common to these personality disorders.

Antisocial personality disorder. Patients with antisocial PD tend to disregard the rights of others and are prone to unethical behaviour. Antisocial PD is often associated with drug and alcohol problems and criminal behaviour. Persons with antisocial PD tend to be irresponsible, and do not "learn" from previous mistakes. For example, they are often unable to keep a job or meet adult financial responsibilities. Typically of low frustration tolerance, antisocial PD patients can be quite aggressive and impulsive, but there are also more cunning and planful variations. More often than not, remorse and guilt are absent for the negative consequences their behaviour may have for others; in fact, some may derive pleasure from the suffering of others. The DSM's conceptualization of antisocial PD heavily emphasizes the antisocial behaviours, which sets it apart from the concept of psychopathy. Chapter 10 discusses the similarities and differences between these concepts in more detail. Three (or more) out of the seven criteria need to be met to satisfy the formal DSM-IV diagnosis.

DIAGNOSTIC CRITERIA FOR 301.7 ANTISOCIAL PERSONALITY DISORDER

A. There is a pervasive pattern of disregard for and violation of the rights of others occurring since age 15 years, as indicated by *three (or more)* of the following:

    (1) failure to conform to social norms with respect to lawful behaviours as indicated by repeatedly performing acts that are grounds for arrest

    (2) deceitfulness, as indicated by repeated lying, use of aliases, or conning others for personal profit or pleasure

    (3) impulsivity or failure to plan ahead

    (4) irritability and aggressiveness, as indicated by repeated physical fights or assaults

    (5) reckless disregard for safety of self or others

    (6) consistent irresponsibility, as indicated by repeated failure to sustain consistent work behaviour or honour financial obligations

    (7) lack of remorse, as indicated by being indifferent to or rationalizing having hurt, mistreated, or stolen from another.

B. The individual is at least age 18 years.
C. There is evidence of Conduct Disorder with onset before age 15 years.
D. The occurrence of antisocial behaviour is not exclusively during the course of Schizophrenia or a Manic Episode.

Source: Reprinted with permission of APA.

Mike, a 28-year-old, charming, handsome man, was expelled from high school for truancy and disruptive behaviour, including physical fights. Since then, he has had as many jobs as girlfriends, both types of "relationships" usually very shortlived. After one of these jobs, he was arrested because of a physical assault on his boss. Mike had never been seriously involved with any girl, although he promised them rosegardens. Quickly bored, he would leave the girls after one or a few nights. He would never go out in the streets without a gun, "because it may come in handy". Put on a waiting list for treatment of his gambling, he was arrested for bank robbery.

Borderline personality disorder. Central to the borderline PD is a pervasive pattern of instability across multiple domains, including affect, inter-personal relationships, and self-image. Borderline PD patients can be extremely angry at one time, despondent the next, and these intense mood shifts are hard to predict and most often short-lived. Likewise, in relationships, they may feel that their partner is "perfect" on any particular day, yet totally worthless the next day. Abandonment fears often predominate. Borderline PD is probably best known for its associated self-destructive impulsivity, which includes (but is not limited to) deliberate self-harm, or parasuicidal behaviours (such as self-cutting, burning, etc.). Their sense of self is compromised, with many borderline PD patients reporting feelings of emptiness, or not knowing who they really are. Five (or more) out of the nine criteria need to be met to satisfy the formal diagnosis.

DIAGNOSTIC CRITERIA FOR 301.83 BORDERLINE PERSONALITY DISORDER

A pervasive pattern of instability of interpersonal relationships, self-image, and affects, and marked impulsivity beginning by early adulthood and present in a variety of contexts, as indicated by *five (or more)* of the following:

(1) frantic efforts to avoid real or imagined abandonment. Note: Do not include suicidal or self-mutilating behaviour covered in Criterion 5.
(2) a pattern of unstable and intense interpersonal relationships characterized by alternating between extremes of idealization and devaluation
(3) identity disturbance: markedly and persistently unstable self-image or sense of self
(4) impulsivity in at least two areas that are potentially self-damaging (e.g., spending, sex, substance abuse, reckless driving, binge eating). Note: Do not include suicidal or self-mutilating behaviour covered in Criterion 5.
(5) recurrent suicidal behaviour, gestures, or threats, or self-mutilating behaviour
(6) affective instability due to a marked reactivity of mood (e.g., intense episodic dysphoria, irritability, or anxiety usually lasting a few hours and only rarely more than a few days)
(7) chronic feelings of emptiness
(8) inappropriate, intense anger or difficulty controlling anger (e.g., frequent displays of temper, constant anger, recurrent physical fights)
(9) transient, stress-related paranoid ideation or severe dissociative symptoms.

Source: Reprinted with permission of APA.

The nursing staff were happy to see the therapist. "That's one for you", they said, referring to a loud howling sound all over the closed unit. This concerned the Dialectical Behaviour Therapist, specialized in the care of borderline PD patients. To his surprise, it was Dianne, one of his outpatients, who had been doing quite well lately, but had rapidly turned suicidal after her (physically abusive) boyfriend decided "it was not working". Sitting with a large stuffed rabbit on her bed, arms in bandages because of self-injury, Dianne, a usually quite competent and intelligent young woman, was in an inconsolable crisis.

Histrionic personality disorder. A key feature of individuals with histrionic PD is the lability and shallowness of their affect: histrionic PD patients may quickly change from being very sad to very cheerful, and express both feelings equally dramatically. To others, however, these feelings may seem unreal or shallow. Histrionic PD patients seek to be the centre of attention, and are unhappy when they are not. To attract attention they may be overly emotionally expressive or use their appearance, perhaps by being flirtatious or inappropriately playful in interpersonal contact. They are quite extraverted and tend to perceive their relationships with others as more special than these others do. Five (or more) out of the eight criteria need to be met to satisfy the formal diagnosis.

DIAGNOSTIC CRITERIA FOR 301.50 HISTRIONIC PERSONALITY DISORDER

A pervasive pattern of excessive emotionality and attention seeking, beginning by early adulthood and present in a variety of contexts, as indicated by *five (or more)* of the following:

    (1) is uncomfortable in situations in which he or she is not the centre of attention
    (2) interaction with others is often characterized by inappropriate sexually seductive or provocative behaviour
    (3) displays rapidly shifting and shallow expression of emotions
    (4) consistently uses physical appearance to draw attention to self
    (5) has a style of speech that is excessively impressionistic and lacking in detail
    (6) shows self-dramatization, theatricality, and exaggerated expression of emotion
    (7) is suggestible, i.e., easily influenced by others or circumstances
    (8) considers relationships to be more intimate than they actually are.

Source: Reprinted with permission of APA.

Claire, a 52-year-old woman, reported for treatment because of "total despair". She was a TV personality who in both her private and public life was known for her sexually provocative outfits and intense emotional displays. Lately, younger colleagues were asked to do the shows she felt were hers. Moreover, in bars and cafés Claire had to work much harder than before to get the attention she wanted; others felt she more than once humiliated herself in the process. During therapy sessions, Claire switched from being deeply despondent over these developments to, only minutes later, being rather seductive towards the therapist. She reported a history of usually short-lived intimate relationships with men who showered her with attention and care until she or they grew tired of this pattern. Despite the unique and deep feelings Claire reported for these partners at one time ("this is the One"), they were quickly replaced.

Narcissistic personality disorder. Narcissistic PD patients are characterized by their self-centredness and preoccupation with success, achievement, and greatness. They demand admiration and are often experienced by others as arrogant. They believe they deserve special attention and considerable privileges, as they consider themselves more accomplished and important than others. In relationships, they tend to have little empathy for others and may be prone to exploitative behaviour if this furthers their causes. Narcissistic PD patients may report for treatment following an experience of failure or disappointment: the discrepancy between their ambitions and ability may give rise to depression. ICD-10 does not include narcissistic PD. Five (or more) out of the nine criteria need to be met to satisfy the formal diagnosis.

DIAGNOSTIC CRITERIA FOR 301.81 NARCISSISTIC PERSONALITY DISORDER

A pervasive pattern of grandiosity (in fantasy or behaviour), need for admiration, and lack of empathy, beginning by early adulthood and present in a variety of contexts, as indicated by *five (or more)* of the following:

(1) has a grandiose sense of self-importance (e.g., exaggerates achievements and talents, expects to be recognized as superior without commensurate achievements)
(2) is preoccupied with fantasies of unlimited success, power, brilliance, beauty, or ideal love
(3) believes that he or she is "special" and unique and can only be understood by, or should associate with, other special or high status people (or institutions)
(4) requires excessive admiration
(5) has a sense of entitlement, i.e., unreasonable expectations of especially favourable treatment or automatic compliance with his or her expectations
(6) is interpersonally exploitative, i.e., takes advantage of others to achieve his or her own ends
(7) lacks empathy: is unwilling to recognize or identify with the feelings and needs of others
(8) is often envious of others or believes that others are envious of him or her
(9) shows arrogant, haughty behaviour or attitudes.

Source: Reprinted with permission of APA.

Dr M. was known to come to psychotherapy conferences surrounded by an entourage of graduate students and junior faculty, labelled by others as his "disciples" for their submissive and admiring behaviour. Dr M.'s writings frequently included case histories remarkable for accounts of how notoriously treatment-resistant patients benefited greatly from his unique insights. Generally, Dr M. did not display interest in other people; he treated them as an audience for his thoughts. Once, when a colleague had openly challenged his views, he had exploded in a fit of intense anger, and refused to talk to this person ever again. His students were worked hard for his benefit, and when they did not meet his expectations, were discarded radically. For some time now, he had been expecting a lifetime award for the outstanding quality of his work, and did not understand how several, in his mind inferior, colleagues were bestowed with these honours while he was passed over. This was probably all due to envy, in his mind. Recently, Dr M. was bragging that he was invited during a conference to sit at the dinner table of the Mayor of the city. "Quite an honour", a student remarked. "Well, I don't know if the Mayor fully realized that", was his reply.

Cluster C

Cluster C includes the avoidant, dependent and obsessive-compulsive personality disorders and is referred to as the "anxious" cluster, presumably because anxiety is a central feature in all three of its constituent personality disorders.

Avoidant personality disorder. What is most striking about patients with avoidant PD is their sensitivity to criticism, disapproval, and rejection. For these reasons, they tend to avoid interpersonal contact. They tend to harbour feelings of inferiority about their abilities and appearance, and feel mistrustful and alienated from other people. Their mood is generally anxious, scanning the environment for signs of rejection, avoiding risk of embarrassment. The differential diagnosis with generalized social phobia is particularly difficult; distinguishing features may be age of onset and the extent to which the patient believes the expectations are reasonable. Avoidant PD is akin to an extreme variation of normal shyness. A patient may report for treatment because of dysphoria over loneliness and isolation, or because of problems with alcohol abuse associated with efforts to mitigate social anxiety. Four (or more) out of the seven criteria need to be met to satisfy the formal diagnosis.

DIAGNOSTIC CRITERIA FOR 301.82 AVOIDANT PERSONALITY DISORDER

A pervasive pattern of social inhibition, feelings of inadequacy, and hypersensitivity to negative evaluations, beginning by early adulthood and present in a variety of contexts, as indicated by *four (or more)* of the following:

  (1) avoids occupational activities that involve significant interpersonal contact, because of fears of criticism, disapproval, or rejection
  (2) is unwilling to get involved with people unless certain of being liked
  (3) shows restraint within intimate relationships because of the fear of being shamed or ridiculed
  (4) is preoccupied with being criticized or rejected in social situations
  (5) is inhibited in new interpersonal situations because of feelings of inadequacy
  (6) views self as socially inept, personally unappealing, or inferior to others
  (7) is unusually reluctant to take personal risks or to engage in any new activities because they may prove embarrassing.

Source: Reprinted with permission of APA.

George, a 45-year-old computer specialist, lived a relatively isolated life. Being highly socially anxious for as long as he could remember, he was only able to hold a job in which contact with people was minimal. Afraid of being criticized, he went to great lengths to avoid people. If avoidance were not possible, he would use alcohol as self-medication to cope with his anxiety. When he was required to attend social gatherings he would drink about five beers in a row, before being able to leave the house. He avoided formal meetings at his work place. Recently being forced by his new boss to attend the weekly department meeting, he had used large quantities of alcohol, which had led to a referral for treatment by the company's occupational health service for his "addiction".

Dependent personality disorder. Patients with dependent PD are characterized by excessive needs for guidance, reassurance, and assistance. They tend to feel incompetent and lack self-confidence when it comes to many everyday choices, chores, and responsibilities. They believe they cannot manage on their own (at all), and fear being alone. Accordingly, they become highly needy and submissive in interpersonal relationships, which can make them vulnerable to exploitation. These individuals may impress as rather immature as a result. Dependent PD patients often report for treatment after an important supporting figure in their social environment has been lost, and they may feel depressed as a result. In therapy, they (again) prefer a directive stance from the therapist. Five out of the eight criteria need to be met to satisfy the formal diagnosis.

DIAGNOSTIC CRITERIA FOR 301.6 DEPENDENT PERSONALITY DISORDER

A pervasive and excessive need to be taken care of that leads to submissive and clinging behaviour and fears of separation, beginning by early adulthood and present in a variety of contexts, as indicated by *five (or more)* of the following:

(1) has difficulty making everyday decisions without an excessive amount of advice and reassurance from others
(2) needs others to assume responsibility for most major areas of his or her life
(3) has difficulty expressing disagreement with others because of fear of loss of support or approval. Note: Do not include realistic fears of retribution.
(4) has difficulty initiating projects or doing things on his or her own (because of a lack of self-confidence in judgement or abilities rather than a lack of motivation or energy)
(5) goes to excessive lengths to obtain nurturance and support from others, to the point of volunteering to do things that are unpleasant
(6) feels uncomfortable or helpless when alone because of exaggerated fears of being unable to care for himself or herself

continues overleaf

Michelle had great difficulty deciding what the nature of her presenting complaint was. She was hoping her therapist would tell her instead. The usually effective questions of the therapist were met with a lot of "I don't knows". Becoming slightly desperate and impatient at the same time, he asked Michelle to tell him what types of things she had done in her previous therapy. Her therapist "had her do experiments". "He would have me go to a shopping mall to buy a pair of earrings. I had to sample a lot of different pairs and then select two pairs I more or less liked. I then had to ask the saleswoman which one she liked best, and then buy the other pair." "And did you?" the therapist asked. "No, she said, "I ended up buying both pairs."

Obsessive-compulsive personality disorder. The most prominent feature of individuals with obsessive-compulsive PD is their behavioural discipline, a counterproductive preoccupation with details, and deep-felt obedience to rules and regulations. These are very scrupulous individuals, who tend to be perfectionist and rigid. As a result, they have difficulty delegating tasks to others, as others are seen as lacking in conscientiousness. They place high value on being controlled, typically at the expense of openness and flexibility. Obsessive-compulsive PD patients may report for treatment when they can no longer keep up their self-imposed levels of perfection and have succumbed to work-related stress complaints. The obsessive-compulsive PD has to be differentiated from the obsessive-compulsive syndrome, which is characterized by repeated intrusive thoughts and rituals. Four (or more) out of the eight criteria need to be met to satisfy the formal diagnosis.

(3) is excessively devoted to work and productivity to the exclusion of leisure activities and friendships (not accounted for by obvious economic necessity)

(4) is overconscientious, scrupulous, and inflexible about matters of morality, ethics, or values (not accounted for by cultural or religious identification)

(5) is unable to discard worn-out or worthless objects even when they have no sentimental value

(6) is reluctant to delegate tasks or to work with others unless they submit exactly to his or her way of doing things

(7) adopts a miserly spending style towards both self and others; money is viewed as something to be hoarded for future catastrophes

(8) shows rigidity and stubbornness.

Source: Reprinted with permission of APA.

The current conceptualization of obsessive-compulsive PD bears remarkable similarity to description of the anal character by Freud in 1908 published in his collected works (Freud, 1959):

> The persons whom I am about to describe are remarkable for a regular combination of the three following peculiarities: they are exceptionally orderly, parsimonious, and obstinate. Each of these words really covers a small group or series of traits which are related to one another. "Orderly" comprises both bodily cleanliness and reliability and conscientiousness in the performance of petty duties: the opposite of it would be "untidy" and "negligent." "Parsimony" may be exaggerated up to the point of avarice; and obstinacy may amount to defiance, with which irascibility and vindictiveness may easily be associated.
>
> (pp. 45–46)

A somewhat irreverent summary of each of the 10 personality disorders is provided in Figure 1.1 (reprinted with permission of Rapidpsychler).

Personality disorder not otherwise specified (PD-NOS)

In clinical practice, comorbidity is often dealt with by assigning the patient the residual DSM-IV-TR category of PD-NOS. However, this practice is not consistent with the DSM guidelines. The PD-NOS label should be assigned when the patient meets the general criteria for a personality disorder and (a) when the patient meets several criteria across personality disorders, but does not reach threshold for any personality disorder in particular ("mixed personality disorder"), or

Figure 1.1.
Cartoon describing
personality disorders.

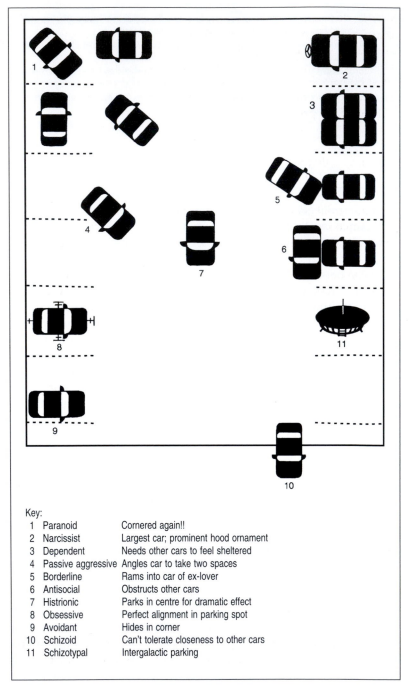

Key:

1	Paranoid	Cornered again!!
2	Narcissist	Largest car; prominent hood ornament
3	Dependent	Needs other cars to feel sheltered
4	Passive aggressive	Angles car to take two spaces
5	Borderline	Rams into car of ex-lover
6	Antisocial	Obstructs other cars
7	Histrionic	Parks in centre for dramatic effect
8	Obsessive	Perfect alignment in parking spot
9	Avoidant	Hides in corner
10	Schizoid	Can't tolerate closeness to other cars
11	Schizotypal	Intergalactic parking

(b) when the patient has a personality disorder that is not among the officially recognized personality disorders ("other personality disorder"; e.g., depressive personality disorder or negativistic personality disorder), or (c) when they have a clinically significant but subthreshold version of a specific diagnostic category ("atypical personality disorder"). Verheul and Widiger (2004) conducted a meta-analysis of the prevalence and usage of the PD-NOS diagnosis. Their findings support the idea that PD-NOS is a highly prevalent (ranging from 8 to 13% in patient samples) but very inconsistently applied diagnostic category. Individual clinicians use various heuristics to decide on the PD-NOS diagnosis, but even semistructured interviews for personality disorder differ substantially in their guidelines for diagnosing PD-NOS. These findings support the perception that PD-NOS functions as a wastebasket diagnosis: it is heterogeneous in content, and inconsistently applied. Accumulating data suggest that PD-NOS may be the most common personality disorder diagnosis in clinical practice when the PD symptoms are systematically assessed (Johnson, First, et al., 2005; Verheul & Widiger, 2004; Westen & Arkowitz-Westen, 1998): another sign that the coverage of the diagnostic system leaves much to be desired.

Concluding remarks

Again, we want to emphasize that most patients that meet diagnostic criteria for one personality disorder, meet criteria for several. Several studies have shown (e.g., Morey, 1988; Oldham et al., 1992) that a patient who receives one personality disorder diagnosis typically receives four to six personality disorder diagnoses. This phenomenon of (within-axis) comorbidity requires explanation. Comorbidity may reflect chance co-occurrence: basic statistics dictates that independent classes will overlap by the degree of the product of their base rates. In other words, some overlap is predicted by chance alone. However, co-occurrence significantly beyond the product of the base rates is in need of clarification, and this is clearly the rule for the Axis-II disorders. Some additional overlap may be due to artefacts of the DSM-IV diagnostic system. For example, criteria overlap yields arti-ficial covariation. To illustrate, in DSM-III, both narcissistic PD and borderline PD included reference to "relationships characterized by idealization and devaluation" (DSM-III-R dropped this optional expression of interpersonal relationship features from narcissistic PD). Such explicit overlap will be reflected in comorbidity. Other explanations likely involve various imperfections of the diagnostic system, a topic reserved for the next chapter, or may point to common aetiological pathways, further discussed in Chapter 4.

Comorbidity complicates treatment planning. In that respect, the treatment resistant (Type R) versus treatment seeking (Type S) typology, presented by Tyrer and colleagues (Tyrer, Mitchard, Methuen, & Ranger, 2003), likely has significant clinical utility. Type S, consisting of PD patients who recognize their abnormal personality functioning and wish to change it, was more often encountered in Cluster C patients than in the other clusters. Motivation for change was lowest in Cluster A. The distinction may be valuable as some interventions may convert Type R to Type S and allow interventions to be used that would otherwise be denied (e.g., pharmacotherapy, combination therapies).

In reading the various descriptions, the reader may have experienced the pain or pleasure of recognition of some of the symptoms or even entire disorders in self or others, respectively. Indeed, personality pathology is ubiquitous; about 12% of the normal population meets criteria for one or more personality disorders (see Chapter 3 for more detail), which may still be a conservative estimate given that significant personality pathology oftentimes does not neatly fit the available DSM slots (Verheul & Widiger, 2004; Westen & Westen-Arkowitz, 2003). On the other hand, one should be careful not to fall prey to the *medical student's syndrome* of too readily perceiving symptoms and signs in oneself or others; for a personality disorder to be present, there needs to be evidence of persistence, pervasiveness, and significant impairment and/or distress.

Adolescent personality disorders

ICD-10 states that a "personality disorder tends to appear in late childhood or adolescence and continues to be manifest into adulthood. It is therefore unlikely that the diagnosis of personality disorder will be appropriate before the age of 16 or 17 years." Likewise, the DSM cautions against diagnosing personality disorders until the patient reaches the age of 18 (unless there is unequivocal evidence of enduring problematic behaviours). Some cautions about diagnosing adolescent personality disorders are indeed in order. In adolescence, it is more common and normative to go through emotionally turbulent times and motivational shift than during adulthood. Accordingly, one runs a significantly elevated risk of false positives (i.e., overdiagnosis). The challenge is to distinguish enduring personality pathology from more or less normative adolescent transitional pains and emotional volatility ("Sturm und Drang"). Moreover, there likely are developmental differences in the expression of the same traits between adolescents and adults that should be taken into account during assessment. On the other hand, both diagnostic systems recognize that personality disorders begin in childhood and that personality pathology is not limited to adulthood. These guidelines are consistent with evidence from longitudinal studies that show that personality is quite consistent across the lifespan (Caspi & Silva, 1995).

Recently, notable researchers have joined ranks with developmental psychologists to investigate the early development of personality pathology (e.g., Bernstein, Cohen, Skodol, Bezirginian, & Brooks, 1996; Westen & Chang, 2000). Several strands of evidence suggest continuity between adolescent and adult personality disorders. First, personality disorders occur at similar frequencies in adulthood and adolescence (Grilo et al., 1998). Second, joint analyses of measures of normal personality variation and of dimensional representations of personality disorder symptoms are quite similar for adult and adolescent groups (de Clerq & de Fruyt, 2003). Third, the structure of Axis-II disorders in adolescents resembles that outlined in DSM-IV (Durrett & Westen, 2005). Fourth, Cluster B symptoms demonstrated high stability across an 8-year interval from adolescence to adulthood, more so than well established Axis-I symptom clusters (Crawford, Cohen, & Brook, 2001). Moreover, research has shown that adolescent personality disorders too are associated with impairment, distress, disturbed family relationships, romantic partner conflict, and general poor outcomes during adulthood (Bernstein et al., 1993; Chen et al., 2004; Johnson, Chen, & Cohen, 2004; Johnson, Cohen, Smailes, et al., 2000; Kasen, Cohen, Skodol, Johnson, & Brook, 1999; Levy et al., 1999). Early intervention models may make an important contribution to improving the odds for better outcomes for adolescents with personality pathology.

Summary

A personality disorder is an enduring pattern of inner experience and behaviour that deviates markedly from the expectations of the individual's culture, is pervasive and inflexible, has an onset in adolescence or early adulthood, is stable over time and leads to distress or impairment (APA, 2000, p. 685). The hallmark of personality disorders is the enduring pattern of disturbed interpersonal relationships. Substantial evidence suggests that individuals with personality disorders are at substantially elevated risk for a wide range of adverse outcomes. With the adoption of a multi-axial system of diagnosis for mental disorders in DSM-III (APA, 1980), the presence or absence of personality disorders has received separate, mandatory attention in addition to Axis-I psychopathology. The consequences for clinical practice and diagnostic thinking have been enormous: personality pathology should now be integrated in any comprehensive diagnostic assessment of every patient. The current version of the DSM distinguishes 10 supposedly discrete personality disorders, a residual personality disorder-NOS category, and two provisional diagnoses; prototypical descriptions and selected case vignettes have been presented. It is emphasized that these descriptions are prototypical rather than reality based: comorbidity and mixed personality pathology are the rule rather than the exception. Much of the literature has been focused on two personality disorders in particular (borderline PD and antisocial PD), leaving the empirical data on the other eight personality disorders still quite scarce (Blashfield & Intoccia, 2000). Several strands of evidence suggest continuity between adolescent and adult personality disorders; interest in pathogenesis and early intervention models heighten the interest in this area of research. The next chapter focuses on the construct validity of the DSM-IV personality disorders. Integral to the appraisal of construct validity is an examination of the extant assessment measures and strategies.

Diagnosis and assessment 2

> Even the psychologist who honestly desires not to under-
> estimate the complexities of personality finds himself
> limited by the crudity of the tools within his professional
> store.
>
> (Allport, 1937, p. 215)

Validity of the concept of personality disorder

Do personality disorders exist? What distinguishes normal and
abnormal personality variation? Are normal and abnormal personality qualitatively different, or merely quantitatively? How many
personality disorders are there, and how can you tell? Such questions
concern the construct validity of personality disorders. In examining
the construct validity of personality disorders, there are at least three
levels to consider (Clark, Livesley, & Morey, 1997): (a) the conceptualization of the constructs themselves, (b) the formulation of the
constituent (DSM) diagnostic criteria sets, and (c) the instruments
used to assess the constructs.

The constructs

Are normal and abnormal personality (personality pathology) qualitatively different, or is the difference a matter of degree? Categorical,
all-or-none formulations of personality disorders imply that there
should be an identifiable, nonarbitrary cut-off point to demarcate
where normal personality ends and abnormal personality begins
(Strack & Lorr, 1997). Several approaches have tried to tackle this
issue. Paul Meehl (1992, 1995) has contributed to empirically resolv-
ing the dimensions or categories question by developing taxometrics.

Simply put, taxometrics describes a family of statistical procedures that test between categorical (taxonic) and dimensional (nontaxonic) models. A review of taxometric studies to date (Haslam, 2003) suggests that the personality disorders represent a mix of latent categories and dimensions, so that neither dimensional nor categorical models of latent structure are likely to have generalized applicability throughout Axis II. For schizotypal PD and schizotypy, the evidence favours taxonicity, i.e., a categorical construct. For antisocial PD, there is also evidence of taxonicity. For borderline PD, the evidence is clearly in favour of dimensionality. To our knowledge, the other seven DSM-IV personality disorders are still awaiting taxometric testing.

Rather than seek a cut-off point, another approach is to define personality pathology by the nature and associated domains of impaired functioning. Millon (1986) has argued for the three-step criterion of functional inflexibility, self-defeating circles, and tenuous stability under stress. Livesley (2003) also proposed a tripartite criterion for personality pathology comprising (a) the failure of the self-system to establish stable and integrated representation of self and others, (b) maladaptive functioning in interpersonal relationships, and (c) failure to develop and maintain prosocial and cooperative relationships. Parker et al. (2002) presented 17 diverse, nonexclusive markers, which together help define disordered personality functioning. This set of constructs comprises: disagreeableness, inability to care for others, lack of cooperation, causing discomfort to others, ineffectiveness, lack of empathy, failure to form and maintain interpersonal relationships, failure to learn from experience, impulsivity, inflexibility, maladaptivity, immorality, extremes of optimism, self-defeating, lack of self-directedness, lack of humour, and tenuous stability under stress.

Is personality pathology (Axis II) different from clinical syndromes (Axis I), enough to warrant a separate axis? Several distinguishing features have been proposed including early onset, stability and persistence, pervasiveness, interpersonal focus, and impairment (e.g., Hirschfeld, 1993). Recently, Krueger (2005) provided a fresh review of the evidence regarding the putative bases for the distinctions between Axis I and Axis II (see also Chapter 9). He distinguished six broad areas, including stability, age of onset, treatment response, insight, comorbidity and symptom specificity, and aetiology. His conclusion was that these criteria do not survive empirical tests; they do not work well to separate the clinical disorders from the personality disorders. Moreover, several authors have suggested that certain personality disorders are probably better conceptualized as variants of major clinical syndromes such as the affective disorders and schizophrenias (e.g., Rutter, 1987). On the other hand, while each of these criteria is insufficient alone, in combination they may capture (some of) the distinctive quality of (some of) personality pathology (Hirschfeld, 1993).

In conclusion, it is has been an elusive goal to come up with a clinically useful demarcation criterion for personality pathology, and various dimensional models have been developed instead. There is little empirical evidence to justify a separate axis for personality pathology, as the differences with the Axis-I disorders appear rather unsystematic.

The DSM personality disorders

A somewhat different, more specific question is whether the specific set of DSM-IV personality disorders as such "exists", that is that empirical evidence backs up its putative nature and structure. Consistent with the medical tradition, the DSM opted for a categorical, all-or-none representation of the personality disorders, although in fairness one could argue that the PD-NOS label and subthreshold diagnoses allow for some dimensionality in clinical judgement. Such categories have practical appeal in that categories fit how clinicians think, categories guide clinical decision making (e.g., treatment planning), and categories can serve as convenient and efficient short-hand communication. To diagnose personality disorder, the DSM-IV-TR requires a two-step procedure. First, sometimes erroneously forgotten, one has to establish that the patient meets the general criterion for the particular personality disorder. These general descriptions are short narratives that describe the core features of the disorder. For example, for paranoid personality disorder, the general criterion is "[a] pervasive distrust and suspiciousness of others such that their motives are interpreted as malevolent" (DSM-IV-TR; APA, 2000, p. 685). Second, each personality disorder has its set of specific constituent diagnostic criteria, as exhibited in Chapter 1. The clinician is to evaluate each of these for their presence or absence, count the hits, and compare the total number of hits to the preset cut-off for each personality disorder.

The DSM has considerably evolved over its versions. In the DSM-II, personality pathology did not receive a separate axis, and involved narratives rather than operational criteria. DSM-III (APA, 1980), in search of more reliable diagnoses, started the operational criteria formulation. Its revision, the DSM-III-R (APA, 1987), emphasized discriminant validity by fine-tuning these diagnostic criteria. It also afforded provisional status to two controversial diagnoses (masochistic/self-defeating and sadistic personality disorder). DSM-IV (APA, 1994) dropped the (deemed objectionable by some; see for example Caplan, 1987) provisional diagnoses again, and adopted instead the negativistic and depressive personality disorders as provisionals. The gradual evolution of criteria sets can have quite an accumulative effect: when comparing DSM-III and DSM-IV criteria sets for paranoid personality disorder, for example, the number of constituent items has dropped from sixteen to seven, and, conversely, for dependent personality disorder, the number of items has increased from three to eight. It seems unlikely that the DSM-IV(-TR) will be the final word on optimal diagnostic criteria for personality disorders.

At the time of DSM-III, there was no compelling reason why Axis II should contain exactly 11 personality disorders, nor for the number or precise nature of the constituent criteria. No substantial body of empirical research was available to guide the inclusion of the 11 personality disorders at the exclusion of all possible others. A panel of experts came to a consensus, compiling considerable clinical expertise with unfortunately scant empirical data (see for example Kroll, 1988, for a particularly revealing discussion). Subsequently, several revisions have been made, based on an accumulating body of evidence (culminating for now in the current set of 10 personality disorders).

In a sense, the issue at this level of observation is to decide on optimal levels of "lumping" and "splitting" when inspecting the spectrum of personality pathology. Take, for example, the distinction between schizoid personality disorder and avoidant personality disorder, introduced in the DSM-III. As noted by Frances (1980), these individuals may closely resemble each other, but the difference resides in the motivation for social isolation. The avoidant PD craves closeness but is terrified of rejection and criticism, while the schizoid personality disorder has no desire or need for it. Is that sufficient justification for separating ("splitting" rather than "lumping" together) these similar clinical pictures? It may be, when the evidence indicates that the family histories of psychiatric problems differ (more neurotic-like versus more psychotic-like), and typical response to treatment differs. The DSM working groups had little reliable evidence available to them to base their conjectures on.

A standard way to empirically investigate the structure of personality pathology as operationalized by the DSM is to employ cluster and factor analytic techniques. To date, numerous factor analytic studies have attempted to map the latent structure of the personality disorders and/or to identify the dimensions of personality that may underlie the DSM personality disorders. These studies differ widely in the specifics of the techniques used, the type of ratings analyses, the nature of the samples, the DSM version employed, etc., which probably accounts for a significant portion of the obtained inconsistent findings. There have been cluster analyses, exploratory and confirmatory factor analyses of DSM personality disorder ratings (e.g., Arntz, 1999; Blais, McCann, Benedict, & Norman, 1997; Ekselius, Lindstron, von Knorring, Bodlund, & Kullgren, 1994; Kass, Skodol, Charles, Spitzer, & Williams, 1985; Widiger, Trull, Hurt, Clarkin, & Frances, 1987), factor analyses of personality disorder symptoms according to various theoretical models (e.g., Clark, Livesley, Schroeder, & Irish, 1996; Harkness, 1992; Livesley, Jackson, & Schroeder, 1986), and factor analyses of dimensional models of normal personality variation (e.g., Cloninger, Przybeck, & Svrakic, 1991; Dyce & O'Connor, 1998), to name a few. Regarding the structure of DSM, the results have been decidedly mixed: while some claim good fit (e.g. Arntz, 1999), others have noted results that are more consistent with factor solutions that include a higher number of factors. Quite recently, an internal validation study was conducted that tested whether the criteria specified in the diagnostic interview International Personality Disorder Examination (see instrument section) for the DSM-IV personality disorders were consistent with single and PD-specific latent dimensions (Nestadt et al., 2006). In a large community sample ($N = 742$), only the dependent and avoidant PDs satisfied commonly used criteria of fit for a one-factor model. As well, the overall latent structure of DSM-IV was examined. When all personality disorder criteria were entered in an exploratory factor analysis, five underlying factors emerged, four of which were associated with diminished functioning. The factors were labelled *compulsive* (not maladaptive), *neurotic avoidant, aloof, impulsive callous*, and *egocentric*.

DSM criteria sets

The DSM-IV manual reads: "A categorical approach to classification works best when the members of a diagnostic class are homogeneous, when there are clear boundaries between classes, and when the different classes are mutually exclusive" (APA, 1994, p. xxiii). Consider then the challenge of producing a brief list of specific diagnostic criteria to capture the broad and complex patterns of inner experience and behaviours we call personality disorder. Seeking a workable, economic set of indicators, the committee had to negotiate the aims of maximizing the internal consistency within each disorder while minimizing overlap across disorders. Meanwhile, to promote reliability in diagnosis, directly observable behaviour was emphasized.

The current DSM-IV-TR uses polythetic criteria that carry equal weight towards a categorical (all-or-none) diagnosis. Several choices and decisions underlie this procedure. First, as discussed before, personality pathology is classified as a dichotomous, categorical phenomenon; it is considered something one has or has not, much like being pregnant or having a broken leg (or not). This in turn implies that a specified minimum number of diagnostic criteria can be defined to demarcate when normal personality ends and personality pathology begins. Second, each criterion is weighted equally towards the diagnosis and no criteria are essential for (as in necessary for) the diagnosis. Let us look closer at the consequences of these various implicit choices, because choices they are.

Polythetic criteria of equal weight: Issues of heterogeneity and diagnostic efficiency. The DSM criterion sets for the personality disorders use polythetic criteria. That is, no single criterion is absolutely required or essential to the disorder, but they are alternative definers of the disorder, with a certain critical minimum number for the diagnosis to be present. What polythetic criteria invite is heterogeneity within diagnostic classes. To illustrate, meeting five or more out of nine symptoms can be done in 246 different ways. Accordingly, there are 246 ways to meet criteria for a diagnosis of borderline, narcissistic, or schizotypal personality disorder. In turn, this means that, particularly for personality disorders that have diverse diagnostic criteria, quite a diversity of individuals share the same diagnosis. For example, antisocial PD individuals may or may not show impulsivity or failure to plan ahead, may or may not show lack of remorse, may or may not exhibit deceitfulness; it is likely that a person who exhibits all three criteria will impress differently to one who does not exhibit any. Moreover, in the current assessment scheme of DSM, all criteria are of equal importance, i.e., receive equal weight towards the diagnosis. It deserves mentioning that the equal weighting of criteria is a matter of choice, made by the consensus committee. One might also have decided to differentially weight criteria, or to declare certain criteria as essential, as for example in major depression, where depressed mood and/or anhedonia are a *conditio sine qua non* for the diagnosis.

Alternative models exist, for example additive models (more criteria met leads to a higher probability of the presence of the diagnosis), or weighting models (consistent with the idea that some criteria are more equal than others in contributing to accurate diagnosis) (Davis, Blashfield, & McElroy, 1993).

In fact, there is evidence that some criteria are more equal than others. Individual criteria differ in their sensitivity and specificity. For example, Kalus, Bernstein, and Siever (1995) reported that the DSM-III-R criterion for schizoid personality disorder "has no close friends or confidants (or only one) other than first-degree relatives" demonstrated high sensitivity but relatively low specificity, that is, may help pick up most of those who meet the diagnosis, but also many others who do not. Such items may contribute relatively heavily to the overlap observed among personality disorders. On the other hand, the criterion "is indifferent to the praise and criticism of others" has maximal specificity, but low sensitivity, meaning that many schizoid personality disorder patients will not endorse this item, but it is highly characteristic of a subgroup. The item "neither desires nor enjoys close relationships, including being part of a family" has both high sensitivity and high specificity, and is thus deemed highly "prototypical" for the disorder.

Coverage: Symptoms versus traits. The DSM-IV personality disorders are an admixture of symptoms, behavioural expressions of traits, and traits themselves. For some disorders, the emphasis is on symptoms and behavioural expressions. For example, borderline PD includes reference to symptoms (e.g., transient paranoid ideation) and behavioural expressions of traits (frantic efforts to avoid real or imagined abandonment). In contrast, paranoid personality disorder consists largely of seven trait-like criteria. A major advantage of operationalized behavioural criteria is that minimal inference is needed on the part of the diagnostician, which promotes interrater reliability. On the other hand, operationalized criteria tend to favour behavioural expressions at the expense of characteristic patterns of inner experience. Motivation, affective experience, and cognitive style may, however, be essential to the concept of a personality disorder and omitting reference to them may represent an unfortunate narrowing of criteria (Westen & Shedler, 1999a, 1999b). This issue goes to the heart of the content validity of the criteria sets; do they capture the target concepts well? Another consequence of symptom and behaviour dominated criterion sets is that the temporal stability of the diagnosis may suffer unduly. Patients with borderline PD, for example, may lose diagnostic status because they no longer exhibit the specific behavioural expressions during the index period, but they may not be functioning much differently or better than before as they remain unchanged at the trait level. Some of this state of affairs has come about because, to quote Tyrer (1995, p. 37), "so much worship [took] place at the altar of reliability". On the other hand, this was a defensible choice by the DSM committees, given that meaningful research is impossible when reliability of the essential categories is absent. Subsequent fine-tuning towards increasing construct validity was an optimistic attempt to look to the future.

Comorbidity. To derive a set of clean, separable disorders was the aim of the DSM personality disorder working group. Stated differently, the aim was to articulate mutually exclusive personality disorders with a specific aetiology, course, and response to treatment. As is evident from the discussion in Chapter 3, this aim was not realized, as no sharp boundaries between the personality disorders are evident in reality. Instead, there is substantial heterogeneity within each personality disorder category as well as excessive comorbidity across personality disorder diagnoses. In fact, mixed personality disorder is the rule rather than the exception; to illustrate, only between 3 and 10% of borderline PD diagnoses are single diagnoses (see Chapter 3), and formal diagnostic assessments yield a modal number of three personality disorders (see Chapter 3 for more detail). In a classificatory system, excessive comorbidity signals failure (Tyrer, 2001).

Of course, even for perfectly independent disorders some co-occurrence is expected (to be precise, the co-occurrence should then be the product of their respective prevalence base rates). However, when epidemiological data indicate that many patients show features of several disorders while few show all the characteristics that define a disorder, and that patients who receive any personality disorder diagnosis typically receive several (Shedler & Westen, 2004a, 2004b), then something is awry with the classificatory system. More than likely, too many separate personality disorders have been proposed.

In the DSM's defence, the personality disorders may have extensive overlap among themselves, but the pattern of comorbidity is not entirely random. For example, histrionic personality disorder and borderline personality disorder co-occur very frequently, while obsessive-compulsive PD and antisocial PD rarely co-occur. For a discussion of this topic, see Chapter 3.

Assessment instruments and construct validity

Construct development and construct validation inherently involve the use of assessment instruments. It is widely recognized that current instruments for the assessment of personality disorders have several limitations. Alternative instruments often have high reliability, but leave much to be desired in terms of convergent and discriminant validity (Clark & Harrison, 2001; Perry, 1992). Undesirable differences may be due to raters, interview occasions, data sources, (different sensitivity to) state effects, or format. The consequences can hardly be overstated. For example, in clinical practice, this means that the *same* patient may receive a *different* diagnosis when diagnosed by a *different* instrument (i.e., problems of convergent validity). Considering that the diagnosis is a principal input for the formulation of an individualized treatment plan, this state of affairs is highly undesirable. In research, cumulative science is hindered, as we are seeking commonalities among possibly different species (due to low convergent validity), or, conversely, calling the same species by different names (low discriminant validity) (Clark et al., 1997). This raises the difficult question of separating method error from construct error. Inconsistent findings may be caused by inconsistent lumping and splitting of groups by instruments with inadequate convergent and discriminant validity, but may also be due to poorly defined constructs that are not in fact present in reality (Clark et al., 1997). Second, most popular instruments are closely linked to the existing criteria sets and consist of items that were selected on the basis of their association with the DSM-IV criteria. How can these items help identify shortcomings and blind spots of the criteria sets they were based on?

In sum, the set of personality disorders on Axis II of the DSM-IV so neatly presented in Chapter 1 suffers from excessive comorbidity across diagnoses (or, alternatively, poor demarcation of the individual personality disorders) and substantial heterogeneity within diagnoses. Moreover, personality disorder diagnoses exhibit modest diagnostic stability and reliability across instruments, and provide limited coverage of the personality pathology seen in clinical practice. For balance, it is important to realize what the DSM has yielded. Prior to the introduction of specific diagnostic criteria, the reliability of personality disorder diagnoses was notoriously low, effectively placing an upper limit on the validity of diagnoses, and in turn effectively preventing advancement of the field. Also, in fairness, most of the objections raised are not unique to the second axis of the

DSM (Arntz, 1999): clinical syndromes like major depression also follow dichotomous decisions with arbitrary cut-offs (yielding much the same problems). More importantly, there is no doubt that the inclusion of a separate axis in the diagnostic system has been a major impetus for researchers and clinicians alike. The body of knowledge on epidemiology, prognosis, aetiology, and efficacious treatments has dramatically increased since, and patients have stood to benefit from all this activity. Finally, in spite of its limitations, we hold that a solid working knowledge of the categorical personality disorder diagnoses will be a good starting point for clinicians in their treatment planning and clinical decision making. More fine-grained psychological case formulations can rely on additional sources of information, as indeed is common in clinical practice.

Dimensional representations of personality disorders: Not whether, but when and which?

The previously reviewed empirical evidence strongly suggests that a categorical conceptualization of personality pathology does not adequately fit reality. In fact, from its inception, influential theorists have argued that a dimensional conceptualization of personality pathology has many theoretical and psychometric advantages (Widiger, 1992; Widiger & Frances, 1985; Widiger, Frances, Spitzer, & Williams, 1988). Dimensional models view personality traits as continuously distributed in populations and personality psycho-pathology as extreme variants of these personality traits. A forceful proponent of dimensional diagnosis of personality disorder is Widiger, who wrote on the practice of categorical personality dis-order diagnoses: "continuing this illusion will not only contribute to the distortion of individual cases but will in fact hinder research and further scientific progress by imposing distinctions and stereotypes that have little empirical validity" (Widiger, 1993, p. 135). In his paper, Widiger reviewed putative advantages of the categorical model – familiarity, tradition, simplicity, ease, and consistency with clinical decision making – and argued that each of these arguments were unconvincing or, as argued by Clark (1993b), even antiscientific. Frances (1993) substantively concurs with Widiger's conclusions as he stated, "that categorical diagnosis establishes a procrustean bed based on an inherently futile attempt to type a continuum that is without clear boundaries. The categorical method results in lost information, reduced reliability, and a cumbersome and artificial comorbidity" (p. 110). However, Frances titled his commentary "dimensional diagnoses of personality – not whether but when and which?" to discuss obstacles to widespread acceptance in clinical practice and to note that there is no true consensus evident on which dimensional model one should base this alternative conceptualization of Axis II.

Not whether, but when to introduce it and which dimensional model therefore seem to be the more pertinent questions when it comes to replacing or augmenting the current categorical system (Frances, 1993). Indeed, if one accepts that the personality disorders classification should be augmented or replaced with dimensions, which dimensions should be selected? Ample evidence suggests that personality traits are hierarchically organized (Trull & Durrett, 2005), and several levels can be examined for their heuristic value in describing personality disorders. Prevailing models include neurobiological models (e.g., Cloninger, 1987, chap. 3; Siever & Davis, 1991), evolutionary models (Millon, 1990), interpersonal models (Benjamin, 1996), and various models describing normal personality variation (e.g., Costa & McCrae, 1992; Eysenck & Eysenck, 1975; Tellegen, 1982, 1985).

The choice to adopt one specific model should be based on its relative superiority in covering the fundamental personality traits, its ability to accommodate behavioural, neurobiological, genetic, and epidemiological data, and its clinical and predictive utility (Trull & Durrett, 2005; Verheul, 2005). Recently, Widiger and Simonsen (2005) reviewed 18 of the most likely candidates among the dimensional models, and showed that most of these disparate models can be integrated in a general hierarchical structure. At the highest level, they proposed the internalizing versus externalizing spectra of psychopathology as presented by Krueger (1999), and immediately below four or five broad personality traits (or 5 ± 2, as succinctly put by Verheul, 2005). Trull and Durrett (2005) reached a similar conclusion in their review of these models, and proposed four core dimensions that seem to be common factors across models. These factors were labelled (a) neuroticism/negative affectivity/emotional dysregulation, (b) extraversion/positive emotionality, (c) dissocial/ antagonism, and (d) constraint/compulsivity/conscientiousness. A fifth factor may be included that is related to the openness to experience from the Five-Factor Model (see next section), but with a twist in the direction of Tellegen's (1993) Unconventionality dimension. This hierarchical rendering of traits, with more or less consensus at the level of a set of four or five traits, seems most promising in contributing to the DSM-V Axis-II formulation (Widiger, Simonsen, Krueger, Livesley, & Verheul, 2005). On the lower levels of the trait hierarchy, consisting of more specific traits, the dimensional models of Clark (1993a), Harkness (1992), Livesley et al. (1989), and Westen and Shedler (1999a, 1999b) have gained prominence, but consensus and integration is less forthcoming at this level. Behaviourally specific diagnostic criteria might be at the bottom of this hierarchy.

The Five-Factor Model and the personality disorders

A particularly strong candidate among the dimensional models is the Five-Factor Model (FFM), sometimes referred to as the "Big Five". In brief, the FFM consists of five dimensions of individual differences: Neuroticism (proneness of the individual to experience unpleasant and disturbing emotions and to have corresponding disturbances in thoughts and actions); Extraversion (preference for social interactions and lively activity); Openness to Experience (receptiveness to new ideas, approaches and experiences); Conscientiousness (organization and achievement motivation); Agreeableness (altruism, and trust in relationships). The most prolific contemporary advocates of the FFM are Costa and McCrae (1992a, 1992b) who codeveloped the most popular operationalization of the FFM, i.e., the NEO-PI question-naires. The revised NEO-PI-R also includes six rationally developed facets that decompose each of the five factors (for a total of 30 facets), and has informant and interview versions in multiple languages (Costa & McCrae, 1995).

Probably no other model of normal personality has inspired as much empirical research, and its track record of replication across many different populations, languages, cultures, and methodologies (Goldberg, 1993; McCrae & Costa, 1997), is impressive. The FFM makes claims to comprehensiveness (i.e., not to overlook important traits) and universality (across languages, cultures, and subpopulations). Moreover, for each of the five dimensions, substantial heritability and longitudinal stability has been observed, suggesting that the traits may have neurobiological underpinnings (Costa & McCrae, 1992a). The FFM is tied to the lexical hypothesis, which dictates that meaningful dimensions of individual differences in daily transactions between people will become encoded into language. Factor analyses of adjectives have consistently revealed the five factors noted earlier.

Likewise, joint factor analyses of various other personality assessment instruments have yielded similar dimensions. Proponents argue that the FFM captures the essential features of personality and that any personality construct can ultimately be mapped onto the factors. This does not mean that the Big Five is a comprehensive list of all personality traits, but they do constitute "five domains that ... include those traits that people consider important and reasonably sufficient in describing themselves and others" (Widiger, 1998, p. 865) and which seem to provide a robust structure in the hierarchical description of personality traits (Markon, Krueger, & Watson, 2005; Trull & Durrett, 2005).

Numerous researchers have attempted to map the DSM personality disorders onto the FFM (e.g., Blais, 1997; Dyce & O'Conor, 1998; Lynam & Widiger, 2001; Widiger & Costa, 1994). The rationale for this endeavour is straightforward: we can as yet not be certain that we have comprehensively collected the symptoms and signs of personality pathology, but we do have substantial evidence suggesting that we have a comprehensive grasp of normal personality variation. As most evidence to date seems to support the idea of continuity between normal and abnormal personality variation, why not take the (five-factor) model of normal personality as a point of departure in deriving a dimensional description of personality and the diagnosis of associated problems (Costa & McCrae, 1992a)?

This line of research has shown that experts can agree in their five-factor description of the DSM-IV personality disorders, and that the hypothesized relationships between the facets of the FFM and the personality disorders are generally consistent with the empirical evidence. Accordingly, specific personality disorders can be described as constellations of maladaptive variants of normal FFM personality traits. For example, from this perspective, antisocial PD may be characterized by the combination of high antagonism (facets of A); low deliberation, dutifulness, and self-discipline (facets of C); low anxiety and self-consciousness (facets of N); and high impulsiveness (N), excitement seeking (E), and angry hostility (N). Likewise, borderline PD may be represented by high anxiousness, angry hostility, depressiveness, impulsivity and vulnerability (N), high openness to feelings and ideas (O), and low deliberation (C) (Lynam & Widiger, 2001). Moreover, Lynam and Widiger (2001) showed that the covariation between the dimensions of the FFM matches the pattern of comorbidity among the personality disorders, suggesting that much of comorbidity probably reflects the covariation of the underlying personality dimensions.

Although the FFM is sometimes presented as a consensus model, alternative models have not been hastily withdrawn and notable dissidents remain who take issue with various fundamental assumptions underlying the methodology and factor partitioning of the FFM (e.g., Block, 1995; Tellegen, 1993), or point to the limited clinical utility of the broad FFM (e.g., Ben-Porath & Waller, 1992a, 1992b; Shedler & Westen, 2004a). Moreover, not all FFMs are equal; particularly the interpretation of the fifth factor (referred to as intellect, culture, openness, or unconventionality) and the factorial home of impulsiveness seem variable across versions. As well, the NEO-PI-R facets were not part of the original model that can claim the record of replication and universality. Others have objected that the FFM does not adequately capture more severe manifestations of personality psychopathology, for example the deliberate self-harm behaviours of borderline individuals (Morey & Zanarini, 2000; Morey et al., 2002). To the extent that consensus is building, it seems to be on the idea that the FFM poses a good starting point for further elaboration of the fundamental structure of personality and its link to personality pathology.

In the context of personality traits and personality disorder, a final point is worth noting. As recently reiterated by Lilienfeld (2005), there is a distinction between basic tendencies (traits) and the characteristic adaptations individuals find for themselves (Harkness & Lilienfeld, 1997). Personality pathology is probably found in the latter, rather than in the former. Put differently: people may (or may not) find relatively healthy solutions and niches for their extreme trait levels. This may in part explain the observed incremental validity of some of the more specific personality pathology measures over the FFM: item content of the former may include specific (maladaptive) characteristic adaptations, whereas the latter is limited to basic tendency/trait descriptors. The ultimate test of the FFM representation of personality pathology (or any other conceptualization, for that matter) is the extent to which it is able to reproduce the important clinical and theoretical components of the personality disorders' presumed interrelations with salient constructs (Trull, Widiger, Lynam, & Costa, 2003).

Starting over: The Shedler and Westen Assessment Procedure

Westen and Shedler codeveloped a particularly radical and innovative alternative model, proposing a dimensional profile to describe the personality disorder categories (Shedler & Westen, 2004a, 2004b; Westen & Shedler, 1999a, 1999b). These authors have noted several limitations of the DSM-IV Axis-II criterion sets. Primary among these is that they believe the criterion sets are too narrow. According to Westen and Shedler, this is a necessary result of trying to do too much with too few (all or none) items. They argue it is a priori impossible to negotiate the simultaneous aims of domain coverage, distinctiveness, and reliability in assessment with a set of 8 to 10 criteria. What suffered in the progressive quest for reliability were items that refer to domains that require more clinical inference than behavioural expressions: patterns of inner experience, including motivation, cognition, and affective experience. Prevailing categorical personality disorder assessment instruments are closely coordinated with the DSM, and as a result they often provide inadequate coverage for the spectrum of personality pathology encountered in clinical practice. Regarding dimensional accounts of personality disorders, Shedler and Westen suggest that FFM descriptions often lack the specificity to characterize complex personality disorders as the item content is limited to the common language included in the self-descriptions of laymen. Shedler and Westen would also like to profit from expert opinion and clinical wisdom in capturing the complexity of personality pathology. Therefore, Westen and Shedler started over with the aim to develop a more comprehensive and clinically relevant instrument: the Shedler–Westen Assessment Procedure-200 (SWAP-200; Westen & Shedler, 1999a, 1999b). The SWAP-200 is a clinician-rated instrument of 200 personality-descriptive statement or items, each printed on a separate index card (an online version can be inspected on http:// www.psychsystems.net/guest.cfm). The items consist of Axis-II and Axis-I symptoms, personality constructs from the clinical and research literature, and clinical observations. According to the authors, the item pool does more justice to the multifaceted nature of personality pathology, and provides richer prototypic descriptions. The SWAP-200 underwent iterative changes over its 7-year developmental period, and clinicians using the instrument were consistently asked to indicate whether they felt able to describe the important psychological aspect of their patients with the instrument. As such, the SWAP-200 not only contains items from the universe of personality descriptors used by laypersons in everyday language, but also from the universe of personality descriptors used by professionals who treat personality pathology. Recently, the same procedure was followed for the assessment of adolescent personality pathology, yielding the SWAP-200-A (Westen, Shedler, Durrett, Glass, & Martens, 2003).

To describe a patient, a clinician sorts the statements into eight categories, according to a prespecified or fixed distribution, from least descriptive to most descriptive. Take for example the first two statements of the SWAP-200: "Tends to feel guilty (e.g., may blame self or feel responsible for bad things that happen)" and "Is able to use his/her talents, abilities, and energy effectively and productively." The clinician is asked to judge how descriptive these statements are for his/her client, essentially on a 0 (minimum) to 7 (maximum) basis, but with preset quota for how many statements can be assigned a zero, seven, or intermediate value.

In a series of studies, experienced clinicians used the SWAP-200 to describe real or prototypical patients with specific personality disorders. Accordingly, SWAP-200 ratings have been used to (a) obtain empirical groupings of personality pathology by Q-analysis, seeking psychological similarity over subjects (rather than similarity over variables, as in factor analysis) (Westen & Shedler, 1999a, 1999b), to (b) yield composite descriptions of these empirical groupings, by averaging the values assigned to each item for a given grouping, to (c) derive prototypical descriptions of DSM-IV Axis-II personality disorders by asking clinicians to describe prototypical personality disorder patients (Westen & Shedler, 2004b), to (d) index the similarity of a given patient to these prototypes, by computing the alpha coefficient between the prototype ratings and the patient ratings, and to (e) examine lower level dimensions of personality pathology by examining the factor structure of the SWAP item pool itself (Shedler & Westen, 2004a). Factor analysis of the SWAP-200 item set yielded 12 factors: psychological health, psychopathy, hostility, narcissism, emotional dysregulation, dysphoria, schizoid orientation, obsessionality, thought disorder, oedipal conflict, dissociation, and sexual conflict (Shedler & Westen, 2004a).

In the Westen and Shedler prototype matching approach to diagnosing personality disorders (Shedler & Westen, 2004b), the clinician is to rate on a 5-point scale the extent to which their patient matches or resembles the narrative descriptions of the various personality disorder prototypes. This approach allows for both dimensional (1 to 5) ratings and for categorical use; starting at level four (corresponding to "good match, the patient has the disorder"), caseness begins.

The SWAP-200 does not neatly fit the emerging consensus regarding four to five underlying dimensions with multiple lower order traits, although its item set encompasses the FFM (Shedler & Westen, 2004a). The SWAP is not without its critics. First, methodological issues have been raised regarding the Q-sort methodology. An advantage of the Q-sort methodology is that it eliminates measurement error associated with differences in calibration among different raters; all clinicians have to use each value the same number of times, according to a carefully picked fixed distribution. On the other hand, in the Westen and Shedler studies, clinicians using the SWAP had to declare exactly half (i.e., 100) of the items as not descriptive of the patients, which, according to Widiger (2002, p. 459), is equivalent to "requiring that persons administering a DSM-IV personality disorder semistructured interview rate half of the diagnostic criteria as absent, no matter what the respondents say in response to an interviewer's questions", which indeed sounds Procrustean. Second, Livesley (2001) has questioned whether prototypes represent the way personality is organized in reality or merely represent information processing structures and heuristics that clinicians use to organize information about their patients. Finally, some of the proposed personality pathology dimensions underlying the SWAP-200 seem rather idiosyncratic and need independent replication (e.g., "Oedipal conflict").

Personality disorder assessment instruments

An exhaustive review of relevant instruments for the assessment of personality disorders is (far) beyond the scope of this chapter. We refer the interested reader to a number of up-to-date and excellent comprehensive reviews, which include a discussion of key characteristics and specific strengths and weaknesses for each individual instrument (see Clark & Harrison, 2001; Widiger, 2002; Widiger & Coker, 2002). This section provides a global overview of frequently used measures. In line with the reviews, we will discuss interviews and self-report questionnaires, and within each class distinguish diagnosis-oriented versus trait-oriented instruments for the assessment of personality disorder.

Structured interviews for diagnosis and trait assessment

Semistructured interviews provide specific, carefully selected questions to operationalize each diagnostic criterion. For example, to assess the first criterion of dependent PD "has difficulty making everyday decisions without an excessive amount of advice and reassurance from others", the SCID-II (see below) interviewer would ask "do you need a lot of advice or reassurance from others before you can make everyday decisions?" For the paranoid PD, to assess "suspects, without sufficient basis, that others are exploiting, harming, or deceiving him or her", one would ask, "do you often have to keep an eye out to stop people from using you or hurting you?" Affirmative answers are followed up with (in part provided) additional questions to ascertain whether the patient's examples meet criteria. As such, the fixed format ensures comprehensive assessment and promotes consistency across clinicians. At the same time, it leaves room for the clinician to decide whether or not the patient's answers constitute sufficient evidence for the criterion in question. A drawback is that these structured diagnostic interviews take considerable time and require specialized training in administration, scoring, and interpretation. Perhaps as a result, they are more frequently used in research settings than in daily clinical practice. There currently are five semistructured interviews coordinated explicitly with the diagnostic criteria provided within DSM-IV:

- Diagnostic Interview for Personality Disorders (DIPD; Zanarini, Frankenburg, Chauncey, & Gunderson, 1987)
- International Personality Disorder Examination (IPDE; Loranger, 1999)
- Personality Disorder Interview–IV (PDI-IV; Widiger, Mangine, Corbitt, Ellis, & Thomas, 1995)
- Structured Clinical Interview for DSM-IV Axis-II Personality Disorder (SCID-II; First, Gibbon, Spitzer, Williams, & Benjamin, 1997)
- Structured Interview for DSM-IV Personality Disorders (SIPD-IV; Pfohl, Blum, & Zimmerman, 1997).

There are substantial differences between these interviews in format, degree of empirical support, and quality of supporting manual. Moreover, not all interviews have yet been adapted for the DSM-IV criterion sets. By most accounts, the structured clinical interviews have gained the status of the "gold standard" for assessing personality disorders. Generally, the within interview interrater reliability is quite good, especially after careful interview training, and the coverage of personality disorder criteria is comprehensive. However, empirical studies show that different structured interviews often do not intercorrelate highly (e.g., Clark & Harrison, 2001; Perry, 1992), suggesting that they may not be measuring identical constructs. The diversity across interviews and the observed, associated lack of convergent validity are in part responsible for discrepant findings across studies (i.e., unwelcome method variance). We agree with Widiger (2002) that rather than foreclosing on uniformity of assessment batteries now, the field first needs more data on the relative psychometric qualities of the available instruments.

Several trait-based interviews have been developed. Some of these are disorder specific (especially Cluster B diagnoses), some assess all personality pathology. Frequently used instruments include:

- Diagnostic Interview for Borderline Patients–Revised (DIB-R; Zanarini, Gunderson, Frankenburg, & Chauncey, 1989)
- Diagnostic Interview for Narcissism (DIN; Gunderson, Ronningstam, & Bodkin, 1990)
- Psychopathy Checklist–Revised (PCL-R; Hare, 1991)
- Personality Assessment Schedule (PAS; Tyrer, 1988)
- Structured Interview for the Five-Factor Model (SIFFM; Trull & Widiger, 1997).

Self-report instruments for diagnosis and trait assessment

Self-report instruments also have some relative strengths, including efficiency, comprehensive domain coverage, and the availability of normative data. Moreover, self-report instruments can detect response sets and biases that may compromise the validity of clinical assessment, provided they contain validity scales to do so (a particular strength of the MMPI-2, for example; see Butcher, Dahlstrom, Graham, Tellegen, & Kaemmer, 1989). On the other hand, self-report assessment of personality pathology contains an inherent risk: personality pathology by definition is ego-syntonic, and personality-disordered individuals may thus be liable to produce biased self-portrayals. For example, a narcissistic person may not feel that his excessive demands on his social environment present a "sense of entitlement"; to him they may seem appropriate and reasonable claims. Likewise, the paranoid person will feel that her mistrust and suspicion of other people is justified by (his appraisal) of the facts, and will therefore not endorse items indicating undue suspiciousness.

There are currently five self-report inventories that are commonly used for the diagnostic assessment of the DSM-IV personality disorders. These are:

- Coolidge Axis II Inventory (CATI; Coolidge & Merwin, 1992)
- Millon Clinical Multiaxial Inventory–III (MCMI-III; Millon, Davis, & Millon, 1994)
- Personality Disorder Questionnaire–IV (PDQ-4; Hyler, 1994)
- Personality Assessment Inventory (PAI; Morey, 1991)
- Schedule for Nonadaptive and Adaptive Personality (SNAP; Clark, 1993a)
- Wisconsin Personality Inventory (WISP; Klein, Benjamin, Rosenfeld, et al., 1993).

In addition to self-report instruments that capture the categorical assessment of personality disorders, there are also trait-based instruments, consistent with the various dimensional models of personality pathology (discussed before). These instruments tap overlapping constellations of maladaptive personality traits. Frequently used trait-based inventories include:

- Dimensional Assessment of Personality Pathology–Basic Questionnaire (DAPP-BQ; Livesley & Jackson, in press)
- Extended Interpersonal Adjective Scales (IASR-B5; Trapnell & Wiggins, 1990)
- Inventory of Interpersonal Problems–Personality Disorders scales (IIP-PD; Pilkonis, Kim, Proietti, & Barkham, 1996)
- Minnesota Multiphasic Personality Inventory-2, Psy-5 scales (MMPI-2; Harkness & McNulty, 1994)
- NEO-Personality Inventory–Revised (NEO-PI-R; Costa & McCrae, 1992b)
- Personality Adjective Check List (PACL; Strack, 1987)
- Schedule for Nonadaptive and Adaptive Personality (SNAP; Clark, 1993a)
- Shedler and Westen Assessment Procedure-200 (SWAP-200; Shedler & Westen, 1999a, 1999b); clinician report rather than self-report
- Tridimensional Personality Questionnaire (TPQ; Cloninger et al., 1991); Temperament–Character Inventory (TCI; Cloninger, Przybeck, Svrakic, & Wetzel, 1994).

Issues pertinent to the clinical assessment of personality disorders

When conducting assessments of personality disorders, several specific issues warrant extra attention. Those issues have been referred to by Zimmerman (1994) as the "who, what, and when" questions of personality disorder assessment. We present a slight variation in order and content.

Who should be assessed?

The case can be made (see Tyrer, 1995) that assessment of personality disorder should rely heavily on informants, or one might rely on clinician-rated methods, such as the SWAP-200. Presumably, these informants are, in contrast to the personality disorder patients themselves, not *qualitate qua* suspect in their appraisals, nor do they run the risk of colouring their report due to the current (mood) state or Axis-I condition. On the other hand, the notion that personality disorder patients present biased self-appraisals is largely untested (Clark & Harrison, 2001). In other words, it may seem plausible (and consistent with the DSM) that personality disorder patients do not present entirely accurate views on their thoughts, feelings, and behaviours, but we have no empirical data to back this up. Also, we know very little about who makes good versus bad informants, but we do know that the correspondence between self- and informant assessments tends to be modest at best (e.g., Klonsky, Oltmanns, & Turkheimer, 2002; Zimmerman, Pfohl, Coryell, Stangl, & Corenthal, 1988). In sum, there appears to be quite a bit of validity in the old adage that "Everyman has three characters: (1) that which he has, (2) that which he thinks he has, (3) that which others think he has" (in Allport, 1937, p. 221). This begs the question how disagreement should be resolved; one option is to attempt to obtain consensus ratings (Zimmerman et al., 1988), or (gently) reinterview the patient on discrepancies. To make matters yet more complicated, however, agreement between self- and informant assessment should not be mistaken for validity; people can agree perfectly on something that is inaccurate (Kamphuis, Emmelkamp, & de Vries, 2004).

When to assess?

Criterion E of the DSM-IV (APA, 1994, p. 689) general diagnostic criteria specifies that "the enduring pattern [the personality disorder]

... is not better accounted for as a manifestation or consequence of another mental disorder". It is not uncommon, and in clinical practice is in fact the rule rather than the exception, for a personality disorder patient to have a comorbid Axis-I disorder. Many personality disorder patients present for treatment specifically because of acute suffering associated with their comorbid Axis-I clinical syndrome; think of the depressed patient with narcissistic or avoidant PD, the substance-dependent patient with borderline PD, etc. This issue presents a specific difficulty with assessing personality disorders: what is the effect of trait (i.e., personality disorder) and what part of the report may be determined by current mental state (i.e., clinical disorder)? In theory, the clinician is required to ensure that the current clinical picture represents an enduring pattern across a wide array of situations. In practice, it can be quite challenging to disentangle the effects of acute clinical disorders and the "true" premorbid personality pathology in a time-limited cross-sectional evaluation. Zimmerman's (1994) review of studies suggested that both interviews and self-report are susceptible to overreporting bias due to the acute psychiatric state, and that subsequent normalization of personality ratings was partly accounted for by Axis-I symptom reduction. In such (and other) cases, good interview training helps, and the clinician may also seek help from informants close to the patient, especially if they knew the person before the onset of the Axis-I condition. As well, personality disorder diagnoses should generally be considered preliminary and be confirmed or corrected by prospective observations.

What to assess?: General diagnostic strategy

Recently, in a special issue of *Assessment* on evidence-based assessment, Widiger and Samuel (2005) presented a general, evidence-based strategy for the assessment of personality disorders. They proposed a practical two-step procedure that combines the complementary strengths of self-report instruments and structured interviews. In the first step, a self-report instrument erring on the side of false positives is administered to narrow down the range of potential personality disorders. In the second step, this information is used to select relevant parts of a structured interview. The interview then comprehensively assesses the presence or absence of the selected personality disorders. Of note, a similar two-step approach to the assessment of personality disorders was tested in a large student sample (Lenzenweger, Loranger, Korfine, & Neff, 1997). The procedure yielded near perfect specificity, suggesting that the self-report screener did its job very well; almost no student received a diagnosis when the screener had indicated that no personality disorder was present. Additional recommendations by Widiger and Samuel include a careful consideration of the following topics when assessing personality disorders: clinicians need to establish the age of onset, be alert for distortions of self-perceptions and presentation, be sensitive to gender bias and the influence of culture and ethnicity, and expect a degree of change in personality pathology over time and treatment.

Summary

"An empirically sound diagnostic system should facilitate reliable and valid diagnoses: independent clinicians should be able to arrive at the same diagnosis, the diagnoses should be relatively distinct from each other, and each diagnosis should be associated with unique and theoretically meaningful correlates, antecedents, and sequelae" (Shedler & Westen, 2004b, p. 1350). The available evidence suggests that the current DSM-IV personality disorders are lacking in this respect: excessive comorbidity points to poor demarcation and, to date, no disorder-specific aetiological agents have been identified, while only few personality disorder specific treatment packages have been developed (most notably for borderline PD). The DSM-IV-TR diagnostic scheme is a categorical system of diagnoses based on specific sets of polythetic criteria of equal weight, most of which are symptoms, behavioural expressions of traits, or traits themselves. To meet criteria for a personality disorder diagnosis, patients should meet the general personality pathology criterion and a minimum number of specific diagnostic criteria. The consequences of the choices underlying these guidelines were reviewed, and it was concluded that a dimensional model of personality pathology has a better fit with evidence-based diagnosis. Quite a few candidate models for dimensional classification of personality disorders are extant, and most empirical research has been conducted on the Five-Factor Model (FFM) or "Big Five". A radical alternative is the proto-type matching approach proposed by Westen and Shedler (1999a, 1999b; Shedler & Westen, 2004b). Most trait models have associated assessment instruments to tap the putative dimensions. The most popular interview and self-report instruments were presented and pertinent issues to the assessment of personality disorders – i.e., use of informants, separating state versus trait, general assessment strategy; or the who, when and what to assess – were reviewed. The next chapter examines the prevalence and course of personality disorders in more detail.

Epidemiology and course 3

> Until fairly recently, almost everyone who learned about . . . personality disorders was taken by the notion that personality disorder was a stable entity whose main characteristic was persistence, at least between the time of adolescence to middle age.
>
> (Tyrer, 2005, p. 573)

The purpose of this chapter is to provide an overview and a synthesis of the information available on the epidemiology of personality disorders, comorbidity with other mental disorders, and current conceptual models to explain the co-occurrence of personality disorders and Axis-I disorders. Next, we will discuss the impact of personality disorders on treatment outcome of anxiety disorders, depression, and substance use disorders.

Prevalence of personality disorders

Community samples

In contrast to Axis-I disorders, few epidemiological studies have been conducted to establish the prevalence of personality disorders. Two reviews (Mattia & Zimmerman, 2001; Torgersen, 2005) have addressed studies on the prevalence of personality disorders in communities, the results of which are summarized in Figure 3.1. The studies reviewed show a wide variation of prevalence of all as well as of the specific PDs. In Figure 3.1 the median of these studies is reported. Both reviews included studies that made use of the criteria of DSM-III , DSM-III-R, or DSM-IV (one study). Generally, the rate of personality disorders tended to be higher according to DSM-III versus DSM-III-R criteria, irrespective of personality disorder studied.

Figure 3.1.
Prevalence of
personality disorders in
community studies;
OCPD = obsessive-
compulsive personality
disorder (Mattia &
Zimmerman, 2001;
Torgersen, 2005).

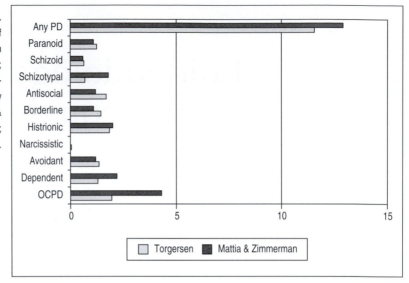

Four of the sixteen studies reviewed by Mattia and Zimmerman (2001) are included in the review of Torgersen (2005). Both reviews concur in that about 12% of the normal population fulfil the criteria for at least one personality disorder. In the cluster of odd personality disorders (Cluster A) both reviews only differ with respect to the prevalence of schizotypal PD. Whether this is due to changes in criteria from DSM-III to DSM-III-R or to methodological differences across studies is not entirely clear. Of note, in the Mattia and Zimmerman review the median for schizotypal PD was 2.2 for DSM-III criteria and only 0.3 for DSM-III-R criteria. Changes in criteria from DSM-III to DSM-III-R may also have affected the rate of occurrence of antisocial PD. Studies using DSM-III criteria found a rather high prevalence of antisocial PD (1.9), while the median of antisocial PD in studies using DSM-III-R was only 0.3. Obsessive-compulsive PD is another personality disorder where large differences in prevalence are found between both reviews, the differences not being easily explained. In clinical settings the prevalence of personality disorders differs dramatically from the prevalence in community studies. In clinical settings avoidant and dependent personality disorders are highly prevalent, followed by obsessive-compulsive, borderline, and histrionic PDs (Torgersen, 2005).

Recently, two large community studies were reported investigating the prevalence of personality disorders in national samples in the UK and the USA respectively. Data from the National Epidemiologic

Survey on Alcohol and Related Conditions (NESARC; Grant et al., 2004) revealed that 14.8% of adult Americans fulfilled criteria for at least one personality disorder. The most common personality disorder was obsessive-compulsive PD (7.9%), followed by paranoid PD (4.4%), antisocial PD (3.6%), schizoid PD (3.1%), avoidant PD (2.4%), histrionic PD (1.8%), and dependent PD (0.5%). Unfortunately, the prevalence of borderline PD, narcissistic PD, and schizotypal PD was not assessed in this study.

In the recent community study in the UK (Coid, Yang, Tyrer, Roberts, & Ullrich, 2006), the rates of personality disorders were generally lower than in the surveys reviewed by Torgersen (2005) and Mattia and Zimmerman (2001) and the rates reported in the NESARC study (Grant et al., 2004). Rather than reflecting true differences, the difference might be explained by differences in diagnostic instruments, and sampling procedures used. In the British sample of individuals the weighted prevalence of any personality disorder was 4.4%. The obsessive-compulsive PD was the most frequent, and the dependent and schizotypal disorders the least frequent. In this community study no cases of narcissistic and histrionic PD were identified.

Cluster A personality disorders. Cluster A disorders are more common among individuals who are separated, unemployed, and of lower social class (Coid et al., 2006). Paranoid PD is more common in individuals with less education (Torgersen et al., 2001), and more common among relatives of individuals with schizophrenia than among relatives of controls (Coid, 2003). Schizoid PD was found to be twice as frequent in men than in women (Torgersen, Kringlen, & Cramer, 2001; Zimmerman & Coryell, 1990). Finally, it has been suggested that schizotypal PD does not belong to the personality domain, but could better be conceptualized as a syndrome (e.g., Parnas, Licht, & Bovet, 2005). Indeed, in ICD-10 schizotypal PD is not diagnosed as a personality disorder.

Cluster B personality disorders. Cluster B disorders are more common in younger age groups and in individuals who are separated, and of lower social class (Coid et al., 2006). Narcissistic PD appears to be the least prevalent PD in community surveys, with most studies actually reporting that none of the participants met criteria for narcissistic PD (e.g., Black, Noyes, Pfohl, Glodstein, & Blum, 1993; Coid et al., 2006). Narcissistic PD is more prevalent among males than among females. Research in community and clinical populations found histrionic PD to be more common in women than in men. In one study the female:male prevalence was 12% versus 0%, but other studies found less extreme sex-related differences in prevalence of histrionic PD (Stone, 2005; Torgersen, 2005). In women histrionic PD is often associated with unexplained medical conditions (Coid, 2003). Borderline PD is more prevalent in younger age groups (20–35 years). Antisocial personality disorder is four times more common in men than in women. Antisocial PD is associated with marital and occupational instability and low education (Cloninger, 2005). Nearly half of male prisoners meet the criteria for antisocial PD (Coid, 2005). Although no hard data are available, psychopathy is believed to occur in approximately 1% of the general population, and in 15–25% of the male and female prison population (Hare, 2003; Hare, Cooke, & Hart, 1999).

Cluster C personality disorders. Generally, Cluster C disorders are hardly associated with demographic characteristics (Coid et al., 2006). A notable exception is obsessive-compulsive PD, which is more common in males than in females. Further, Cluster C disorders are more prevalent among more educated people (Coid, 2003; Torgersen, 2005), but persons with avoidant PD had less education than those without this disorder in one study (Torgersen et al., 2001).

Clinical populations

Although epidemiological studies have reported high prevalence rates of personality disorder in the community, only a small proportion of individuals with a personality disorder (less than 10%) have severe personality disorder (Tyrer & Mulder, 2006). Severe personality disorder is defined as covering many different personality categories and often several clusters of personality disorder, including at least one disorder from Cluster B (Tyrer & Johnson, 1996).

Surprisingly few reliable data are available with respect to the prevalence of the various personality disorders in community mental health settings and hospital patients. Generally, Cluster B disorders, especially borderline and antisocial PD, are more prevalent in mental health settings than in community samples (e.g., Oldham & Skodol, 1991). In a study by Kantojärvi et al. (2004) the prevalence of different personality disorders was investigated in Finland in hospital settings and a representative sample of the community. Cluster B personality disorders were more prevalent in hospital-treated patients than in the community, whereas Cluster C personality disorders were more common in the community sample.

Rates of personality disorders among patients treated in psychiatric outpatient care are high. It is estimated that about one-third of patients attending a community mental health service have a DSM-IV personality disorder (Zimmerman, Rothschild, & Chelminski, 2005). Similar figures are reported in addiction treatment centres (Emmelkamp & Vedel, 2006).

Course

Although DSM holds that personality disorder "is an enduring pattern of inner experience and behaviour ... has an onset in adolescence or early adulthood, is stable over time ..." (APA, 2000, p. 685), actually very few studies have addressed the course of personality disorders and the studies that are available present a less gloomy picture of the course of personality disorders than depicted in DSM and ICD. Most information is available concerning borderline PD.

Borderline personality disorder

Longitudinal studies indicate that borderline PD is most severe in patients' mid-20s, then gradually improves over a long time period with a number of studies reporting a substantial proportion of patients showing remittance of the borderline PD in their late 30s (Coid, 2003; Paris & Zweig-Frank, 2001; Stone, 2005; Zanarini, Frankenburg, Hennen, & Silk, 2004). In clinical samples, patients with borderline PD are more likely to seek treatment than patients with other PDs and patients with depressive disorder (Bender et al., 2001). In hospitalized borderline PD a number of studies have retrospectively assessed the course of the disorder after hospitalization. Three to ten per cent of patients had committed suicide. Factors associated with poor outcome and suicide include parental emotional and sexual abuse, impulsivity, continued substance abuse, and antisocial traits. Of the remaining patients most functioned reasonably well. The high-risk years are from adolescence to the early 30s. Most patients started to improve after the age of 30 (Stone, 2005), and continued to improve in late middle age (Paris & Zweig-Frank, 2001), but whether these improvements are due to treatment received or delayed maturation is unclear. In a follow-up study of patients with borderline PD (Gunderson et al., 2003), 10% of patients with borderline PD remitted in the first 6 months, which suggest that the prognosis of borderline PD is better than often assumed. Improvement in these cases was associated with situational changes and remissions of co-occurring Axis-I disorders.

In a study by Zanarini et al. (2004), who conducted follow-ups of patients with borderline PD 6 years after hospitalization, only one-third were hospitalized during the final 2 years of the 6-year follow-up. Further, the use of daycare facilities had also decreased dramatically. However, most patients were still taking psychotropic drugs and/or were in psychological treatment at the 6-year follow-up. The longest follow-up to date has been reported by Paris and Zweig-Frank (2001). Patients were followed up 27 years after index hospitalization. Most patients showed significant improvement as compared to a previous 15-year follow-up, with only five (8%) still meeting criteria for borderline PD. Further, there was a low rate of depressive disorders. On the negative side, over 10% of the original cohort had committed suicide and of the remaining patients less than half of the patients were living in an intimate relationship. Results suggest that for a substantial number of patients with borderline PD good outcome is associated with avoidance of intimate relationships.

It should be noted that the figures presented above are based on borderline patients who have been hospitalized and cannot necessarily be generalized to individuals with borderline PD in the community.

Antisocial personality disorder

Few data are available with respect to the course of antisocial PD. Ninety per cent of juvenile delinquents had conduct disorder as children (Scott, 1998). A 30-year follow-up of delinquent children shows that delinquency in youth predicts antisocial behaviour in adulthood (Sampson & Laub, 1993). However, most individuals with recurrent antisocial behaviour as a child or adolescent do not persist in antisocial behaviour as adults (Cloninger, 2005). As with borderline PD, there is evidence that some individuals with antisocial PD may "mature out" of the disorder over a long time period (Black, Monahan, Baumgard, & Bell, 1997), perhaps due to reduced levels of impulsiveness. In their follow-up study of hospitalized patients with antisocial PD up to 30 years after hospitalization, Black et al. (1997) reported "burn-out" of antisocial personality disorder to occur at a rate of approximately 1% per year. Factors associated with good long-term outcome in individuals with antisocial PD are job stability, no alcohol abuse, and a stable marriage arrangement (Black et al., 1997; Sampson & Laub, 1993). On the other hand, early substance abuse and more severely antisocial behaviour are associated with worse late life symptoms (Reid & Gacono, 2000).

Unfortunately, the buffer and risk factors do not say much about causation. Rather than causing good long-term outcome, the factors associated with good outcome may already be early indications of improvement. Further, the decreasing gradient with increasing age may also be partly accounted for by early mortality from violence, accidents, and cardiovascular disease. In a follow-up study by Black, Baumgard, Bell, and Kao (1996) a 24% mortality rate was reported. Antisocial men younger than 40 years were at excessive risk for premature death as compared to individuals from the general population. In a large epidemiological study in Sweden (Rydelius, 1988) into the course of antisocial youngsters who were in probation at age 16, 13% of boys and 10% of girls had died 18 years later, the youngest being still in their teens when they died. Eighty-five per cent of the subjects had died "sudden violent deaths", including accidents, suicides, murder, or substance abuse.

Many clinicians report that psychopathy burns out as well with increasing age. However, research indicates that psychopaths more than individuals with antisocial PD remain at high risk for violent offences much later in life (Reid & Gacono, 2000).

Other personality disorders

Recently, results of the Collaborative Longitudinal Personality Disorders Study have been reported (Grilo et al., 2004). The main purpose of this multisite study is to examine the short-term and long-term stability of four highly prevalent personality disorders: avoidant, borderline, schizotypal, and obsessive-compulsive PDs. Assessment conducted 24 months after baseline revealed remission rates ranging from 50% for avoidant PD to 61% for schizotypal PD. In a community-based longitudinal investigation, PD traits were assessed in adolescents at ages 14, 16, and 22. Personality disorder features declined steadily in prevalence during late adolescence and early adulthood. Overall, personality disorder traits declined 28% during this period (Johnson, Cohen, Kasen, et al., 2000). Also in the UK, individuals with personality disorders have been found to improve over time, the avoidant PD being a notable exception (Seivewright,

Tyrer, & Johnson, 2002). Individuals with an avoidant PD had become more severely distressed 12 years later.

Finally, there is some evidence that the anxious cluster of personality disorders becomes more pronounced with increasing age (Tyrer, 2005). In a study by Seivewright et al. (2002), individuals with Cluster B PDs tended to improve with age, but individuals with Cluster C PDs became more disordered. Further, obsessive-compulsive PDs are more prevalent among elderly than among younger age groups (Engels, Duijsens, Haringsma, & van Putten, 2003).

Concluding remarks

Summarizing results of the long-term course and outcome of the impulsive personality disorders, as antisocial and borderline PDs are sometimes called, there is some evidence that in a number of patients the symptoms become less over time and that patients continue to improve in late middle age. Whether this is due to biological maturation, to learning more adequate coping skills, or due to continued treatment is unclear at present. Further, there is some evidence that personality disorder traits tend to be only moderately stable during adolescence and that from adolescence through adulthood "maturation and socialization may contribute to the gradual development of less and less problematic patterns of personality" (Johnson, Cohen, Kasen, et al., 2000, p. 272).

Impairment

By definition impairment in psychosocial functioning is a *conditio sine qua non* for the diagnosis of personality disorder. Patients with personality disorders have to experience emotional and behavioural problems. According to DSM-IV-R, a diagnosis of personality disorder can only be provided when an enduring pattern of personality leads to clinically significant distress or impairment in social, occupational, or other important areas of functioning. Although it is generally assumed that personality disorders are associated with impairment and low quality of life, actually few studies investigated this issue and most of these studies involved the severe end of the continuum, i.e., borderline and antisocial personality disorder.

Generally, personality disorder has been found to be associated with impairment in occupational, relationship, and leisure functioning.

In the NESARC study (Grant et al., 2004) avoidant, dependent, schizoid, paranoid, and antisocial personality disorders were each significant predictors of disability. Obsessive-compulsive PD and histrionic PD were hardly associated with impairment. In the community study of Torgersen et al. (2001) in Norway, quality of life was assessed by interview and included, amongst others, subjective well being, social support, and negative life events. Results revealed that nearly all personality disorders were associated with reduced quality of life, the obsessive-compulsive PD being a notable exception (Cramer, Torgersen, & Kringlen, 2006). Schizotypal, borderline, and avoidant PDs were associated with the most reduced quality of life in Cluster A, Cluster B, and Cluster C, respectively. Further, there was a perfect linear and negative relationship between number of criteria of personality disorder fulfilled and quality of life, independent of any specific personality disorder.

Skodol et al. (2002) compared the impairment associated with schizotypal, borderline, obsessive-compulsive, and avoidant personality disorder with the impairment associated with major depression. Functional impairment associated with schizotypal, borderline, and avoidant personality disorder was severe. Obsessive-compulsive personality disorder was associated with least impairment, in line with the findings of Cramer et al. (2006) and Grant et al. (2004). Schizotypal and borderline disorders had greater degrees of functional impairment than did patients with major depressive disorder.

In the Skodol et al. (2002) study the impairment of avoidant PD was intermediate between the impairment associated with borderline and schizotypal PD on the one hand and obsessive-compulsive PD on the other, but it is unclear whether this impairment is associated with the avoidant personality disorder per se or due to the generalized social phobia often associated with avoidant PD. Van Velzen, Emmelkamp, and Scholing (2000) found patients with generalized social phobia and avoidant PD reporting more depressive symptoms, and being more impaired in both social and occupational functioning as compared with those with generalized social phobia without avoidant PD.

Results so far suggest that personality disorders are associated with impairment, but these studies involved a limited time-span (1 year). One prospective study has been reported that assessed the impairment associated with DSM-III personality disorder traits 13–18 years earlier (Hong et al., 2004). The results of this study revealed that apart from narcissistic and obsessive-compulsive PD, all other PDs were associated with significant impairment about 15 years later. In a number of instances impairment increases when the PD continues into older adulthood. For example, dependent PD may have existed across the lifetime, but the functional impairment can become more evident in older adulthood, particularly if adult children have left home and the partner dies. Finally, when personality disorders are associated with depression, this may enhance the impairment. Individuals with personality disorders and comorbid depression reported more impairment than those with depression without personality disorders (Skodol et al., 2005; Trompenaars, Masthoff, van Heck, Hodiamont, & de Vries, 2006).

Cross-cultural aspects

Personality disorders are often seen as the result of not only biological and environmental psychological precursors, but of sociocultural experiences as well. Despite popular assertions to the contrary, there is no evidence that in western cultures the prevalence of personality disorders is on the rise as a result of increased importance put on achievement and competition. Further, the increase in antisocial PD found in some ghettos of cities in Europe and the US may be accounted for by a large increase in substance abuse and dependence, resulting in criminal behaviour in order to get the drugs needed, rather than by a true increase of antisocial PD in the last decades. This "confound" should also be considered when interpreting the difference in prevalence figures across various cultural and ethnic groups in addition to genetic and environmental influences.

Ethnicity

A recent study compared the prevalence of personality disorders in the National Epidemiologic Survey on Alcohol and Related Conditions (NESARC; Huang, et al., 2006) across five ethnic subgroups of the US population: Caucasians ("whites"), African Americans ("blacks"), Native Americans, Asians, and Hispanics ("latinos"). Rates of current personality disorders were greater among African Americans (16.6%) than among Caucasians (14.6%) or Hispanics (14.0%). The rate of personality disorders among Asian persons was lowest (10%). These results suggest that differences in the prevalence of personality disorders between race-ethnic minorities may be just as important as differences in prevalence that exist between Caucasians and ethnic minorities in the United States (Huang et al., 2006).

Similarly, it has been suggested that cultural differences may be reflected in the prevalence of *specific* personality disorders. In the study of Chavira et al. (2003), borderline PD was more prevalent among Hispanic than among Caucasian and African American patients. This was particularly true for the symptoms of affective instability, unstable relationships, and intense anger. On the other hand, schizotypical PD was found to be more prevalent among African Americans than among Caucasians.

Social class differences

Although it has been suggested (Millon & Grossman, 2005; Paris, 1996a) that some personality disorders are more prevalent in Western upper social classes (obsessive-compulsive, narcissistic, histrionic, and borderline PDs) and others are more prevalent in lower socio-economic layers of society (avoidant, antisocial, schizotypal, schizoid, and paranoid PDs), the results from epidemiological studies are far from conclusive.

Religion

It has been suggested that religion may "shape" specific personality traits in individuals, which might be reflected in specific personality disorders. For example, Okasha, Saad, Khalil, Seif El Dawla, and Yehia (2004) found that Christian patients had half the rate of obsessive-compulsive PD of Muslim patients, which they ascribed to the ritualistic upbringing of Muslim patients. Similarly, it has been suggested (Alarcon, 2005) that a strict Catholic upbringing, empha-sizing guilt and shame, would render Catholics more susceptible to avoidant and dependent PD, but this hypothesis has not yet been empirically confirmed.

Are prevalence rates of antisocial PD related to culture?

In large epidemiological studies conducted in the US the prevalence of antisocial PD was 2.1% (Robins & Regier, 1991), 2.7% (Kessler et al., 1994), and 3.6% (Grant et al., 2004), respectively. Antisocial personality disorder is especially prevalent in US inner-city locations, which may be related to poor living conditions and substance abuse. In Europe and East Asia, the prevalence of antisocial PD is lower than in

US studies (Paris, 1996). In community surveys in the UK (Coid et al., 2006; Singleton, Bumpstead, & O'Brien, 2001) and Norway (Torgersen et al., 2001) prevalence rates were 0.6, 0.6, and 0.7, respectively. Whether this reflects true "cultural differences" or is associated with the sampling methods or assessments methods used is unclear. Interestingly, psychopathy as assessed with the Hare Psychopathy Checklist–Revised (PCL-R) has been found to vary across cultures (Cooke, Michie, Hart, & Clark, 2005; Hildebrand, 2004). In the study of Cooke et al. (2005) a comparison was made between large samples in the UK and the USA. Scores on the PCL-R obtained in the UK were not directly comparable with those obtained in North America: the same level of psychopathy was associated with lower PCL-R scores in the UK. On the other hand, in the USA the same structure of psychopathy was found across Caucasian, African American, and Hispanic male adolescents (Jones, Cauffman, Miller, & Mulvey, 2006).

Concluding remarks

Results are difficult to interpret at face value, given that a number of factors other than "culture" or ethnicity may be involved, such as education, poor living conditions, substance abuse, and socioeconomic factors. One problem with comparing prevalence figures in different countries is that, apart from true "cultural" differences, differences in the prevalence of personality disorder reported may be accounted for by other factors such as availability of treatment facilities. For example, as shown by Zanarini et al. (2004), a substantial number of individuals with borderline PD in the US when improved may stay in remission. The results of this study suggest that the majority of borderline patients continue to use outpatient treatment in a sustained manner through 6 years of follow-up. As suggested by Tyrer (2005), results in less developed countries could be different, given that the "remitted" patients in the US continue to use mental health services unavailable in less well-resourced areas of the world.

Effects of gender

Generally, apart from schizotypal PD, odd/eccentric PDs appear to be more common among men than among women, while the reverse is true for Cluster C (anxious) PDs apart from obsessive-compulsive

PD. This picture parallels findings from epidemiological studies into Axis-I disorders (Torgersen, 2005). In these studies anxiety and depressive disorders are more common among females. The picture with respect to Cluster B (dramatic/emotional) is more complex. Antisocial PD and narcissistic PD are much more common among males, while histrionic PD is more common among females. In contrast to clinical lore, borderline PD is equally common among men and women both in community surveys (Torgersen et al., 2001; Zimmerman & Coryell, 1990) and in clinical samples (e.g., Fossati et al., 2003). Generally, females and males are equally impaired from a personality disorder (Skodol et al., 2002).

Since the appearance of DSM-III there has been controversy over whether (some) personality disorders may be gender biased. More specifically, it has been argued that dependent, histrionic, and borderline PDs are more frequently diagnosed in women and that antisocial, narcissistic, and obsessive-compulsive PDs are more frequently diagnosed in men and that these differential sex prevalence rates are largely an artefact of a diagnostic gender bias. However, as noted by Widiger (1998), "the purpose of the DSM-IV is to provide an accurate classification of psychopathology, not to develop a diagnostic system that will, democratically, diagnose as many men with a personality disorder as women" (p. 98).

Already in 1983 Kaplan argued rather provocatively that, given that members of the DSM-III committee had been predominantly male (9 out of 10), the criteria for dependent and histrionic PD could be considered stereotypic traits of femininity such as emotionality (histrionic PD) and submissiveness (dependent PD). Thus, it would not come as a surprise that these disorders are more frequently diagnosed in females than in males. Some have even proposed to add to DSM personality disorders that would represent stereotypically "masculine" traits. As noted by Widiger (2000), however, these diagnoses already exist. Obsessive-compulsive personality is characterized by such stereotypically masculine traits as "devotion to work" and a "restricted emotional expression". Further, individuals with a narcissistic personality are characterized by disregard for other people's feelings, also considered by many to characterize males. Another typical masculine trait is the aggressive behaviour that is associated with the antisocial personality disorder.

Since this discussion started in 1983, a number of studies have investigated whether (some) personality disorders are gender biased. Typically, clinicians are presented with the same case histories, but information with respect to the gender of the patient is varied. Results of these studies show that if clinicians are led to believe that the patient is female they are more likely to provide the diagnosis histrionic than when they have been informed that the patient is male (Garb, 1997). The reverse is true in the case of antisocial personality disorder (e.g., Becker & Lamb, 1994; Garb, 1997).

Of course, it may be desirable to define personality traits and personality disorders independent of gender, but studies show that men and women differ, on average, with respect to many traits (Widiger, 2000). Thus, given that personality disorders are characterized by dysfunctional variants of these traits, it should not come as a surprise that some personality disorders are more prevalent in females than in males and vice versa.

Co-occurrence with other disorders

Comorbidity refers to the coexistence of two or more clinical and/or personality disorders in one patient. First, we will discuss the co-occurrence of various personality disorders. Next we will discuss the literature with respect to the co-occurrence of personality disorders with other psychiatric disorders.

Co-occurrence with other personality disorders

There is a high level of comorbidity among the various personality disorders. In clinical samples co-occurrence of other personality disorders is the rule rather than the exception. For example, in studies by Widiger and colleagues over 80% of individuals who fulfilled the criteria for one personality disorder also qualified for at least one other personality disorder (Widiger, Frances, Pincus, Davis, & First, 1991). In community studies there is also a high rate of co-occurrence of personality disorders. In studies by Zimmerman and Coryell (1990) and Torgersen et al. (2001), 25–29% of those with at least one personality disorder met criteria for at least one other. In a large ongoing study in the USA (the Collaborative Longitudinal Personality Disorders Study), the mean number of co-occurring PDs was 1.4 (McGlashan et al., 2000). In the national British community study (Coid et al., 2006) co-occurrence of personality disorders was even higher, 54% having one disorder only, 22% having two disorders, 11% having three disorders, and 14% having 4–8 personality disorders.

There is considerable "within-cluster" comorbidity. For example, within the anxious personality disorder cluster there is high overlap (e.g., Alden, Laposa, Taylor, & Ryder, 2002; van Velzen & Emmelkamp, 1999), especially among avoidant and dependent PDs. Stuart et al. (1998) found that 59% of patients with dependent PD also met critera for avoidant PD. Histrionic PD is often associated with borderline PD (Oshima, 2001). Schizotypal PD is significantly associated with paranoid and schizoid PDs. In over two-thirds of patients diagnosed with schizotypal PD, other PD diagnoses are common, especially paranoid PD and schizotypal PD (Fossati et al., 2001).

To complicate matters further, the co-occurrence of personality disorders is not limited to specific clusters. Although it is more common to have "within-cluster" comorbidity, a substantial number of individuals qualify for personality disorders from different clusters. For example, comorbidity of Cluster B personality disorders with personality disorders from Clusters A and C is quite common (Ekselius et al., 1994; McGlashan et al., 2000; van Velzen & Emmelkamp, 1999). In the the Collaborative Longitudinal Personality Disorders Study, borderline PD was associated with antisocial and dependent PDs (McGlashan et al., 2000), but other studies found borderline PD to be associated with most other personality disorders apart from schizoid PD (Oldham et al., 1992; Stone, 2005). Finally, in forensic samples, paranoid PD is frequently comorbid with antisocial PD and borderline PD (Coid, 2005).

Co-occurrence with Axis-I disorders

Comorbidity of mental (Axis-I) and personality disorders is common in clinical and community samples. Approximately half of individuals in the community with a personality disorder also meet criteria for at least one other lifetime mental disorder, while about half of individuals with a lifetime mental disorder also fulfil criteria for one or more personality disorders. Studies of clinically referred samples reveal even higher rates of comorbidity of personality disorders and other psychiatric disorders. Thus, in clinical cases comorbidity is the rule rather than the exception and is a pervasive clinical problem. In the Collaborative Longitudinal Personality Disorders Study the mean number of co-occurring lifetime Axis-I disorders in the sample was 3.4; schizotypal PD and borderline PD had more co-occurring disorders than avoidant PD and obsessive-compulsive PD (McGlashan et al., 2000). Most studies have focused on the comorbidity of personality disorders with substance use disorders and mood and anxiety disorders, which will be discussed below. In addition, the Cluster A personality disorders (paranoid, schizoid, and schizotypal) are thought to be related to autism spectrum disorders, but results of studies investigating this relationship are not yet conclusive (Wolff, 1991). Similarly, there is no convincing evidence yet that psychopathic features are related to autism spectrum disorders (Soderstrom, Nilsson, Sjodin, Carlstedt, & Forsman, 2005).

Substance abuse and dependence

The rates of personality disorders are particularly high for patients treated for drug and alcohol abuse. For example, Bowden-Jones et al. (2004) reported that more than one-third of patients attending drug services and over half of patients attending alcohol services fulfilled criteria for personality disorders. Substance abuse and dependence are particularly common in individuals with borderline PD and antisocial PD (Emmelkamp & Vedel, 2006).

Borderline PD. Given the defining characteristics of borderline PD, which include self-damaging impulsivity (e.g., sex, substance abuse, binge eating), it does not come as a surprise that high comorbidity has been reported between borderline personality disorder and substance abuse. Two-thirds of borderline patients fulfil diagnostic criteria for substance abuse disorder. Additionally, individuals diagnosed with borderline PD are likely to initiate substance use and abuse at a younger age than nonborderline individuals, resulting in more severe substance use disorders (i.e., more severe physical dependence) and more adverse emotional and social consequences (Emmelkamp & Vedel, 2006).

It is hypothesized that shared aetiological factors may account for the high comorbidity between borderline personality disorder and substance use disorders, including impulse disinhibition and adverse family upbringing (Trull, Sher, Minks-Brown, Durbin, & Burr, 2000). A genetic/biological predisposition to impulsivity and a family history of mood disorders and impulsivity are important aetiological factors in both substance use disorders and borderline personality disorders and are likely candidates to account for this comorbidity. Indeed, impulsivity consistently has been shown to be a biologically based, heritable characteristic with emergent psychological properties linked to the development and maintenance of borderline personality disorder and substance abuse (Lejueza, Daughters, Rosenthal, &

Lynch, 2005). A second possible pathway to comorbidity of substance use disorder and borderline personality disorder may be due to a history of (persistent) traumatic childhood experiences (i.e., physical and sexual abuse), which may lead to self-harm (Tyler, Whitbeck, Hoyt, & Johnson, 2003), and substance use. For these individuals, self-harm and substance abuse may serve as a coping strategy to deal with negative feelings.

Antisocial PD. There is also an extremely high comorbidity between substance abuse and antisocial PD. In the NCS community study, the odds ratios for comorbidity between antisocial PD and substance use disorders and drug use disorders were 11.3 and 11.5 respectively. In another large epidemiological study in the United States (NESARC), many highly positive associations between antisocial personality disorder and specific substance use disorders were found (Compton, Conway, Stinson, Colliver, & Grant, 2005; Grant et al., 2004). Based on earlier community studies it is estimated that up to 80% of people with antisocial PD meet lifetime criteria for at least one substance use disorder (Moran, 1999). With respect to the personality-based rather than the behaviour-based formulation of antisociality, it has been estimated that 10–15% of substance abuse populations fulfil the criteria for psychopathy (Alterman, Cacciola, & Rutherford, 1993).

The high comorbidity between antisocial PD and substance abuse has been accounted for by shared genetic risk and by a shared neurobehavioural disinhibition leading to impaired executive decision making (Compton et al., 2005). Alternatively, as in the case of borderline PD, this high comorbidity may be partly due to the defining characteristics of antisocial personality disorder, including impulsivity and reckless disregard for safety of self or others.

Anxiety and mood disorders

A number of studies have addressed the prevalence of personality disorders among patients with Axis-I anxiety disorders or mood disorders, but the results of a number of these studies are difficult to interpret given the small sample sizes involved and different diagnostic criteria used.

Anxiety disorders. In anxiety disorders, the median prevalence rates of any PD with panic disorder (with or without agoraphobia), social phobia, generalized anxiety disorder, and obsessive-compulsive disorder varied between 50 and 60% (van Velzen and Emmelkamp, 1999). More recent studies found an association between posttraumatic stress disorder and personality disorders, including paranoid, schizotypal, avoidant, dependent, and borderline PD (Gomez-Beneyto, Salazar-Fraile, Marti-Sanjuan, & Gonzalez-Luan, 2006; Shea et al., 2000; Yen et al., 2002). Those with the more severe PDs (paranoid, schizotypal, borderline PD) reported more types of traumatic exposure and higher rates of being physically/sexually molested when compared to other personality disorder groups (Gomez-Beneyto et al., 2006; Yen et al., 2002).

Mood disorders. Studies of comorbid personality disorder in patients with depression show high rates. A review (Mulder, 2004) found that between 40 and 50% of depressed patients have at least one personality disorder. Most studies into the relationship between personality disorders and depression, however, have been cross-sectional. A growing number of studies, however, show that personality disorders may contribute to elevated risk for the development or recurrence of depressive disorders. For example, Johnson, Cohen, Kasen, and Brook (2005) investigated the association of personality disorder traits and the risk for development of depressive disorders by middle adulthood in individuals without a history of depression, using data from the Children in the Community Study, a prospective longitudinal investigation. A number of personality disorder (i.e., dependent, borderline, histrionic, antisocial, and schizotypal) traits were significantly associated with an elevated risk for dysthymia or major depressive disorder in the 30s age group. Moreover, individuals identified as having a DSM-IV Cluster A or Cluster C personality disorder in their early 20s were at elevated risk for recurrent depression. The relationship between personality traits in adolescence and depressive disorder in adulthood is not specific. The same research group (Johnson, Cohen, Kasen, & Brook, 2006a) found that individuals with at least one personality disorder assessed in late adolescence were at markedly elevated risk for agoraphobia, generalized anxiety disorder, obsessive-compulsive disorder, and panic disorder by middle adulthood. The findings of this study suggest that some types of PD traits that become evident by early adulthood may contribute to increased risk for the development of depressive disorders, anxiety disorders, and even eating disorders (see Johnson, Cohen, Kasen, & Brook, 2006b) by middle adulthood.

Grant et al. (2005) investigated the prevalence and co-occurrence of DSM-IV personality disorders among individuals with current DSM-IV mood and anxiety disorders in the US population and among individuals who sought treatment for such mood or anxiety disorders. This is a very strong study in that structured interviews were held with more than 40,000 individuals in the community. Odds ratios were calculated to determine the prevalence and associations between current DSM-IV Axis-I and Axis-II disorders. Associations between mood, anxiety, and personality disorders were all positive and statistically significant. Nearly half of individuals with a current anxiety or mood disorder had at least one personality disorder. Personality disorders were no less prevalent among individuals with anxiety disorders than among individuals with mood disorders. Personality disorders from the anxious Cluster C were more strongly related to mood and anxiety disorders than other personality disorders, particularly dependent PD and avoidant PD. Personality disorders from the odd cluster (paranoid and schizoid PD) were most strongly related to dysthymia, mania, panic disorder with agoraphobia, social phobia, and generalized anxiety disorder. With respect to Cluster B personality disorders, histrionic and antisocial were most strongly associated with mania, panic disorder with agoraphobia, social phobia and generalized anxiety disorder. Prevalences of personality disorders were very high among individuals who sought treatment for a specific mood or anxiety disorder, often much higher than among all individuals with a current mood or anxiety disorder. Unfortunately, borderline PD was not assessed in this study. Other studies, however, found borderline PD comorbid with anxiety disorders and depression (Coid, 2003; Stone, 2005).

In sum, looking at the average picture it can be concluded that roughly half of the patients with an anxiety or mood disorder have a comorbid personality disorder. As expected, there is a strong relationship between specific anxious and mood disorders and the personality disorders from anxious Cluster C, but the associations are clearly not limited to this conceptually related cluster.

Conceptual models to explain co-occurrence

A variety of conceptual and theoretical models have been advanced regarding the associations of specific types of personality disorders with Axis-I disorders (van Velzen & Emmelkamp, 1996), which will be briefly discussed:

- *Vulnerability model:* Personality disorders may predispose to the development of an Axis-I disorder. For example, Cluster C personality disorders form a risk factor for unipolar depression and anxiety disorders in middle adulthood (Johnson, Cohen, Kasen, & Brook, 2006b).
- *Continuity model:* Personality disorders are viewed as the subclinical manifestation of a slowly developing Axis-I disorder. For example, borderline pathology may predispose individuals to have a major depression. Improvements in borderline pathology were considerably more often followed by improvements in major depression than vice versa (Gunderson et al., 2004), which could be taken as some support for the continuity model.
- *Complication model:* Personality disorders develop as a result of an enduring Axis-I disorder. For example, depression in childhood may enhance the risk of a personality disorder in adulthood. Kasen et al. (2001) found that depression at age 12 increased the risk of dependent, antisocial, and histrionic PDs substantially.
- *Coeffect model or shared risk model:* Personality disorders and Axis-I disorders are two separate structures, but they co-occur as a result of a third common factor or causal process. For example, personality disorders commonly co-occur with mood and anxiety disorders because of a common third factor, e.g., inadequate or abusive parenting. Physical and sexual abuse are common in many Axis-I and Axis-II disorders. High rates of abuse have been reported not only in borderline and antisocial PDs, but also in anxiety disorders, schizophrenia, and substance use disorders.
- *Attenuation model:* Both disorders are alternative expressions of the same genetic or constitutional liability. For example, it has been suggested that some personality disorders and mood disorders (e.g., borderline PD and unipolar depression) may occupy different points along a common affective or depressive spectrum. In a study by Kendler, Prescott, Myers, and Neale (2003), who analysed comorbidity in twin pairs, separate internalizing (major depression, generalized anxiety disorder, phobia) and externalizing (conduct disorder, antisocial personality disorder, alcohol dependence, drug abuse, and dependence) genetic factors explained most of the comorbidity of individual disorders.

Two remarks should be made concerning the above-mentioned models. First, they suggest causal relationships between personality disorders and Axis-I disorders. These models can only be properly investigated in longitudinal designs, which has hardly been done until now (but see Johnson, Cohen, Kasen, & Brook, 2006a, 2006b). Second, although these models do not differentiate between the specific personality disorders, it is tempting to assume that different types of personality disorders co-occurring with the same Axis-I disorder lead to different clinical pictures and, consequently, demand specific treatment strategies, which will be illustrated below.

In clinical practice, the comorbidity models may have a heuristic value. An analysis of related problems (a macroanalysis; Emmelkamp, 1982), in which the Axis-I disorders and personality disorders are conceptualized, may determine which treatment strategies should be chosen and whether specific attention should be paid to the personality disorder in that particular case. Take, for example, the comorbidity of bulimia and personality disorder. Is bulimia a consequence of an underlying personality disorder (vulnerability hypothesis) or are both disorders related to the same genetic or constitutional liability (impulsivity in case of borderline PD)? What is the function of binge eating? Avoiding unpleasant feelings? Or is the bulimic patient unable to control her impulsive behaviour in general? The answer to such questions will determine which specific treatment strategy has to be chosen in a particular case. The presence of a borderline PD in a bulimic patient may demand specific attention for impulsive behaviour in treatment, whereas for bulimic patients with an avoidant PD it may be necessary also to focus on avoidance behaviour. The same questions have to be addressed in the assessment and treatment planning of patients with personality disorders and concurrent substance use disorders. For a detailed discussion of these issues see Emmelkamp and Vedel (2006).

Effects of personality disorders on treatment of Axis-I disorders

In clinical practice it is often assumed that patients with comorbid personality pathology benefit less from treatment targeting Axis-I disorders than patients without additional personality pathology, but what is the evidence to support this clinical lore? Most studies into the effects of personality disorders have involved anxious, depressed, or substance abusing patients. Therefore, we will limit the discussion to these disorders.

Anxiety disorders

Comorbid personality disorders are common in patients with anxiety disorders, the avoidant and dependent PDs being most frequently found (van Velzen & Emmelkamp, 1999). Although there is some evidence that some personality traits are associated with poorer outcome (Mennin & Heimberg, 2000; van Velzen & Emmelkamp, 1996), there is no evidence that the presence of personality disorders per se results in poorer outcome when personality disorder diagnosis is formally established with a structured interview (Dreessen & Arntz, 1998; Dreessen, Arntz, Hendriks, Keune, & van den Hout, 1999; van Velzen, Emmelkamp, & Scholing, 1997; Weertman, Arntz, Schouten, & Dreessen, 2005). Further, the negative effects of personality disorders on outcome are more pronounced in pharmacotherapy studies than in cognitive-behavioural therapy (CBT) studies.

Depression

Recently, a meta-analysis (Newton-Howes, Tyrer, & Johnson, 2006) was published on the effects of personality disorders on the outcome of psychological treatments of depression. Comorbid personality disorder with depression was associated with a doubling of the risk for poor outcome in depression compared to depressed patients without personality disorder. These findings suggest that the treatment of depression with psychotherapy may be less effective among patients with personality disorder.

There is some evidence that the effects on treatment outcome of personality disorders differ between different psychotherapies. In the National Institute of Mental Health (NIMH) Treatment of Depression Collaborative Research Program, concurrent personality disorders hardly affected the outcome of cognitive therapy, but a more pronounced effect was observed for the treatment outcome of interpersonal psychotherapy (Shea et al., 1990). A recent study using interpersonal psychotherapy (IPT) as maintenance treatment for women with depression supported this conclusion; higher rates of recurrence and more rapid relapse in a subgroup with personality disorder (Cyranowski et al., 2004).

Whether personality disorders affect the outcome of *pharmacotherapy* in depression is still a matter of debate. Earlier review articles concluded that concurrent personality pathology was associated with significantly worse outcome in social functioning and poorer treatment response (Ilardi & Craighead, 1995; Reich & Green, 1991; Shea, Widiger, & Klein, 1992). More recent reviews, however, concluded that the best-designed studies reported the least effect of personality pathology on treatment outcome of depression (Kool et al., 2005; Mulder, 2002). In the meta-analysis of Newton-Howes et al. (2006) the negative effects of personality disorder on treatment outcome of pharmacotherapy in depressed individuals were less pronounced than on psychotherapy outcome. One of the reasons that outcome of pharmacotherapy is less negatively affected by personality pathology is presumably due to the direct effects of newer medications on personality pathology (e.g., Fava et al., 2002). Another reason, which may account for the discrepant findings between earlier studies and more recent studies, may be that earlier reviews relied heavily on uncontrolled naturalistic studies. In routine clinical care, patients with comorbid personality pathology may be less likely to receive adequate drug therapy for their depression. This hypothesis is supported by results of a meta-analysis by Kool et al. (2005), who found that pharmacotherapy conducted in the context of a randomized clinical trial (RCT) design, in which treatment is controlled and carefully protocolized, yields better results than more naturalistic designs.

Substance use disorders

Research into the effects of personality disorders on treatment outcome among patients with substance use disorder was reviewed by Verheul, van den Bosch, and Ball (2005). These authors concluded that patients with personality pathology benefit from treatment for the substance abuse and dependence. Verheul et al. did not specifically address the impact of antisocial PD on treatment outcome. Looking more specifically at studies into the effects of treatment of people with antisocial PD, there is less reason for optimism (see Emmelkamp & Vedel, 2006). Some studies suggest that individuals with antisocial PD do not benefit from substance abuse treatment involving pharmacotherapy (e.g., Leal, Ziedonis, & Kosten, 1994) or treatment in the context of a therapeutic community (Messina, Wish, & Nemes, 1999). Other studies also reported worse outcome for substance-dependent patients with antisocial PD with a variety of treatments (Compton, Cottler, Jacobs, Ben-Abdallah, & Spitznagel, 2003; Galen, Brower, Gillespie, & Zucker, 2000; Havens & Strathdee, 2005; Westermeyer & Thuras, 2005). Only a few studies found psychological treatment to be effective for alcohol-dependent individuals (Kalman, Longabaugh, Clifford, Beattie, & Maisto, 2000) and cocaine-dependent individuals (McKay,

Alterman, Cacciola, Mulvaney, & O'Brien, 2000), irrespective of antisocial PD. Whether the limited effects of substance abuse treatment may be primarily ascribed to psychopathic features rather than to antisocial features per se, as suggested by Taylor and Lang (2005), deserves to be studied.

Concluding remarks

Taken together, a complex picture emerges. Studies that investigated whether one or more personality disorder categories were associated with treatment outcome have led to conflicting results. Definite conclusions are not yet warranted given a number of methodological problems in most of the studies discussed.

First, most studies into the effects of personality disorders on treatment outcome of Axis-I disorders are difficult to interpret because personality disorders were often assessed in patients who were treated in comparative therapy outcome studies, which means that patients in such studies are treated by different treatment methods. As suggested elsewhere (van Velzen & Emmelkamp, 1996) personality disorders may affect the outcome of different treatments in different ways. For example, a specific personality disorder (e.g., avoidant PD) may have a negative effect on behavioural procedures, whereas the effects of the same personality disorder on the outcome of cognitive therapy may be negligible because this treatment, in dealing with cognitive processes, may indirectly also deal with the personality problem. That personality disorders may specifically affect the outcome of different treatments is illustrated in the NIMH study on depression (Shea at al., 1990) discussed above and in a study by Tyrer, Seivewright, Ferguson, Murphy, and Johnson (1993). In the Tyrer et al. study, cognitive and behavioural therapy were found to be more effective in patients without a personality disorder, whereas pharmacotherapy (primarily antidepressants) was found to be equally effective among patients with or without personality disorders.

Further, most studies on the impact of personality pathology on the outcome of treatment did not take into account the severity of personality disorders. In a study that did take into account severity, there was a clear negative influence of personality disorders on treatment outcome (Seivewright, Tyrer, & Johnson, 2004).

Another issue that needs to be addressed is whether personality disorders affect the long-term outcome of treatment of Axis-I disorders, given that the current evidence is limited to short-term effects. As noted by Verheul et al. in the context of substance abuse treatment for individuals with personality disorders: "they often only improve to a level of problem severity that leaves them at considerable risk for relapse" (2005, p. 473). In personality disordered patients, one would expect a greater vulnerability to relapse, a hypothesis that needs further empirical testing.

Finally, when studies reveal that personality disorders negatively influence treatment outcome for Axis-I disorders, it should be noted that no clear evidence for a *causal* role of personality disorder has been established. Most studies simply demonstrate that patients with personality disorder do worse than patients without personality disorder. This does not establish that the presence or absence of personality disorder was the critical factor. Patients with personality disorder, compared to those without a personality disorder, differ on a range of other variables (e.g., severity or duration of the presenting Axis-I disorder). Any of these other variables might be the critical elements influencing treatment outcome.

Summary

Personality disorders are highly prevalent in community studies, estimates ranging from 4.4% to 13%. Obsessive-compulsive PD is the most prevalent; narcissistic disorder is the least prevalent. Longitudinal studies show that in a number of patients the symptoms become less over time. Impairment associated with specific personality disorders varies from mild (obsessive-compulsive PD) to severe (borderline PD). Cultural and gender differences have been found to be related to various personality disorders, but how to interpret these differences is not fully understood yet. There is a high level of comorbidity among the various personality disorders and between personality disorders and mental disorders. A variety of conceptual models have been advanced regarding the associations of specific types of personality disorders with Axis-I disorders, which may have heuristic value for treatment planning. Finally, studies that investigated whether one or more personality disorder categories were associated with treatment outcome have led to conflicting results.

Biological and psychological theories 4

> It is an irony of our times that psychodynamic approaches are disappearing from the academic and therapeutic landscapes just as empirical research has begun to corroborate some of their most important postulates, for example, about the ubiquity of unconscious processes, including implicit affective and motivational processes (and) the importance of early attachment relationships for subsequent development and psychopathology ...
>
> (Bradley & Westen, 2005, p. 927)

Over the past 15 years, the aetiology and developmental psychopathology of personality disorder has received increased attention. While earlier theories, primarily based on clinical observations, stressed the psychosocial origins of personality disorders, more recent research has suggested that genetic, biological, and environmental factors may all play important contributory roles in the development of personality disorder, with each variable on its own accounting for small to moderate outcome variance. Because personality disorders often start during early adolescence, there is a clear need for prospective longitudinal studies to investigate risk factors that contribute to the development of personality disorder, but few longitudinal studies have been conducted so far.

A number of questions will be addressed in this chapter. What are the early precursors to personality disorders? This question is not only of theoretical interest but also has implications for preventive efforts. If prodromal signs (changes in behaviour that occur prior to the onset of a disorder) can be identified in childhood or early adolescence perhaps we might be able to prevent high-risk cases from becoming individuals with full-blown personality disorder. Research has specifically focused on the role of attachment and child abuse, maltreatment, and (early) trauma. Further, are there genetic influences involved and, if so, how do possible genetic predispositions to personality disorders become realized? Other questions addressed are whether there are neurobiological features associated with personality disorder and how developmental and environmental experiences (e.g., trauma) influence the neurobiological features. In our view, an adequate explanation will require approaches that simultaneously examine environmental, biological, genetic, and temperamental variables, which has not been achieved yet.

Genetic contribution

In the last decade the traditional assumption that nurture or environment are primarily responsible for the development of personality disorders has been challenged. Studies into environmental influences as aetiological agents of personality disorders have been criticized by not taking into account the potential role played by genes. For example, although it may be tempting to assume that aggressive and abusive behaviour in adult victims of child abuse is caused by these traumatic experiences in childhood, the evidence is correlational at best, which does not rule out other explanations such as genetic factors or gene–environment interaction. To complicate matters, it is becoming increasingly clear that parents' personality traits, which are heritable, affect the environments they provide for their children. For example, in a Swedish adoption twin study pairs of adult monozygotic twins (identical twins developed from one egg) reared apart were assessed with respect to their own parenting styles. Results revealed that 25% of the variation in parenting was genetically determined (Plomin, McClearn, Pederson, Nesselroade, & Bergeman, 1989).

Behavioural-genetic studies may forward the investigation of personality disorders from risk-factor research to understanding causal relationships. Behavioural genetics attempts to unravel genetic from nongenetic aspects of familial transmission of personality and personality disorders. Given that the genes specifically involved in personality disorders are as yet unknown, data from monozygotic (MZ) and dizygotic (DZ) twin pairs have been used to study the relationship between environmental and genetic risk factors with respect to personality traits and personality disorders. Contrasting the similarity of MZ and DZ twins provides a means of estimating the influence of genetic contributions on phenotypes; if genetic factors influence a phenotype, then MZ twins would be more similar than

DZ twins. It is generally assumed that a child's genetic risk for a specific personality trait or personality disorder is high if his or her MZ co-twin is characterized by this trait or has the disorder and low if his or her MZ co-twin is not characterized by this trait or does not have the disorder. The degree of genetic influence can be expressed in a statistic known as heritability. This "heritability" statistic reflects a percentage of the total variation in the phenotype.

Personality traits

Research has revealed that genetic factors significantly contribute to the determination of human personality traits although environmental influence is also important. Personality traits assessed by self-report questionnaires show moderate heritability (e.g., Bouchard, Lykken, McGue, Segal, & Tellegen, 1990; Eaves et al., 1999; Keller, Coventry, Heath, & Martin, 2005; Lykken, 2006), but it is less clear which specific genes or interaction between specific genes are involved (Kusumi et al., 2005).

In addition to research on the heritability of the Big Five personality dimensions Neuroticism, Extraversion, and Agreeableness, which consistently have been found to be related to personality disorders, another line of research has focused on the heritability of Impulsivity. This personality trait is characterized by response inhibition failure, reduced information processing, and intolerance to the delay of reward. Impulsivity has been associated with borderline and antisocial personality disorders. Impulsive aggression may be directed to others but may also be directed towards the subject himself or herself as in self-injurious or suicidal behaviour. Presumably, dysfunctions of such inhibitory processes in impulsive personalities may be accounted for by both environmental and genetic variables. In twin studies, a higher concordance in impulsivity has been found in monozygotic twins than in dizygotic twins (Coccaro, Bergeman, & McClearn, 1993), thus suggesting moderate heritability of impulsivity. Studies conducted on subjects with aggressive behaviour found impulsivity to be related to diminished levels of serotonin (e.g., Passamonti et al., 2006). Genetic variants of the monoamine oxidase A (MAO-A) have also been associated with impulsive-aggression-related personality traits in several studies. In a study by Jacob et al. (2005) MAO-A genotype was significantly associated with Cluster B personality disorders, but not with Cluster C personality disorders.

The dramatic personality disorders (Cluster B)

Torgersen et al. (2000) used structural equation modelling to estimate the heritability of personality disorders. Data were based on the Structured Clinical Interview for DSM-III-R Personality Disorders (SCID-II) of monozygotic and dizygotic twin pairs. The best-fitting models yielded a heritability of .79 for narcissistic, .69 for borderline and .67 for histrionic PDs, respectively. The low occurrence of anti-social PD in the twin sample precluded any model for this disorder. As concluded by the authors, PDs seem to be more strongly influenced by genetic effects than almost any Axis-I disorder, and more than personality traits.

Borderline PD. Several studies also yielded evidence for a genetic contribution to borderline PD. Results of family studies suggest a familial relationship: probands of patients with borderline PD are at higher risk of borderline pathology than controls (White, Gunderson, & Zanarini, 2003). In a twin study of personality disorders in Norway, Torgersen et al. (2000) found a 35% concordance rate between monozygotic twins and the diagnosis of borderline PD, which was significantly higher than the concordance rate (7%) for dizygotic twins and the diagnosis of borderline PD, suggesting a significant genetic role in the aetiology of borderline PD. Further, family aggregation studies suggest a genetic basis for borderline PD as a diagnosis, but the heritability for dimensions such as impulsivity and affective instability is presumably greater than for the diagnostic criteria (Siever, Torgersen, Gunderson, Livesley, & Kendler, 2002). More than likely, genes do not act directly on personality disorders, but indirectly. Some genotypes may increase children's sensitivity to environmental adversities such as physical maltreatment, whereas other genotypes may promote children's resistance to trauma (Moffitt, 2005).

Antisocial PD. Conduct disorder is also influenced by genetic factors (e.g., Slutske et al., 1998). Adoption studies have shown that aggression emerges in children despite the fact that they were separated from their at-risk biological parents at birth and reared by "normal" adoptive parents (Moffitt, 2005). Further, twin studies have shown that genetic factors influence antisocial behaviour in childhood (Arseneault et al., 2003; van den Oord, Verhulst, & Boomsma, 1996). This genetic influence on antisocial behaviour increases from childhood through to adulthood (Lyons et al., 1995). Early onset conduct disorder has a stronger genetic link than does adolescent onset of conduct disorder (Eaves et al., 1997; Taylor, Iacono, & McGue, 2000).

Although many twin and adoption studies have been published, it is difficult to estimate the magnitude of genetic and environmental influences. In an attempt to integrate the existing literature, Waldman and Hyun Rhee (2005) conducted a meta-analysis and concluded that genes accounted for slightly less variance than shared and nonshared environmental influences. As far as psychopathic traits were concerned, however, the meta-analysis revealed a substantially higher heritability factor, thus raising the possibility that psychopathic features mediate part of the genetic influences on the development of antisocial PD. Viding, Blair, Moffitt, and Plomin (2005) examined the heritability of the core psychopathic feature "callous and unemotional tendencies" in 3500 twin pairs within the Twins Early Development Study. The results revealed that this feature is more strongly heritable than overt antisocial behaviour. Early warning signs of lifelong psychopathy, callous-unemotional traits and high levels of antisocial behaviour, were identified in children at the end of the first school year. Dividing children with antisocial behaviour into those with high and low levels of callous-unemotional traits showed striking results. In children with both high levels of antisocial behaviour and high levels of callous-unemotional traits they found an extremely strong heritability and no influence of shared environment, whereas in children who were only antisocial and showed no signs of callous-unemotional traits shared environmental influences were more important; in this group of children they found only a modest contribution of heritability.

There is emerging evidence of gene–environment interaction effects on antisocial behaviour. Button, Scourfield, Martin, Purcell, and McGuffin (2005) investigated the interaction of genes and family dysfunction in contributing to conduct problems in children and adolescents. Both main and gene–environment interaction effects were highly significant. The authors suggest that it is highly likely that a risk genotype conferring susceptibility to family dysfunction is responsible for most of the variance in antisocial symptoms in youngsters.

Twin studies show substantial genetic overlap among "externalizing disorders", including conduct disorder, adult antisocial behaviour, and alcohol and drug dependence, suggesting that most familial resemblance for externalizing disorders is due to a highly heritable *general* vulnerability, rather than a disorder-specific vulnerability.

Further, large epidemiological studies consistently show a broad dimension of risk underlying the comorbidity of conduct disorder, antisocial personality disorder, and substance dependence (e.g., Vollebergh et al., 2001). Results from recent twin studies (e.g., Hicks, Krueger, Iacono, McGue, & Patrick, 2004; Kendler et al., 2003) reveal that the source of the comorbidity in these syndromes can be attributed to common genetic factors. However, exactly what is inherited, and how the disorders are transmitted, is unclear. As suggested by Hicks et al. (2004), the results of the studies so far indicate that genetic factors influence a broad behavioural system or psychopathological process characterized by behavioural undercontrol that underlies all the disorders in the externalizing spectrum.

Studies into the molecular genetics in antisocial PD are just taking off. One study found monoamine oxidase A (MAO-A) polymorphism related to antisocial behaviour in the presence of childhood maltreatment (Caspi et al., 2002). Generally, however, the results with respect to studies into specific genes involved in antisocial behaviour are as yet inconclusive (Moffitt, 2005).

Cluster A personality disorders

There is also some evidence for a genetic contribution to Cluster A personality disorders, although the heritability is estimated to be slightly less than for Cluster B disorders. Torgersen et al. (2000) estimated the heritability of Cluster A personality disorder as .37. Increasing evidence from family and adoption studies suggests a familial association between schizophrenia and Cluster A personality disorders (i.e., schizotypal, schizoid, and paranoid PDs). An early study reported that schizotypal PD is common in relatives of probands with schizophrenia (15%) (Baron, Gruen, & Rainer, 1985). This has been confirmed in more recent studies, although the prevalence figures reported are lower. Studies on first-degree relatives of schizophrenic patients found that first-degree relatives had a significantly higher rate of Cluster A personality disorder than community controls (see Shih, Belmonte, & Zandi, 2004).

In the study by Torgersen et al. (2000), the best-fitting model had a heritability of .61 for schizotypal, .29 for schizoid, and .28 for paranoid PDs. Another study of this group (Torgersen et al., 2002) investigated whether schizotypal PD within the genetic spectrum of schizophrenia could be differentiated from schizotypal PD outside the genetic spectrum of schizophrenia. Schizotypals with and without schizophrenic co-twins and first-degree relatives were compared with controls. Odd communication, inadequate rapport, social isolation, and delusions and hallucinations appeared to be the genetic core of schizotypy as it is related to schizophrenia. Schizotypals outside the schizophrenic spectrum, however, scored higher than schizotypals inside the schizophrenic spectrum on ideas of reference, suspiciousness, paranoia, social anxiety, self-damaging acts, chronic anger, free-floating anxiety, and sensitivity to rejection. Torgersen et al. (2002) conclude that psychotic-like schizotypal features and a number of "borderline traits", especially affective, anxious, aggressive, self-destructive, and "neurotic" sensitive features, indicate a nonschizophrenic schizotypal disorder.

Further evidence for genetic influence on schizotypal PD comes from the Finnish Adoptive Family Study of Schizophrenia. This study revealed that in adoptees whose mothers had schizophrenia there was an enhanced risk of schizophrenia spectrum disorder: schizotypal PD was found significantly more often in high-risk than in low-risk adoptees (Tienari et al., 2003). Finally, Coolidge, Thede, and Jang (2001, 2004) found high heritability of Cluster A traits in a twin study. The heritability coefficient decreased from schizotypal traits (.81) and schizoid traits (.73) to paranoid traits (.50).

Anxiety-related personality disorders (Cluster C)

There have been few studies of the genetics of Cluster C personality disorders. There is some evidence of a general genetic basis of anxiety-related traits, given that avoidant and dependent personality traits were more common in first degree relatives of patients with panic disorder as compared to controls (Reich, 1991). There is only "circumstantial evidence" for a genetic basis of avoidant personality disorder. The key feature of avoidant personality disorder is a pervasive pattern of social inhibition, feeling of inadequacy, and hypersensitivity to negative evaluation. Given the high comorbidity between social phobia and avoidant PD (e.g., van Velzen & Emmelkamp, 1999), social phobia and avoidant PD are considered to lie on a continuum, with specific social phobia at the mild end and avoidant PD at the severe end (see Chapter 6). There is some evidence for a genetic basis of behavioural inhibition in childhood, which may be considered a precursor of social anxiety in adolescence and – in more severe cases – avoidant PD in adulthood (Emmelkamp & Scholing, 1997). In the study of Torgersen et al. (2000) the best-fitting models yielded heritabilities of .62 for the fearful cluster, .78 for obsessive-compulsive PD, .57 for dependent PD, and .28 for avoidant PD.

A few molecular genetic studies have been reported, investigating candidate genes for personality disorders from the anxious cluster. Joyce, Rogers, et al. (2003) found that the family of dopamine receptors (DRD4 and DRD3) was related to avoidant and obsessive-compulsive traits. Given that this sample was depressed when evaluated and differential gene effects may be operative in distinct normal and clinical populations, a replication is needed in non-depressed samples before conclusions can be drawn. Another study failed to demonstrate a general association between the serotonergic system (allelic variation in 5-HT function) and anxiety-related traits in patients with personality disorders (Jacob et al., 2004).

Concluding remarks

Although behavioural genetic studies have demonstrated a small to strong heritability component in personality disorders, they provide little information on the nature of what is inherited. Molecular genetic studies are emerging, but the evidence to date does not support the view that specific genes are related to specific personality disorders. Presumably, multiple genes are involved in each personality disorder, some of which will overlap with other personality disorders and/or Axis-I disorders. In order to understand the interplay between genes and environment in personality traits and personality disorders, multivariate genetic studies are needed that take into account the genetic and environmental factors and gene–environment interaction.

Cloninger's biosocial theory of personality

In his Unified Biosocial Theory of Personality, Robert Cloninger (1987) posited three temperament dimensions, which are presumed to be genetically independent: harm avoidance, novelty seeking, and reward dependence. The three temperament dimensions are defined in terms of individual differences in behavioural learning mechanisms, explaining responses to novelty, danger, or punishment and cues for reward, avoiding aversive stimuli, and reactions to rewards. Harm avoidance is the tendency to inhibit responses to signals of aversive stimuli that lead to avoidance of punishment and nonreward and is related to behavioural inhibition. Individuals high on harm avoidance are assumed to be particularly reactive to unpleasant stimuli. Novelty seeking is related to behavioural activation and is described as the tendency to respond actively to novel stimuli leading to pursuit of rewards and escape from punishment. Individuals high on novelty seeking are expected to be more sensitive to pleasant stimuli. Finally, reward dependence is the tendency for a positive response to conditioned signals of reward that maintain behaviour. These three temperament dimensions are held to be associated with the activity of one of the three major monoamine neurotransmitter systems in the brain. Harm avoidance is posited to be mediated by serotonergic neurotransmission, novelty seeking by dopaminergic activity, and reward dependence is said to be mediated by noradrenergic activity.

Unfortunately, the three temperament dimensions were not specifically related to the personality disorders, which led to a revised model. In this revised biosocial model of personality, Cloninger, Svrakic, and Przybeck (1993) distinguish seven domains of personality, which are either *innate temperaments* or *acquired characters*. Cloninger et al. assume that character is less heritable than temperament and matures with age. Cloninger et al. (1993) added a fourth temperament domain, persistence, which is defined as perseverance despite frustration and fatigue. In addition, three character domains were added (self-directedness, cooperativeness, and self-transcendence). Self-directedness measures individual self-acceptance and adaptation of behaviour to the requirements of a situation, cooperativeness measures acceptance of other persons, while self-transcendence reflects the degree to which someone feels a part of nature and the universe at large and is associated with spirituality. In Cloninger's view, the temperament and character domains, although distinct, interact with each other in shaping behaviour. The character dimensions of self-directedness and cooperativeness have been found to be strongly linked to the presence of personality symptoms, while the temperament dimensions were more sensitive in differentiating among the various personality disorders: individuals with Cluster A disorders are primarily characterized by low reward dependence, individuals with Cluster B disorders by novelty seeking, and individuals with Cluster C disorders by harm avoidance (Svrakic, Whitehead, Przybeck, & Cloninger, 1993). More recently, Cloninger (2000) defined personality disorders by low scores on self-directedness, cooperativeness, and self-transcendence. In addition, to qualify for a personality disorder, the individual should be characterized by low affective stability.

The Temperament and Character Inventory (TCI) was developed with the goal of assessing the seven factors of the psychobiological model of personality. The TCI is a 240-item true/false questionnaire measuring the four dimensions of temperament and the three dimensions of character; 25 facets are also measured as subscales of the seven main TCI dimensions. There is a considerable body of research attesting to its stability (test–retest) and construct validity. Factor analytic studies have supported Cloninger's revised seven-factor model of personality (e.g., Hansenne, Delhez, & Cloninger, 2005; Miettunen et al., 2004; Pelissolo et al., 2005), although it has been suggested that a five-factor solution, in which harm avoidance is combined with low self-directedness and reward dependence is combined with cooperativeness, may be a better psychometric solution (Herbst, Zonderman, McCrae, & Costa, 2000). As noted by Herbst et al. (2000), if the subscales of the TCI share some genetic basis, they should covary to define a common factor. Based on this criterion, there is some evidence for a common genetic basis for harm avoidance, but neither for novelty seeking nor for reward dependence.

Although it has been claimed that the model of Cloninger et al. (1993) as assessed with the TCI is superior to the Big-Five personality dimensions (Costa & McCrae, 1992a) as assessed with the NEO-PI-R in terms of describing personality disorder differences, the results so far are far from conclusive (Saulsman & Page, 2004). For example, the presumed greater descriptive specificity of the TCI traits could not be demonstrated in a recent study of de Fruyt, DeClercq, van de Wiele, and van Heeringen (2006); neither of the models did better in explaining personality symptomatology at the higher order level. Actually, at the level of the lower order traits, the NEO-PI-R predicted more personality disorders than the TCI.

The most interesting aspect of Cloninger et al.'s (1993) model of personality dimensions is the proposed relationship with genetically determined activity in monoamine neurotransmission in the brain. Further research is needed, however, to support this biological orientation of Cloninger's personality model (e.g., Herbst et al., 2000). According to these authors, there is no evidence of a "simple genetic architecture", as Cloninger and colleagues claimed. They base this conclusion on molecular genetics and factor analysis of the TCI. In a twin study, multivariate genetic analyses showed that several subscales used to define one dimension shared a common genetic basis with subscales defining others (Ando et al., 2004), thus also not supporting Cloninger's model. Further, molecular genetic studies have found some support for a link between the dopaminergic system and novelty seeking and between the serotonergic system and harm avoidance, but the results are far from conclusive (Ebstein, 2006; Paris, 2005b; Savitz & Ramesar, 2004).

Neurobiology

As argued by Depue and Lenzenweger (2001) and many others, personality disorders may be considered a maladaptive expression of normal personality traits. In this view personality disorders are understood as fluid, multidimensional entities, produced by a mixing of personality traits on neurobehavioural dimensions existing in the domain of normal personality. Most of the studies into the neurobiology of personality disorders have focused on borderline PD. Fewer studies have investigated antisocial and schizotypal PDs. The neurobiology of anxious personality disorders has hardly been addressed in empirical studies.

Borderline personality disorder

In the past two decades accumulating evidence from serotonergic (5-HT) system challenge studies have implicated hypofunctioning of the serotonergic system in the pathophysiology of borderline PD and characteristics associated with borderline PD, including impulsivity, self-mutilation, and affective instability (see Resnick, Goodman, New, & Siever, 2005). Of the many neurochemical factors, which may play a role in the pathophysiology of borderline traits, the evidence for involvement of the 5-HT system is most robust.

Another line of research has studied whether psychosocial events may result in persisting biological alterations in the brain. For example, different forms of maltreatment during childhood have been found to promote adaptations in particular brain structures as well as elevated neurotransmitter levels that persist into adulthood (Glaser, 2000). There is some evidence that early childhood trauma may lead to a chronic sensitization of the hypothalamic-pituitary-adrenal (HPA) axis, which may be related to hypersecretion of corticotrophin releasing factor (CRF) (Heim & Nemeroff, 2002; Stein, Yehuda, Koverola, & Hanna, 1997). Frequent increases in cortisol over the course of time may affect the 5-HT system by blunting serotonergic activity, thereby linking chronic exposure to stress to borderline PD through biological mediators (e.g., HPA and 5-HT systems). Rinne et al. (2002) found in patients with borderline PD that a history of childhood abuse is associated with hyperresponsiveness of ACTH (adrenocorticotrophic hormone) release. Because the HPA axis is linked with serotonergic function, these studies provide some support for using serotonin reuptake inhibitors in patients with borderline PD. Impulsivity and suicidal behaviour, which are often related to borderline PD, are both associated with indices of diminished central serotonergic function (Putnam & Silk, 2005).

Neuroimaging. Neuroimaging studies provide insight into anatomical and functional alterations in the brain. The results of neuroimaging research in borderline PD suggest that a hallmark of the disorder is general dysfunction of the frontal and limbic circuitry. This fronto-limbic network consists of anterior cingulate cortex, orbitofrontal and dorsolateral prefrontal cortex, hippocampus, and amygdala (see Baird, Veague, & Rabbit, 2005, and Schmahl & Bremner, 2005, for reviews of research in this area). The results of structural imaging studies show smaller hippocampal as well as reduced amygdala volumes in (female) patients with borderline PD. These range from a 13 to 21% reduction in the hippocampus and an 8 to 25% reduction in the amygdala. Reduced hippocampal volume (but not reduced amygdala volume) has also been found in patients with post-traumatic stress disorder. Whether the differences in hippocampal volume are a relatively generic risk factor for psychopathology, or the result of stressful and traumatic events, is not clear yet.

In sum, although in patients with borderline personality disorder structural changes in the amygdala may enhance vigilance and threat perception, this may also be the other way around. As a result of the frontal deficits, however, patients with borderline PD are unable to correctly evaluate such reactions and to cope adequately with them (Baird et al., 2005).

Antisocial personality disorder and psychopathy

Studies into the neurobiological underpinnings of antisocial PD and psychopathy are currently inconclusive. Studies by Soderstrom and colleagues found serotonergic abnormalities in individuals with psychopathy (e.g., Soderstrom, Blennow, Sjodin, & Forsman, 2003), but this was not confirmed in other studies with more representative samples (e.g., Dolan & Anderson, 2003). Although an association between reduced serotonergic response and increased levels of aggression was found, this was not found to be related to the affective-interpersonal core features of psychopathy. In addition, there have been a series of reports that high levels of antisocial conduct/conduct disorder are associated with reduced norepinephrine levels. Others have suggested that the norepinephrine system may be involved in psychopathy (Blair, Peschardt, Budhani, Mitchell, & Pine, 2006).

Another line of research has studied whether frontal brain lesions are implicated in antisocial PD. Damage to the frontal lobe appears to be associated with some symptoms and cognitive impairments that may also be found in individuals with antisocial PD. The most notable neurological case study is that of the railroad worker Phineas Gage, whose case was described by Harlow in 1848 (cited in Damasio, Grabowski, Frank, Galaburda, & Damasio, 1994). After a trauma to the prefrontal cortex, Gage changed from a responsible railroad manager to an impulsive, irresponsible, sexually promiscuous, verbally abusive person, a typical case of what we now would classify as antisocial PD. A number of studies found reduced frontal lobe functioning to be associated with aggression and antisocial behaviour (see Raine, 2002). Studies of patients with prefrontal lobe damage suggest that the orbital frontal cortex plays a role in mediating some behaviours related to antisocial PD. Damage to the orbital frontal cortex leads to a condition termed "acquired sociopathic personality" characterized by problems with reactive aggression, motivation, empathy, planning and organization, impulsivity, irresponsibility, insight, and behavioural inhibition (Kiehl, 2006). Finally, dysfunctioning of the orbital frontal cortex is also reflected in impaired performance on neuropsychological measures of executive functioning in individuals with antisocial PD (Morgan & Lilienfeld, 2000).

Neuroimaging. There are fewer neuroimaging studies of people with antisocial PD. Research so far found reductions in the temporal lobe (particularly the amygdala), but results with respect to reductions in the frontal lobes are inconclusive as yet (Barkataki, Kumari, Das, Taylor, & Sharma, 2006). Recently, Kiehl (2006) has suggested that psychopathy is associated with the paralimbic system. Indirect evidence in favour of this hypothesis is provided by studies of behavioural and cognitive deficits associated with brain damage. These studies suggest that in addition to the orbital frontal cortex, anterior insula, and anterior cingulate of the frontal lobe, the amygdala and adjacent regions of the anterior temporal lobe are also implicated in psychopathic symptomatology. This hypothesis is further supported by recent cognitive neuroscience studies in psychopathy (Blair et al., 2006; Kiehl, 2006; Laakso et al., 2002).

Schizotypal personality disorder

Many brain imaging studies have been conducted with schizophrenic patients, but only a few with patients with schizotypal PD or with subjects who score high on schizotypy. The cingulate gyrus, which is part of the limbic cortex, and is involved in affect, attention, memory, and higher executive functions, has been implicated as a dysfunctional region in schizophrenia. A recent neuroimaging study (Takahashi et al., 2006) confirms an abnormality in the cingulate gyrus in schizophrenia, with schizotypal PD patients demonstrating a pattern lying in between schizophrenic patients and normal subjects. In other studies schizotypy was associated with decreased grey matter concentration in key areas of the cortex, particularly the prefrontal and temporal cortices (Diwadkar, Montrose, Dworakowski, Sweeney, & Keshavan, 2006). Finally, the results of a recent study suggest altered frontotemporal connectivity, corroborating findings in schizophrenia, and intact neocortical-limbic connectivity, which is typically altered in schizophrenia (Nakamura et al., 2005).

Thus, several neuroimaging studies show similarities between schizotypal PD and schizophrenia, suggesting a common predisposition toward neurodevelopmental aberrations. The fact that there is only some overlap between neuroimaging findings in schizotypal PD and schizophrenia suggests that schizotypal PD might be a milder presentation of pathology (Nakamura et al., 2005).

Nutritional deficiencies

Finally, there is some evidence that nutritional deficiencies may enhance the risk of schizoid and antisocial PD. A series of studies in the Netherlands was conducted among male adolescents who were born after the hunger winter at the end of the Second World War. The clear demarcation of the famine in time and place provided a key to identifying exposed males. Any individual could be classed in the group exposed to famine during a specific period in gestation if he or she was born within a given calendar period in the famine-stricken areas. Results of these studies revealed that the risk for schizoid PD (Hoek et al., 1996) and antisocial PD (Neugebauer, Hoek, & Susser, 1999) doubled compared to subjects who had not been exposed to famine during the hunger winter. Results are interpreted in terms of famine causing neurodevelopmental deficits associated with the development of these personality disorders.

Child abuse and maltreatment

Environmental factors significantly contribute to the development of personality disorders and may modify the expression of genetically inherited personality traits. Among the environmental factors contributing to the aetiology of personality disorders, child abuse and maltreatment have been afforded prominence. Although other factors (e.g., peer influences) may also be important, these factors have hardly been studied. Maltreatment is commonly understood to include physical, emotional, and sexual abuse as well as parental neglect. Among the behavioural consequences of such experiences are increased rates of antisocial behaviour, substance abuse, depression, and poor academic performance. Traumatic childhood experiences such as abuse and neglect have also been investigated as potential risk factors for the development of personality disorders. There is considerable evidence that child physical abuse, sexual abuse, and neglect are related to personality disorders (e.g., Bradley, Jenei, & Westen, 2005; Johnson et al., 2001, 2002; Joyce, McKenzie, et al., 2003; Rogosch & Cicchetti, 2005; Silverman, Reinherz, & Giaconia, 1996). Most evidence is available with respect to borderline PD. A number of studies found that patients with borderline PD reported higher rates of child maltreatment, including sexual abuse, than either patients with other personality disorders or patients with Axis-I disorders (e.g., Battle et al., 2004; Johnson, Smailes, et al., 2000; Rogosch & Cicchetti, 2005). In the Collaborative Longitudinal Personality Disorders Study, patients with schizotypal PD and borderline PD reported more sexual traumas, including childhood sexual abuse and higher rates of being physically attacked, compared to patients with avoidant PD and obsessive-compulsive PD (Yen et al., 2002). Dependent PD was not associated with childhood abuse, nor with parental neglect when controlled for the presence of other PDs (Johnson, Smailes, Cohen, Brown, & Bernstein, 2000).

Whether early trauma is a cause or a symptom of borderline PD can not be concluded on the basis of these studies. An alternative explanation could be that a person who has borderline PD may be more likely to interpret or remember events as traumatic. Although some (e.g., Herman, Perry, & van der Kolk, 1989) have suggested that childhood sexual abuse is highly frequent among patients with borderline pathology and the most important contributory factor to its aetiology, results of a meta-analysis did not support this contention (Fossati, Madeddu, & Maffei, 1999). In this meta-analysis on studies published between 1980 and 1995, including about 2500 cases, childhood sexual abuse only explained a small part (8%) of the borderline pathology.

Most studies in this area were retrospective or cross-sectional, which limits the conclusions to be drawn. To address the limitations inherent in retrospective research, longitudinal studies have been conducted. Results of these longitudinal studies suggest that childhood abuse and neglect may be associated with a variety of personality disorders (Drake, Adler, & Vaillant, 1988; Johnson, Cohen, Brown, Smailes, & Bernstein, 1999; Johnson et al., 2001; Luntz & Widom, 1994). In the community study of Johnson et al. (2001) individuals who had been maltreated or abused were three times more likely to develop a personality disorder as compared to children who had not been abused or maltreated. A major consequence of maltreatment in early childhood is antisocial behaviour, but not all maltreated children develop conduct problems or antisocial PD in adulthood (Lansford et al., 2002). Presumably, antisocial behaviour problems emerge when genetically vulnerable children encounter family environments in which they are maltreated (Moffitt, 2005). Whether such gene–environment interaction also plays a role in the association of maltreatment and other personality disorders (e.g., borderline PD) has not yet been investigated.

Although a number of retrospective and prospective studies have shown that child abuse is a risk factor for the development of personality disorders, relatively few studies have addressed the question of whether more common childhood adversities, such as problematic parenting, may affect the risk for personality disorder. A recent prospective longitudinal study investigated what the effects of behavioural and emotional problems during childhood and parental psychiatric disorders were on offspring risk for personality disorder and whether bad parenting would enhance this risk (Johnson, Cohen, Chen, Kasen, Brown, & Brook, 2006). The results revealed that some types of parenting practices, such as lack of parental affection and care and harsh punishment, enhanced the risk of offspring personality disorders in adulthood, beyond the effects of emotional and behavioural problems during childhood at age 6 and parental psychiatric disorder evident by mean offspring age of 16 years. The effects were still evident at a mean offspring age of 33 years. More specifically, *lack of parental affection and care* was associated with elevated risk in the child for antisocial, borderline, paranoid, schizotypal, schizoid, and avoidant PDs. *Harsh punishment* was found to be associated with elevated risk of borderline, paranoid, and schizotypal personality disorders.

Concluding remarks

Although there is considerable evidence that child abuse and maltreatment are associated with personality disorder, these appear to be two of the many risk factors and to be of more importance in personality disorders from Cluster B than from other clusters. Although these factors have been found to be associated with personality pathology, many individuals who have a history of child abuse or maltreatment do not develop a personality disorder. Although some of them may develop another psychiatric disorder, many do not develop any disorder at all. Some people respond poorly to adversity whereas others are resilient to it. Apparently, other vulnerability factors are involved in moderating adversity, including personality traits and biological factors. Very little systematic evidence is available to explain why children show such marked variation in their response to maltreatment, child abuse, and other traumas. Research into sources of resilience primarily focused on social experiences thought to protect children (e.g., warm parenting, social support), but the protective role of genes has largely been ignored. Recently, it has been suggested that genetically influenced individual differences in susceptibility to environmental experiences like maltreatment play a part in whether or not a child will develop antisocial behaviour (Moffitt, 2005).

Attachment

Attachment theory, originally developed by Bowlby and traditionally regarded as based on psychoanalytic ideas, has developed significantly over the recent years, combining object relations theory with empirical research in developmental psychopathology (Levy, 2005). Attachment theory has long been considered very influential with respect to understanding an individual's personality development, and attachment is now also considered an important aetiological factor in the development of personality disorders.

Bowlby defines his attachment theory as a way of conceptualizing the propensity of human beings to make strong affectional bonds to particular others and deficits in the process of attachment are assumed to be associated with many forms of emotional distress and personality disturbance, including anxiety, anger, depression, and emotional detachment (Bowlby, 1977, p. 201). Attachment is a long-lasting affective bond characterized by proneness to seek and maintain closeness to a specific adult in order to feel safe and secure. Infants form working models of interpersonal relationships based on their attachment experiences with key adults, usually the parents, and these models guide future encounters in new settings.

Attachment is formed very early and is a universal psychobiological process. Activation of the attachment system is related to stress hormones (van Bakel & Riksen-Walraven, 2004). Primary caretakers, usually the parents, play an important role in the development of the attachment representations of the child. Attuned attachment figures who provide comfort and protection based on their ability to respond sensitively to their child's behaviour may provide the basis for secure attachment. By comforting the child when needed, key attachment figures reduce the child's distress, thus enabling the child to learn to organize the information about itself and its social environment. In doing so the child develops an internal network of attachment that directs feelings and behaviours later on in life. Attachment theory suggests that early on in life, before we can talk, we form internal working models about how reliable, responsive, and understanding our caregiver is. It is generally assumed that early parent–child interactions result in the development of relatively stable internalized, affective/cognitive working models of self and others. Such working models are largely out of awareness, are associated with dysfunctional attitudes about self and others, and may contribute to individual vulnerability. In support of this theory, Andersson and Perris (2000) found a relationship between insecure attachment and dysfunctional attitudes about self and others.

Generally four "attachment representations" are recognized: one is secure attachment, also called autonomous; the other three are insecure and are called dismissive, preoccupied, and unresolved. In the case of *secure attachment* the child has received consistent, sensitive caregiving, and later tends to respond in confident and flexible ways to him/herself and others. The three categories of insecure attachment develop in different ways in early childhood: the child develops *dismissive attachment* when the caregiver rejects the child's feelings of need, fear, or anger, which the child, in turn, learns to suppress in order to get along with the attachment figure(s). *Preoccupied attachment* develops in response to inconsistent, even needy caregiving, causing the child to have increased sensitivity to fear, anger, or neediness in order to stay connected to the attachment figure. The fourth category, *unresolved attachment*, results from threats of being abandoned, hurt, or ignored by attachment figures when the child is most needy, or as a consequence of not being able to do anything about loss or hurt.

Attachment may explain important aspects of interpersonal relations later on in life. According to attachment theory, early relationships with parents strongly influence perception of competence, and perception of trustworthiness of others. When the attachment pattern is insecure, problems later on in life are likely to occur. Attachment status can be affected at any stage in life during times of stress, frustration, or anger or by profound influences such as loss, separation, and trauma. For example, van Ecke, Chope, and Emmelkamp (2005) found that emigration was associated with unresolved attachment many years later.

A number of studies support the view that measures of attachment style are associated with mental processes related to close relationships, and behaviours observed in such relationships (Mikulincer, Shaver, & Pereg, 2003). Longitudinal studies demonstrate that insecure attachment in infancy predicts relationship and behavioural difficulties later on in life (Egeland, Weinfield, Bosquet, & Cheng, 2000).

Measures of attachment

In studies investigating attachment representations in adults with personality disorders, the Adult Attachment Interview (AAI; Main & Goldwyn, 1991, 1994) has often been used, an instrument that assesses aspects of adults' internal working models of attachment with regard to their parents. The AAI is a semistructured interview designed to elicit thoughts, feelings, and memories about early attachment experiences, and to assess the individual's state of mind with regard to early attachment relationships. The interview yields one of five primary classifications discussed above: secure/ autonomous, preoccupied, dismissing, unresolved, or cannot classify.

Over the years, many improvements in the measurement of attachment style have been proposed, the most important being the assessment of attachment by using dimensional measures rather than a categorical measure as in the AAI by Main and Goldwyn (1991). The most influential is the model of Bartholomew and Horowitz (1991), who distinguish four attachment types that are conceptualized on two essentially orthogonal dimensions: concept of self and concept of others. *Secure attachment* is characterized by a valuing of intimate friendships, the capacity to maintain close relationships without losing personal autonomy, and a coherence and thoughtfulness in discussing relationships and related issues. A downplaying of the importance of close relationships, restricted emotionality, an emphasis on independence and self-reliance, and a lack of clarity or credibility in discussing relationships characterize the *dismissing attachment* style. The *preoccupied attachment* style is characterized by an overinvolvement in close relationships, a dependence on other people's acceptance for a sense of personal well-being, a tendency to idealize other people, and incoherence and exaggerated emotionality in discussing relationships. The *fearful attachment* style is characterized by avoidance of close relationships because of fear of rejection, a sense of personal insecurity, and a distrust of others (Timmerman & Emmelkamp, 2006).

Brennan, Clark, and Shaver (1998) and Fraley and Shaver (2000) found that a two-dimensional, continuous measure of attachment style (the Experiences in Close Relationships scale, or ECR), comparable to the scheme proposed by Bartholomew and Horowitz (1991), was more reliable than previous measures. The dimensions are called "attachment-related anxiety" representing anxiety about rejection, abandonment, and unlovability and extreme emotional reactivity, and "attachment-avoidance", which reflects strategies of emotional and behavioural distancing in intimate relationships.

The typology of Bartholomew and Horowitz (1991), and Brennan et al. (1998), originates from a social psychological tradition in which attachment is defined as an interpersonal concept, whereas the classification of Main and Goldwyn (1991) stems from developmental psychology in which attachment refers to intrapsychic processes. The measures that are derived from both views, the Adult Attachment Interview (AAI; Main & Goldwyn, 1994) on the one hand, and the Relationship Questionnaire (RQ; Bartholomew & Horowitz, 1991) and the ECR on the other, are therefore not regarded as measures of identical constructs. This implies that when reviewing the literature on the relationship between attachment and personality disorders one has to take note of the attachment measure that is reported on.

Attachment representations and personality

How do attachment representations contribute to personality traits and disorder? A number of studies addressed this issue by comparing attachment styles with measures of the Big-Five personality traits. As reviewed by Noftle and Shafer (2006), the results reveal that attachment security (low scores on both attachment anxiety and avoidance) is moderately negatively correlated with neuroticism and moderately positively correlated with extraversion and agreeableness, modestly positively correlated with conscientiousness, and not correlated with openness. Attachment anxiety is moderately to strongly correlated with neuroticism and not correlated with openness. Attachment anxiety is especially related to the depression, vulnerability, and anxiety facets of neuroticism, which suggests "that anxious attach-ment occurs when a person feels inadequately loved and insufficiently in control of interpersonal events" (Noftle & Shaver, 2006, p. 205), thus supporting Bowlby's (1977) theory. The relation of attachment anxiety to the other three dimensions is equivocal. Although some studies found significant associations with extraversion, agreeableness, and conscientiousness, other studies did not. Further, attachment avoid-ance has been modestly to moderately correlated (negatively) with extraversion and agreeableness, but not correlated with openness. Results with respect to avoidance on the one hand and neuroticism and conscientiousness on the other are inconclusive.

Attachment and personality disorders

Given the relationship between attachment and personality traits discussed above, one may wonder whether there is an association between attachment and personality disorders. Several empirical studies have been conducted on the relationship between attachment on the one hand and personality disorders on the other hand. A number of studies found that disorganized attachment behaviours (unresolved) predict aggression in school-age children with other family factors controlled for (Lyons-Ruth, 1996). In an earlier review into the relationship between attachment and psychopathology, van IJzendoorn and Bakermans-Kranenburg (1996) concluded that there are no systematic relations between clinical diagnosis and type of insecure attachment as assessed by the AAI. More recently, however, a number of studies have found specific associations between attach-ment style and personality disorders. For example, Rosenstein and Horowitz (1996) found that psychiatrically hospitalized adolescents, showing a dismissing attachment organization according to the AAI, were more likely to have a conduct or substance abuse disorder, or a narcissistic or antisocial personality disorder. Patients with a pre-occupied attachment organization were more likely to be diagnosed with an obsessive-compulsive, histrionic, borderline, or schizotypal PD. Most studies have investigated the relationship between attachment styles and borderline and antisocial PDs.

Borderline PD. Given that one of the diagnostic criteria of borderline PD is fear of abandonment, one would expect that patients with border-line pathology are characterized by insecure/unresolved attachment. Patients with a borderline PD diagnosis according to the AAI were characterized more frequently by an unresolved attachment style than matched controls (Fonagy et al., 1996). In another study significant differences on several self-report measures for attachment styles were found between borderline patients and controls (Sack, Sperling, Fagen, & Foelsch, 1996). Borderline patients were found to endorse avoidant, hostile, and resistant/ambivalent attachment styles significantly more frequently than controls according to the Attachment Style Inventory (Sperling & Berman, 1991). According to another self-report attachment instrument, the Reciprocal Attachment Questionnaire (RAQ; West, Sheldon, & Reiffer, 1987), the borderline group was characterized by angry withdrawal. A similar finding was found in a study among male forensic borderline outpatients and outpatient controls who were characterized by avoidant/schizoid PDs: the borderline patients reported an anxious style of attachment that is characterized by angry withdrawal as measured with the RAQ (West, Rose, McDonald, & Hashman, 1996; West et al., 1987).

The same questionnaire was used to compare the attachment styles of patients with borderline PD to the attachment styles of patients with obsessive-compulsive PD (Aaronson, Bender, Skodol, & Gunderson, 2006). The results revealed that patients with borderline PD were more likely to exhibit angry withdrawal and patients with compulsive PD careseeking attachment patterns. Further, patients with borderline PD also scored higher on feared loss of the attachment figure than patients with obsessive-compulsive PD. Finally, in a study by Minzenberg, Poole, and Vinogradov (2006), patients with borderline PD were found to be characterized by elevated scores on each of two fundamental social attachment dimensions on the ECR scale (Brennan et al., 1998). Interestingly, a relationship of adult social attachment to childhood maltreatment was found. Attachment anxiety was specifically related to sexual abuse in childhood, whereas attachment avoidance was related to each of five types of reported childhood abuse. Attachment avoidance scores were associated with depressive symptoms. Attachment-anxiety scores, on the other hand, were related to impulsivity and hostility.

Antisocial PD. Bowlby (1977) noted that emotionally detached individuals are often delinquent. According to attachment theory insecurely attached infants will show increasing noncompliant and antisocial behaviour as they seek responses from uninvolved primary caregivers. Eventually, they will develop mistrustful, aggressive, and chaotic representations of relationships, enhancing the risk of antisocial problems later in life (Londerville & Main, 1981), which has been supported empirically (Shaw & Vondra, 1995).

Results of studies into the relationship between attachment style and antisocial PD are inconclusive. In a longitudinal study (Allen, Hauser, & Borman-Spurrell, 1996), adults aged 25–28 years whose attachment style could not be determined (unresolved according to AAI) and adults with a dismissing attachment style reported significantly more criminal behaviour as well as psychological distress than secure adults. Brennan and Shaver (1998) found in a large group of students some evidence that self-reported attachment (RQ) was unrelated to psychopathy. The other personality disorder factors in their study, however, did show strong associations with attachment.

In a study by Timmerman and Emmelkamp (2006), the relationship between attachment styles, personality pathology, and criminal status was examined in a criminal offender population and in the general population. The results showed that criminal status is negatively associated with a secure attachment style, meaning that criminals in prison and forensic inpatients show more insecure attachment styles than controls from the general population. These findings are consistent with other studies that found that criminal offender populations are insecurely attached (e.g., van IJzendoorn et al., 1997). Criminal status in the Timmerman and Emmelkamp study was significantly linked to only one of the three insecure attachment styles, namely fearful attachment. Persons with a fearful attachment style are characterized by avoidance of close relationships because of fear of rejection, a sense of personal insecurity, and a distrust of others. These findings are consistent with clinical impressions and empirical findings about the learning histories of prisoners and forensic inpatients. Most of them have a history of early traumatic experiences in which often parental figures play a causal role in violating their trust in them.

Finally, a number of studies investigated attachment style in sexual offenders. Generally, attachment style of sexual offenders was characterized as insecure (e.g., Bogaerts, Vervaeke, & Goethals, 2004; Bumby & Hansen, 1997; Jamieson & Marshall, 2000; Smallbone & Dadds, 1998). Of note, not all individuals in these studies necessarily fulfilled criteria of antisocial PD, or any personality disorder at all. A study by Bogaerts, Vanheule, and deClercq (2005), however, found that child molesters are characterized by the antisocial and the schizoid personality disorders. Further, compared to a normal population, child molesters were found to be more insecurely attached. However, given that nearly half of the sample of child molesters was securely attached, insecure attachment is not a necessary condition for child molesting behaviour.

Concluding remarks

Although a number of studies show that poor early attachment is related to borderline PD and antisocial PD, there are a number of limitations, which restrict the conclusions to be drawn. First, only a few studies used the AAI, generally considered the gold standard to assess childhood attachment. Other studies relied on self-report instruments assessing disturbed adult social attachment. Such instruments can be susceptible to reporting biases, and it is not yet clear how self-report attachment measures relate to attachment as assessed with the AAI. Further, apart from the study of Minzenberg et al. (2006), there has been little research that has gone beyond the simple "fact finding" to more closely investigating how and why early attachment is related to personality disorders. Although it is generally assumed that poor parenting should be "blamed" for the development of insecure attachment styles, Baird et al. (2005) have proposed that there may be a subtype of individuals where the failure to develop secure attachment may be due to neurophysiological deficits on the infant side of the parent–infant dyad, rather than to parental characteristics.

In sum, attachment is one of the many variables involved in the development of personality disorders and may interact with other environmental and biological factors. It is likely that a combination of biological factors, personality characteristics, and deficits in attachment is involved in the development of personality disorders. As suggested by Livesley (2005), poor attachment relationships may merely amplify the expression of genetic predispositions.

Summary

Multiple biological and psychosocial variables have been found to be associated with the development of personality disorders, each accounting for only a part of the variance. Most research has been limited to Cluster B disorders, but even here we still do not have the final answer to the question which factors "cause" the personality disorder. A genetically based temperament is probably a key factor in the development of most personality disorders, particularly for Clusters A and B. Such temperamental predispositions may increase the likelihood that negative life events will occur. Negative psychosocial events, in turn, may result in persisting biological alterations in the brain. Biological differences may result from interactions between individual temperamental factors and social and family processes. Functional and structural neuroimaging studies provide some support for dysfunction in frontolimbic circuits in borderline and antisocial PDs, and temporal lobe and basal striatal-thalamic circuits in schizotypal PD. Given the small part of the variance explained by biological, genetic, and psychosocial factors, it is inappropriate to speak of causes (Livesley, 2005). Research is only beginning to identify the factors that are involved in the development of personality disorders. The findings of recent studies into gene–environment interaction suggest that purely environmental aetiological theories of personality disorders are incomplete, as are purely genetic accounts. Presumably, both pathogenic environmental influences (e.g., attachment, child maltreatment) and genetic risk factors are involved in the aetiology of personality disorders.

The anxious/inhibited personality disorders 5

> Among the personality disorders, the anxious cluster is
> relatively neglected. It does not have the same prominence
> that is attached to its flamboyant equivalent, particularly
> borderline personality disorder, and it does not carry the
> hint of excitement ... that schizotypal and paranoid per-
> sonality disorder impart. Nevertheless, it is the largest
> group of personality disorders and it is associated with
> more morbidity than others.
>
> (Tyrer, 2005, p. 366)

The anxious/inhibited personality disorders (Cluster C) include
avoidant PD, dependent PD, and obsessive-compulsive PD. These are
the most prevalent personality disorders in the general population. In
clinical settings the avoidant PD is highly prevalent and as common
as borderline PD; the dependent PD and obsessive-compulsive PD
are less prevalent in clinical settings.

Is Cluster C a clinical entity?

Factor analytic studies of the DSM-III-R and DSM-IV personality
disorders conducted to evaluate the latent dimensions underlying the
various personality disorders have, with respect to Cluster C PDs, led
to conflicting results. Two studies (Nestadt et al., 2006; O'Connor &
Dyce, 1998) were unable to replicate the DSM Cluster C factor. In
these studies obsessive-compulsive PD loaded on a different factor
than avoidant PD and dependent PD, which loaded together on one
factor. Sanislow, Morey, et al. (2002) factor analysed the DSM-IV
avoidant PD and obsessive-compulsive PD features and found that
criteria for both personality disorders loaded on one dimension;
unfortunately, the dependent PD criteria were not included in this

study. A more recent study (Fossati et al., 2006) included all three Cluster C criteria and found support for the latent common structure of the current Cluster C personality disorders. Factor analysis results of this study suggested that avoidant, dependent, and obsessive-compulsive PDs share a common latent dimension. Further, support was found for the three-factor structure of DSM-IV Cluster C personality disorder criteria, albeit that a few items loaded on a different Cluster C factor than in the original DSM-IV Cluster C structure. Thus, there is consistent evidence that avoidant and dependent PDs belong to the same cluster, and the results with respect to obsessive-compulsive PD are currently inconclusive.

Another line of research has dealt with the comorbidity of Cluster C personality disorders and anxiety disorders. As discussed in Chapter 3, generally high co-occurrence of the anxious/inhibited personality disorders and Axis-I anxiety disorders has been found in community and clinical studies. As argued by Krueger (2005), personality disorders and clinical syndromes are highly stable and both have an early onset, which does not support the notion of DSM that personality disorders and clinical syndromes are developmentally distinctive. Further, a number of anxiety-related syndromes and personality disorders share similar symptoms (e.g., dependent PD and panic disorder/agoraphobia; avoidant PD and social phobia). In addition, anxiety disorders (and mood disorders) share significant genetic variance with the personality trait of neuroticism, which is heavily involved in Cluster C pathology. The finding that anxiety disorders and anxiety/inhibited personality disorders have both shared and distinctive features suggests that: "conceptualizing this domain in terms of a set of distinct categories spread across two axes of the DSM ... may not be the most fruitful strategy" (Krueger, 2005, p. 245). Rather than conceptualizing anxious/inhibited PDs and clinical anxiety disorders as different domains, a more fruitful research approach would be to study why these domains are so interlinked.

Cognitive conceptualizations

In cognitive views of personality disorders (Beck, Freeman, & Davis, 2004), personality disorders are conceptualized as the overt expression of underlying dysfunctional beliefs and schemas, which make such individuals vulnerable to negative life experiences. The cognitive model takes as its starting point the idea that it is not the

TABLE 5.1

Basic beliefs and compensatory strategies associated with Cluster C personality disorders

Personality disorder	Beliefs	Compensatory strategies
Dependent	"I am helpless" "I need a strong person to survive"	Attachment Help seeking Clinging
Avoidant	"I may get hurt" "I am unlovable" "I should avoid unpleasant situations at all costs"	Avoidance Unassertiveness
Obsessive-compulsive	"I must not err" "I need order to survive"	Perfectionism Control

event itself but one's interpretation of the event that causes emotional distress and leads to (interpersonal) dysfunctioning in individuals with personality disorders. These false perceptions and interpretations of events are rooted in deeper structures that are central to personality dysfunctioning (Beck et al., 2004). There are remarkable similarities between cognitive and attachment theory conceptualizations of personality disorder. As Beck and Young posited: "the child learns to construe reality through his or her early experiences with the environment, especially with significant others ... sometimes, these early experiences lead children to accept attitudes and beliefs that will later prove maladaptive" (1985, p. 207). Such early experiences "shape" core beliefs or schemas. When activated, such dysfunctional beliefs or schemas lead to the use of maladaptive compensatory strategies in order to deactivate the core beliefs and the anxiety associated with these beliefs. Examples of specific core beliefs and compensatory behavioural strategies associated with dependent, avoidant, and obsessive-compulsive PDs are listed in Table 5.1.

It is assumed that specific sets of beliefs and schemas are associated with each personality disorder. As far as personality disorders from Cluster C are concerned, this specificity has not yet been convincingly demonstrated. A study by Nordahl and Stiles (2000) provided only "circumstantial evidence" for cognitive specificity of Cluster C disorders. Avoidant PD was significantly associated with the sociotropic subscales "concern about disapproval" and "pleasing others", while the results for the dependent PD and the obsessive-compulsive PD were less convincing. More support for the specificity of beliefs in Cluster C disorders was provided by studies of Arntz, Dreessen, Schouten, and Weertman (2004) and Beck et al. (2001).

Although patients with avoidant, dependent, and obsessive-compulsive PDs preferentially endorsed beliefs theoretically consistent with their specific personality disorder, there was also endorsement of beliefs associated with other personality disorders. This suggests that the belief sets may not be as conceptually distinct as proposed by cognitive theory. The dependent and obsessive-compulsive PDs were the most problematic to predict from specific personality disorder belief scales (Arntz et al., 2004).

Interpersonal violence

There is some evidence that individuals with dependent and avoidant PDs are at high risk of becoming victims of violence. In a study by Watson et al. (1997), 12% of victims of domestic violence had avoidant PD. The risk of victimization in persons with dependent PD is even higher. In a recent study, as many as 80% of individuals with dependent PD were victims of violent acts (Cormier, LeFauveau, & Loas, 2006). In contrast to individuals with other personality disorders, individuals with dependent PD often became victims of violence from a family member.

Apart from enhancing the risk of becoming a victim of violence, Cluster C personality disorder (i.e., avoidant PD) has been found to be associated with perpetrating violence.

In the early 1970s one of the authors treated a female patient for her anxiety disorders. In the course of treatment she disclosed that her husband regularly beat her up. The therapist invited her husband for the next session and asked some colleagues to keep an eye out, because he expected a very aggressive antisocial man. To his surprise a rather shy, timid man appeared at the appointment, who tearfully admitted that he regularly had attacked his wife.

Since then, a number of studies have revealed that a substantial proportion of wife batterers are characterized by avoidant personality (e.g., Dutton, 2002). In incarcerated spousal killers, murdering one's wife is better predicted by avoidant personality traits than by psychopathic traits (Dutton & Kerry, 1999).

Dependent personality disorder

Studies have shown that dependent persons are characterized by high trait anxiety. Individuals with dependent personality features react with increased anxiety when confronted with interpersonal conflict (Priel & Besser, 2000). The theory of Blatt (1991) is of some relevance with respect to understanding dependent personalities. Blatt characterized personality development as the integration of a person's capabilities for self-definition (self-criticism) and interpersonal relatedness (dependency). According to Blatt's theory of personality styles, *self-criticism* involves preoccupation with themes of self-esteem, failure, guilt, and lack of self-worth and autonomy, while *dependency* embodies themes of concern with abandonment, feelings of loneliness and helplessness, and a desire to be close to, relate to, and be dependent on others. This personality style of dependency has been found to be associated with strict, controlling, and inconsistent parental rearing (Blatt, 2004). There is considerable evidence that self-criticism and dependency enhance the vulnerability for depression (Flett, Hewitt, Endler, & Bagby, 1995).

Clinically, individuals with dependent PD have an exaggerated fear of making mistakes (associated with catastrophic interpretations) and a deep-seated belief in their own incompetence both to deal with everyday life and also to deal with the catastrophies they anticipate. Tyrer (2005) has argued that dependent PD is the extreme end of generalized anxiety disorder, in much the same way that avoidant PD may be the extreme end of social anxiety as discussed below. However, a recent meta-analysis revealed that dependent PD showed significant comorbidity with PD, social phobia, and obsessive-compulsive disorder, but was *not* significantly related to generalized anxiety disorder (Ng & Bornstein, 2005).

Components of dependent personality

There is some evidence that dependent PD is comprised of two different components: attachment and dependency behaviours (Livesley, Schroeder, & Jackson, 1990). As argued by Arntz (2005b) DSM-IV-TR assesses only one type of dependency, i.e., "functional dependency": the dependent individual sees him/herself as incompetent, lacks self-confidence and wants continuous reassurance and support in practical areas from someone stronger than him/herself. Emotional dependency, on the other hand, refers to the emotional need that somebody else is securely attached to the person: "Without such a person, people high in emotional dependency feel lonely and empty, and they experience a strong longing for a loving person to connect with. With intimate relationships, these people may experience abandonment fears (including panic like states), and they may cling to partners, friends, and family members (including their children)" (Arntz, 2005b, p. 412).

What is the evidence that dependent personality is comprised of two different factors? The results of a study by Gude, Hoffart, Hedley, and Rø (2004) support the idea that the criteria for DSM-IV dependent PD form two distinct components: dependency/incompetence and attachment/abandonment. Two criteria for borderline personality disorder also loaded on the attachment/abandonment component. These two components have only a modest relationship with each other, the correlation between attachment and dependency being only .28. Further support is provided by factor analyses on the Young's Schema Questionnaire, which found psychometric evidence for a distinction between abandonment and dependence/incompetence (e.g., Rijkeboer, van den Bergh, & van den Bout, 2005).

The emotional attachment/abandonment component, characterized by excessive interpersonal dependency, has also been called neediness. Neediness does not only feature in dependent PD, but is also associated with depression and with borderline PD and histrionic PD (Cogswell & Alloy, 2006). This distinction between functional dependency and emotional or attachment dependency is not only of theoretical interest, but may have clinical implications as well. While increasing self-confidence may be targeted in treatment of functional dependency, this will probably be of little avail to patients who are primarily characterized by emotional/attachment dependency. With these patients treatment needs to focus on emotionally correcting pathogenic attachment and early loss (Arntz, 2005b).

Avoidant personality disorder

As discussed in Chapter 1, a central characteristic of avoidant PD is social avoidance, together with hypersensitivity to negative evaluation, fears of rejection, and feelings of inferiority. Although in current nosology of DSM-IV-TR avoidance of interpersonal situations is highlighted, others have argued that avoidance should be broadened to include avoidance of unpleasant emotions and novel situations in addition to avoidance of social situations (e.g., Arntz, 1999; Rettew, 2000).

Two recent studies have investigated whether avoidant PD can better be conceptualized as a blend of two distinctive components. A study by Meyer, Ajchenbrenner, and Bowles (2005) found that avoidant personality features were related to avoidance of aversive situations in general. Compared to individuals with borderline features, individuals with avoidant PD features were inclined to avoid aversive overstimulation. Taylor, Laposa, and Alden (2004) examined whether people with avoidant personality traits avoid thinking about and experiencing emotions. In a series of related studies they investigated whether avoidance of pleasant and negative emotions, avoidance of novel situations, and beliefs about intense emotion were associated with avoidant PD. The results revealed that there is a low to moderate association between avoidant PD and avoidance of emotions and avoidance of novel situations. This clustering of various situations supports the notion that avoidant PD is characterized by a broad pattern of avoidance extending beyond social situations. This series of studies suggests further that individuals with avoidant PD have a low tolerance for emotional distress. In interpreting these results, the authors suggest that avoidance of novelty may be the developmental outcome of the innate temperament of behavioural inhibition.

Taken together, the results of these studies suggest that avoidant personality may be broadened to include avoidance of situations other than social situations, including emotional distress in general and novel situations.

Temperamental vulnerability

There is some research to suggest that temperamental vulnerability might increase risk for avoidant PD. Children who are behaviourally inhibited, shy, or hypersensitive to harmful stimuli might be vulnerable to develop avoidant PD. In support of this idea, Meyer et al. (2005) found that avoidant PD features were associated with a measure of "sensory-processing sensitivity". Sensory-processing sensitivity refers to a core dimension of temperament or personality, which can be defined as a biologically based disposition to respond strongly to emotional stimuli, and sensitivity to potential harm. Individuals who are behaviourally inhibited and hypersensitive to harmful stimuli might be vulnerable to avoidant PD. Such temperamental vulnerability combined with early adversity might increase risk for avoidant PD. As stated by Meyer et al., it appears plausible that one pathway to avoidant PD "involves relatively positive, albeit overprotective, sheltering parenting, in which highly sensitive children are prevented from habituating to the aversive novelty associated with frequent social encounters" (p. 653).

Schema-congruent information processing

According to the cognitive theory of personality disorders (Beck et al., 2004), patients with personality disorders will show schema-congruent information processing. In a study by Dreessen et al. (1999), avoidant personality disorder beliefs were associated with an implicit schema-congruent information processing. In this study, a pragmatic inference task was used to assess an implicit attributional bias. A pragmatic inference is a conclusion drawn by an individual, based on tacit assumptions about information that was not directly stated or logically implied by the original information. Since cognitive theory states that schematic processing may not occur unless schemas are activated, avoidant schemas were primed by a priming task. As predicted from cognitive theory, avoidant personality features were associated with avoidant beliefs and avoidant beliefs were associated with schema-congruent information processing bias. However, avoidant personality pathology in terms of DSM was not associated with schema-congruent information processing bias.

A study by Meyer et al. (2005) provides further support for the notion that individuals with avoidant personality features are characterized by schema-congruent information processing. In this study a vignette task was devised to examine cognitive-affective reactions in ambiguous situations that could be interpreted as signalling rejection. Compared to individuals with borderline features, individuals high on avoidant personality features interpreted such ambiguous social situations with a negative, rejection-implying bias. They had strong negative expectancies and tended to respond with distress and avoidance in such situations.

Although research in this area is just taking off, the studies discussed above suggest that information-processing may be a clinically relevant process in avoidant PD. Of note, studies so far have only included subclinical individuals exhibiting avoidant personality features, rather than fulfilling the criteria of avoidant PD.

Overlap with social phobia

In the last decade a number of studies have addressed the overlap between the clinical syndrome of social phobia and avoidant PD, because of the apparent similarity between both disorders. According to DSM-IV-TR, the main characteristic of both social phobia and avoidant PD is a fear of negative evaluation, resulting in avoidance of social situations or feeling uncomfortable in social situations. In the DSM-III-R, a subtype of social phobia was introduced: the diagnosis of generalized social phobia should be assigned when the anxiety and avoidance is related to most social situations. Introduction of the generalized social phobia subtype resulted in a large conceptual overlap between this disorder and the avoidant PD: six of the seven DSM-IV-TR diagnostic criteria for the avoidant PD are clearly related to the criteria of social phobia. In addition, the age of onset is similar in both disorders: both begin in late childhood or early adolescence, indicating that social phobia may be as chronic as the avoidant PD.

In studies addressing the comorbidity issue of social phobia and avoidant PD, the severity continuum hypothesis has been the dominant hypothesis, stating that social phobia and avoidant PD are not distinctive entities, but only differ in severity. Studies comparing social phobia and avoidant PD have led to the conclusion that both disorders are not qualitatively different, but only differ in severity of dysfunction (see van Velzen et al., 2000). The relationship between social phobia and avoidant PD may be explained by the attenuation hypothesis (see Chapter 3): both disorders are alternative expressions of the same genetic or constitutional liability in terms of underlying personality traits, possible candidates being high introversion (low extraversion) and high neuroticism (low emotional stability).

Obsessive-compulsive personality disorder

The current DSM-IV-TR description of obsessive-compulsive disorder is reminiscent of the anal traits as described by Freud (1959). The anal character traits are supposed to be the result of conflict aroused in the child during toilet training early in life. Thus, problems concerning bowel training were thought to lay the basis for anal fixations. Unfortunately, Freud was not very specific about what environmental factors during toilet training would lead to "anal fixations". The training could be "too early, too late, too strict or too libidinous" (cited by Fenichel, 1977, p. 305). Several studies have attempted to show a relationship between toilet training and anal orientation/obsessive-compulsive personality of the child. Generally, little or no evidence was found to support the psychoanalytic theory, that is, no relationship was found between a child's toilet training and the traits constituting the obsessive-compulsive personality (see Emmelkamp, 1982).

Although many clinicians assume that obsessive-compulsive personality is related to the clinical syndrome obsessive-compulsive disorder (OCD), this is not supported by empirical studies. A recent meta-analysis revealed that the majority of individuals with the syndrome OCD (75%) do not have obsessive-compulsive PD. Similarly, the majority of individuals with obsessive-compulsive PD (80%) do not have the clinical syndrome of OCD. Obsessive-compulsive PD has been found to co-occur with eating disorders (see Lilenfeld, Wonderlich, Riso, Crosby, & Mitchell, 2006) and depression (McGlashan et al., 2000). In the McGlashan et al. (2000) study nearly three-quarters of patients with obsessive-compulsive PD had a concurrent major depression.

Despite being the most prevalent personality disorder in community studies (see Chapter 3), obsessive-compulsive PD has received little attention from researchers. Most research on obsessive-compulsive PD has been conducted in the context of the Collaborative Longitudinal Personality Disorders Study, the results of which have already been discussed in the previous chapters. Generally, as compared to patients with borderline, schizotypal, and avoidant PD, individuals with the obsessive-compulsive PD are the least impaired, impairment being only mild across various areas of functioning (e.g., work, recreation, interpersonal relationships). One of the problems associated with the current DSM diagnostic criteria is that not all have maladaptive consequences (Costa, Samuels, Bagby, Daffin, & Norton, 2005). Given the mild impairment associated with obsessive-compulsive disorder, one may wonder whether obsessive-compulsive disorder is a valid disorder or merely a problem in living.

Evidence-based treatment

Although a number of patients with Cluster C disorders are treated with pharmacotherapy, only three randomized controlled trials (RCTs) have been reported. Results of these studies suggest that monoamine oxidase inhibitors (Fahlen, 1995), tricyclic antidepressants (Tyrer et al., 1993), and selective serotonin reuptake inhibitors (Ekselius & von Knorrig, 1999) may lead to reduction in personality pathology, but more studies are needed before firm conclusions can be drawn. A number of studies have evaluated the effects of psychological treatments (i.e., psychodynamic and cognitive-behavioural therapies), the results of which will be discussed in some detail.

Mixed Cluster C personality disorders

In an earlier open study (Barber, Morse, Krakhauer, Chittams, & Crits-Christoph, 1997) of psychodynamic therapy the effects of supportive expressive psychotherapy with avoidant and obsessive-compulsive PD patients were evaluated. The results were rather modest: slightly better outcomes were achieved with patients with obsessive-compulsive PD. The data are difficult to interpret since half of the avoidant PD patients dropped out of treatment. Further, this study was not controlled.

In a study by Winston et al. (1994) two forms of psychodynamic therapy were contrasted with a waiting-list control group: a more confrontational approach developed by Malan (1979) ($n = 31$) and a more supportive approach developed by the authors ($n = 32$). In that study, patients with predominantly Cluster C disorders (70%) showed significant and equivalent improvement on measures of distress (Sympton Checklist 90; SCL-90) and social functioning after 40 sessions of these two forms of psychodynamic psychotherapy. Furthermore, treated patients did significantly better than waiting list comparison subjects, and gains were maintained at 1.5-year follow-up. No differences were found between the two psychodynamic treatments. Again the data are difficult to interpret, given that both active treatments lasted much longer than the waiting list, which lasted only 4 months. Further, slightly more than half of the patients participated in the follow-up.

A study by Svartberg, Stiles, and Seltzer (2004) extends the study by Winston et al. (1994) by examining the effects of a 40-session, short-term dynamic psychotherapy specifically designed for personality problems and comparing this to cognitive therapy. Fifty-one patients with Cluster C personality disorders were randomly allocated to receive weekly sessions of dynamic therapy (Malan's approach) or cognitive therapy (Beck's approach). Both groups improved and continued to improve after treatment until 2-year follow-up both in distress and in terms of avoidant personality profile (Millon's Clinical Multiaxial Inventory). Psychodynamic therapy proved to be much more effective than the psychodynamic treatments in the Winston et al. study. The effect size in the Svartberg et al. study was $d = 1.76$, compared to $d = 0.59$ and $d = 0.95$ for both forms of dynamic therapy in the Winston et al. study. Two years after treatment, 54% of the short-term dynamic psychotherapy patients and 42% of the cognitive therapy patients had recovered symptomatically, whereas approximately 40% of the patients in both groups had recovered in terms of interpersonal problems and personality functioning. With respect to interpersonal problems, effect sizes for both treatments were large (short-term dynamic psychotherapy: $d = 1.07$; cognitive therapy: $d = 1.29$). None of the differences between dynamic therapy and cognitive therapy were significant.

Avoidant personality disorder

To date, few studies have evaluated the effects of psychological treatments with patients with avoidant PD. Although a number of studies into cognitive-behavioural therapy (CBT) with social phobia included patients with a comorbid avoidant PD, the effects of treatment on the avoidant PD were not established. Further, comparisons between trials with social phobia rather than avoidant personality disorder as primary complaint are fraught with difficulty because of differences in selection criteria, and other characteristics. It is questionable whether patients with a primary diagnosis of social phobia with comorbid avoidant PD are comparable to patients with a primary diagnosis of avoidant PD. Therefore, we will limit our discussion here to studies evaluating treatment for avoidant PD as the primary complaint.

One group has conducted two controlled studies into the effects of behavioural approaches in patients with avoidant PD (Alden, 1989; Cappe & Alden, 1986). The results of these studies show that various behavioural strategies (exposure and social skills training) are more effective than no-treatment control. However, the effects were generally modest. Renneberg et al. (1990), in an uncontrolled study, found that improvement was maintained up to one-year follow-up. Alden (1989) found that skills training did not enhance the effects of exposure in vivo. However, Alden and Capreol (1993) found that interpersonal profiles might be related to outcome. Patients who had interpersonal problems related to distrustful and angry behaviour benefited from the graduated exposure procedure but not from social skills training, whereas patients who experienced interpersonal problems related to being coerced and controlled by others benefited equally from exposure and social skills training.

Given that individuals with avoidant personality features have formed persistent negative representations of others that direct their responses to various social encounters (e.g., Meyer et al., 2005), cognitive therapy dealing with these cognitions and schemata may have something to offer to patients with avoidant PD. Because patients with avoidant PD may misinterpret ambiguous social information and are inclined to infer rejection, they will avoid all kinds of social situations. A variety of cognitive and behavioural strategies can be used to challenge and refute negative expectations and inferences about social encounters, while in vivo behavioural exposure strategies may be used to help patients habituate to aversive social stimulation (Emmelkamp, Bouman, & Scholing, 1992).

Emmelkamp et al. (2006) compared the effectiveness of such a CBT with brief dynamic therapy in outpatients suffering from avoidant personality disorder. Treatment lasted 20 sessions. CBT in general operates from the assumption that adjustment is dependent on accurate information processing. Accordingly, it aims to identify and modify core dysfunctional beliefs that automatically organize biased perceptions of self, others, and the future. CBT in this study was based on the assumption that anxiety and avoidance in avoidant PD are related to individuals' maladaptive beliefs and related thought processes. The model emphasizes collaborative interactions between patient and therapist in conjunction with specific cognitive and behavioural techniques such as Socratic dialogue, monitoring of beliefs, analysis of the advantages/disadvantages of avoidance analysis, activity monitoring and scheduling, graded exposure assignments, behavioural experiments, and role-play (Beck et al., 2004; Emmelkamp et al., 1992). Brief dynamic therapy was based on the assumption that anxiety and avoidance are related to individuals' unconscious psychodynamic conflicts, in addition to which shame plays a major role. Treatment was directed at defence restructuring and affect restructuring. The model emphasizes a therapeutic alliance, on the basis of which the most essential unconscious conflict can be clarified and resolved with the help of expressive techniques like clarification, confrontation, and especially interpretation (Malan, 1979). However, a flexible approach was used. In a number of cases a more supportive attitude and technique was used to bolster threatened equilibrium and to relieve the consequences of unconscious conflict by means of methods such as suggestion, reassurance, and encouragement (Luborsky & Mark, 1991). In these instances, the therapist clarifies rather than confronts defences in order to regulate rather than to provoke anxiety.

At posttest immediately after treatment the most favourable outcome was obtained from CBT: CBT was more effective than waiting-list control and brief dynamic therapy for all primary outcome measures. At 6-months follow-up, CBT was found to be significantly superior to brief dynamic therapy on most measures: only 9% of the CBT patients were still classed as having avoidant personality disorder, whereas 36% of the brief dynamic therapy patients still fulfilled the criteria. In a study on Collaborative Longitudinal Personality Disorders (Shea et al., 2002), 67% of patients with avoidant personality disorder still fulfilled the diagnostic criteria of avoidant PD at 6-months follow-up, despite the fact that most patients had received clinical care. A reduction in avoidant PD of 64% in brief dynamic therapy is substantial and of 91% in CBT is very substantial in comparison with the 33% reduction in the Shea et al. (2002) study. The positive results of CBT are of considerable clinical interest given that of all the personality disorders avoidant PD is found to be the most persistent (Shea et al., 2002), and even tends to worsen over time (Seivewright et al., 2002).

The results of the Emmelkamp et al. (2006) study support earlier studies that evaluated behavioural treatments for patients classified as having avoidant PD (Alden et al., 2002; Renneberg et al., 1990). The behavioural treatments investigated in these studies included social skills training and in vivo exposure to social situations, but none looked at cognitive therapy. Whether cognitive therapy enhances the effects of behaviour therapy deserves further study.

Finally, the differential effects achieved with brief dynamic therapy and CBT in patients with avoidant PD may have important implications for clinical practice. Given that brief dynamic therapy is not more effective than waiting list control and CBT is significantly superior to brief dynamic therapy, CBT seems the treatment of choice for patients with avoidant PD. Given the high prevalence of avoidant PD in the community (Torgersen et al., 2002), the persistence of avoidant PD (Shea et al., 2002), and the high functional impairment related to avoidant PD (Skodol et al., 2002; van Velzen et al., 2000), the robust finding across a number of studies that (cognitive) behavioural treatments are effective with avoidant PD provides an important step forward for community mental health care.

Summary

Among the personality disorders, disorders from the anxious/inhibited cluster are rather neglected in the research literature, despite being the largest group in community studies. Whether the Cluster C is a valid diagnostic entity has been questioned. In particular the position of obsessive-compulsive PD needs further investigation, given conflicting results of factor analyses and the low to mild impairment associated with this disorder. There is some evidence that dependent PD is comprised of two different components: attachment/abandonment and dependency behaviours. Further, research suggests avoidant PD should be broadened to include avoidance of unpleasant emotions and novel situations in addition to avoidance of social situations. Compared to Cluster B disorders, there is less evidence that child abuse is associated with anxious/inhibited personality disorders. In recent years a number of controlled studies have revealed that both cognitive-behavioural and psychodynamic therapy are effective treatments, but results with respect to the comparative effectiveness of these approaches are inconclusive yet. As to avoidant PD, there is consistent evidence that behavioural and cognitive-behavioural approaches are beneficial and might be more effective than psychodynamic therapy.

Borderline personality disorder 6

> Whatever *it* is that the borderlines exploit in us when we
> become caught up in their psychopathology, the *it* is in us.
> (Kroll, 1988, p. xvi)

General description of borderline personality disorder

> The borderline patient is a therapist's nightmare ...
> because borderlines never really get better. The best you
> can do is help them coast, without getting sucked into their
> pathology ... They're the chronically depressed, the deter-
> minedly addicted, the compulsively divorced, living from
> one emotional disaster to the next. ... And they end up
> taking vacations in psychiatric wards and prison calls,
> emerge looking good, raising everybody's hopes. Until the
> next letdown, real or imagined, the next excursion into
> self-damage. What they don't do is change.
> (Kellerman, 1989, pp. 113–114, cited in
> Davison & Neale, 1998)

Evidently, as is illustrated in the above quotation, borderline PD has a
bad reputation, both in the popular media (in, for example, movies
like *Fatal Attraction*), and often in clinical practice too. This probably
has to do with the unique challenges posed by patients characterized
by severe patterns of chronic instability of emotions, cognitions, self-
image, along with heightened, self-detrimental impulsivity. The term
"borderline" is a misnomer based on an outdated, empirically unten-
able notion that this form of psychopathology lies on a border
between neurosis and psychosis; an interesting account of the history
of the psychiatric classification of borderline PD is provided by Kroll

(1988). Prevalence estimates for the general population are between 1 and 2%, but the disorder is clinically quite common, with prevalence estimates of 10–15% for psychiatric outpatient patients, 15–20% for psychiatric inpatients, and 30–60% for clinical populations with a personality disorder (APA, 2001). More than three out of four borderline PD patients receiving therapy are women, though in certain settings the distribution is much more equal over the sexes (e.g., forensic settings; Timmerman & Emmelkamp, 2004).

As one might imagine, borderline PD exacts immense personal suffering and interferes with effective functioning in work, interpersonal relationships, and recreation (Skodol et al., 2002; Zanarini et al., 2005). Treatment utilization has been documented to be the most intense of all psychiatric disorders (Bender et al., 2001, 2006; Zanarini et al., 2004). Several case studies illustrate the individual psychiatric and treatment histories of borderline PD patients in more detail. The interested reader is referred to Oldham (2002), or Linehan and Kehrer (1993).

Up to 10% of borderline PD patients end up committing suicide, which makes borderline PD one of the top risk diagnoses for suicide. However, somewhat against clinical lore, most borderline PD individuals do improve over time. In a prospective study, Zanarini and colleagues (Zanarini, Frankenburg, Hennen, & Silk, 2003) observed that two-thirds of formally diagnosed borderline PD patients no longer met diagnostic criteria 6 years later. Several variables are associated with better or worse outcome. High intelligence, giftedness, and, in females, physical attractiveness appeared to increase the odds of positive outcome, while low education, low socioeconomic status, and ongoing abuse were associated with worse outcome. Stone (1990) cautions that not all borderline PDs are well represented in these long-term follow-up studies; it may well be that the very underprivileged groups never reach mental health facilities. On the other hand, some selection for more severe cases is also evident, as most studies originated from inpatient settings (Stone, 1990). What changes in borderline PD? More than likely it is the symptomatic part of the criteria rather than the more trait-focused criteria. Symptoms can be thought of as extreme, problematic adaptations; in therapy patients can learn more functional ways to deal with their emotional problems. The traits as such, however, may not change much. As Stone (2006, p. viii) puts it: "Symptoms can often be alleviated dramatically; personality is, as it should be, highly resistant to change. ... Psychotherapists do not aim to make radical changes in a patient's personality, but rather smooth down the rough edges with

TABLE 6.1

DSM-IV diagnostic criteria for borderline PD regrouped according to domains of functioning

Affective criteria
- affective instability due to a marked reactivity of mood (e.g., intense episodic dysphoria, irritability, or anxiety usually lasting a few hours and only rarely more than a few days)
- chronic feelings of emptiness
- inappropriate, intense anger or difficulty controlling anger (e.g., frequent displays of temper, constant anger, recurrent physical fights).

Interpersonal criteria
- frantic efforts to avoid real or imagined abandonment that do not include suicidal or self-mutilating behaviour
- a pattern of unstable and intense interpersonal relationships characterized by alternating between extremes of idealization and devaluation.

Behavioural criteria
- impulsivity in at least two areas that are potentially self-damaging (e.g., spending, sex, substance abuse, reckless driving, binge eating) that do not include suicidal or self-mutilating behaviour
- recurrent suicidal behaviour, gestures, or threats, or self-mutilating behaviour.

Cognitive criteria
- transient, stress-related paranoid ideation or severe dissociative symptoms
- identity disturbance: markedly and persistently unstable self-image or sense of self.

fine sandpaper – to make the abrasive person more polite, the impulsive more restrained, and so on." As it is, the possible exception is impulsivity; there is evidence that this trait lessens ("mellows") with age.

As with the other personality disorders, the borderline PD diagnosis follows in two stages. First, it is assessed whether the patient meets the general criterion for borderline PD, that is, whether the patient exhibits "A pervasive pattern of instability of interpersonal relationships, self-image, and affects, and marked impulsivity beginning by early adulthood and present in a variety of contexts" (APA, 2000, p. 706). Next, it is assessed whether the specific diagnostic criteria for borderline PD are met. Several authors have reorganized the set of borderline PD diagnostic criteria in domains of functioning, or in trait-specific domains (e.g., Lieb, Zanarini, Schmahl, & Linehan, 2004; Linehan, 1993a; Paris, 2005a). Depending on the frame of reference, some criteria can be thought of as primarily cognitive versus primarily interpersonal in nature (e.g., unstable self-image), or as impulsivity-related versus interpersonal (e.g., oscillating between extremes in relationships). We align with Lieb et al.'s (2004) listing (see Table 6.1).

In sum, profound instability is the hallmark/essential feature of borderline PD. Indeed, what seems to be stable about borderline PD is its instability. The prototypical borderline PD patient shows a pervasive pattern of instability across the domains of mood, cognition, interpersonal relationships, self-image, and impulse control. Let us examine these domains more closely.

Affective features

Marked emotional reactivity to specific events, especially of an interpersonal nature, characterizes the borderline PD patient. Patients with borderline PD tend to react quickly and intensely, but they do not return quickly to their emotional baseline. As a result, they tend to move from one emotional crisis to the next, sometimes several in a day. In Dialectical Behaviour Therapy, specifically developed for borderline PD, this vulnerability is referred to as having "emotional sunburn", indicating that even minor touch will elicit strong distress reactions. The emotional life of borderline PD patients is perhaps best summarized by Lieb et al. (2004), who stated that "these individuals can be distinguished from other groups by the overall degree of their multifaceted emotional pain" (p. 454). To others, they also seem particularly motivated to convey the extent of their pain. Another characteristic emotional feature is difficulty with anger management, sometimes leading to angry explosive outbursts. Psychopharmacological agents such as anticonvulsants are sometimes used to help stabilize mood, and antidepressants are frequently prescribed during prolonged emotional crises.

Interpersonal features

Borderline PD patients tend to alternate between the extremes of idealizing or devaluing important attachment figures in their environment. Particularly romantic partners tend to be experienced as totally desirable, unique, and terrific, or as utterly inadequate and worthless, and they are treated accordingly. Abandonment fears are prominent among many borderline PD patients; minor rejections are readily perceived as signs of pending relationship dissolution, leading to fearful dependent seeking of reassurance and frantic clinging, sometimes to the point of actually stalking the other person (Kamphuis & Emmelkamp, 2000). The reality is that intimate relationships tend to be short-lived, as partners grow tired of the intense and unpredictable cycles of rejection/hatred and clinging/adoration, or because the borderline PD patient loses respect and interest for the other person.

Cognitive features

Under (interpersonal) stress, some borderline PD patients exhibit transient paranoid ideation or marked dissociative symptoms. Such episodes can set the stage for self-injurious behaviours (i.e., self cutting, scratching, burning, etc.). In general, borderline PD individuals tend to be extreme in their evaluations of others – all good, or all bad. The extreme evaluations tend to oscillate; the constant is that borderline PD patients seem to have difficulty in simultaneously holding positive and negative aspects of the same person in their consciousness, a phenomenon referred to as "splitting" in the psycho-dynamic literature; a topic we will return to later in this chapter. These tendencies can also wreak havoc in the treatment of borderline PD patients; often in inpatient care some of the staff will be "all-bad", while others will be "all-good", creating tensions within the treatment team. With regard to self-image, borderline PD individuals seem to miss a core sense of identity, and may experience themselves quite differently depending on whom they are with. They may report that they "don't know who they really are", and the associated affective component is often verbalized as "feeling empty".

Problems with impulse control

To escape emotional distress, borderline PD patients may engage in many different impulsive and potentially self-destructive behaviours, including alcohol and drug abuse, promiscuous sex, binge eating, and, perhaps worst of all, self-injurious behaviour (SIB). SIB can be defined as all behaviours involving the deliberate infliction of direct physical harm to one's own body without any intent to die as a consequence of the behaviour (Simeon & Favazza, 2001). It has been estimated that about three out of four borderline PD patients have at some point engaged in SIB (Clarkin, Widiger, Frances, Hurt, & Gilmore, 1983). SIB, sometimes referred to as deliberate self-harm or parasuicidal behaviour, takes many forms; most common are self-cutting, scratching, and burning, but more extreme forms include head banging, ingesting or applying toxic chemicals (e.g., antiseptic fluids), etc. A pivotal motivation for SIB seems to be altering sub-jectively experienced affective states (Briere & Gil, 1998; Favazza & Conterio, 1989; Kemperman, Russ, & Shearin, 1997). Patients seem to seek relief from unbearable emotional states, be it over- or under-stimulation. Typically, SIB follows an escalation of subjectively unbearable feelings of tension, anger, despair, loneliness, depression, or emptiness and is continued until usually short-lived relief from these feelings is achieved. However, as noted in a review by Yates (2004), few empirical studies have systematically investigated individuals' motivations for engaging in SIB. Borderline PD patients are often more or less chronically suicidal, which adds considerably to the strain of having these patients in the caseload. Suicide prevalence estimates are generally between 8 and 10% (APA, 2001), which puts borderline PD patients at a 50 times higher risk than persons from the general population. To combat impulsiveness, selective serotonin reuptake inhibitors (SSRIs), mood stabilizers, and low-dose atypical neuroleptics have been prescribed, which can provide limited symptom relief, not remission.

Impulse control problems are very evident in the following vignette:

Rebecca had been chronically suicidal for many years. She had an extensive history of severe parasuicidal behaviours: she regularly cut and burned herself, had ingested chloride, and hit herself with a hammer until a fragment of her wrist broke off. In her group skills training, she had difficulty tolerating that other group members received central attention. One of her (rare) strengths included a strong interest and apparent ability in horse riding; but initiatives to become more involved in this activity were invariably sabotaged by an interpersonal crisis leading to self-injury or hospitalization.

Construct validity of borderline personality disorder

Borderline PD is a recent addition to the DSM, and it is one of its more controversial diagnoses. In the ICD-10, borderline PD does not exist as a separate disorder but is included as a subtype of the emotionally unstable personality disorders, together with the impulsive subtype. The literature on borderline PD has been growing rapidly over the past two decades (Blashfield & Intoccia, 2000), and the diagnosis has been the subject of much criticism. Some authors have advocated deletion of the diagnosis altogether (e.g., Taylor, 1995; Tyrer, 1999), while others proposed various conceptualizations, including borderline PD as extreme neuroticism (e.g., Widiger, 1993), as a complex Post Traumatic Stress Disorder (PTSD)-like syndrome (e.g., van der Kolk, 1996), as a disorder of self-structure (Gunderson, 1984), or as primarily an affective disorder (Akiskal, 1981).

Relevant to this debate, there are many ways to be a borderline patient. In fact, counting all possible permutations, there are 246 ways to meet the five (or more) out of the nine DSM-IV criteria (see Chapter 1). Of course, not every combination of criteria is equally likely, but clinically too, one encounters quite a diversity of patients who satisfy the borderline PD criteria. Severe and chronic PTSD/dissociative symptoms may dominate the clinical picture, but may also be absent. Intense affective and/or cognitive reactivity may be closely tied to (perceived) abandonment, or they may be more chronic and general. Some authors mention subtypes to account for the heterogeneity (Oldham, 2002). Others have argued (e.g., Tyrer, 1999) that the heterogeneity of borderline PD and its associated poor demarcation from other disorders points to "a motley diagnosis in need of reform". Tyrer (1999) suggests that borderline PD in its current shape should be considered a prediagnosis rather than a diagnosis, merely pointing the clinician to "difficult behaviour that requires intervention".

How to decide whether *the* borderline PD diagnosis as such exists, or that the diagnosis is in fact a mixed bag of multiple diagnoses? Evidence to answer the question can be collected from various domains, including phenomenology, neurobiology, family history, response to treatment, course, and comorbidity patterns. For example, do borderlines have distinctive symptomatology? Several studies have compared the clinical features of borderline PD to that of other disorders, seeking demarcation (e.g., Gunderson & Kolb, 1984; Perry & Klerman, 1980; Zanarini, Gunderson, Frankenburg, & Chauncey, 1990). Zanarini and colleagues (1990) compared borderline PD patients to other Axis-II patients on the 22 summary statements of the Revised Diagnostic Interview for Borderlines (DIB-R). Most symptoms were not specific to borderline PD. However, seven features were found to be somewhat specific to borderline PD: quasipsychotic thought, self-mutilation, manipulative suicide efforts, abandonment/engulfment/annihilation concerns, demandingness/entitlement, treatment regressions, and countertransference issues. However, the authors also commented that the overall pattern of clinical features was probably more distinctive than any one feature taken alone.

Another approach is to tackle this issue by factor analytic studies. Five studies were conducted to determine the factor structure of the borderline PD criteria (Clarkin, Hull, & Hurt, 1993; Fossati, Maffei, et al., 1999; Rosenberg & Miller, 1989; Sanislow, Grilo, & McGlashan, 2000; Sanislow, Grilo, et al., 2002). The findings were inconsistent, suggesting one, two, or three latent factors. Differences may be due to differences in the severity of the study groups, the specific assessment instruments used, etc. Sanislow and colleagues seem to have a particularly strong case for a three-factor solution (Sanislow et al., 2000). In their first study, a principal components factor analysis on the DSM-III-R borderline PD criteria yielded three factors, corresponding to disturbed relatedness, behavioural dysregulation, and affective regulation. Using confirmatory factor analytic techniques, Sanislow, Grilo, et al. (2002) were able to confirm these factors in a second study using an independent sample, using DSM-IV criteria. The factors were highly intercorrelated, supporting the construct validity of the borderline PD diagnosis. The identified factors can account for some of the heterogeneity encountered among borderline PD patients, and may ultimately inform treatment strategies by elucidating the interplay of underlying pathogenic processes.

The heterogeneity of borderline PD is reflected in its extensive comorbidity (as reported on in more detail in Chapter 3). Almost as a rule, borderline PD co-occurs with other psychiatric problems, most notably other personality disorders, substance abuse, and affective disorders. Borderline PD overlaps substantially with the other Cluster B personality disorders and, by virtue of the shared fear of object loss, also with dependent PD. Its excessive comorbidity with substance use disorders suggests a shared impulse control problem. Other common comorbid diagnoses include major depression, eating disorders, and PTSD. Evidence from family history reviews, and investigations of course and treatment response, suggest that borderline PD is more similar to affective disorders than to schizophrenia. The extreme and rapid emotional shifts present differential diagnostic issues with bipolar II disorder. In unipolar and bipolar depression, however, the same mood usually predominates for weeks, whereas in borderline PD patients may experience intense bouts of depression, anxiety, or anger for a couple of hours.

Diathesis-stress models

Many, but not all, individuals with borderline PD report a childhood history of traumatic experiences, and childhood abuse and neglect have frequently been proposed as important factors in the aetiology of borderline PD. However, as stated in Chapter 3, not everybody who experiences such adverse experiences while growing up develops borderline PD, some being more vulnerable than others. This conclusion points to the role of individual differences, or person variables. What is needed then is theorizing that incorporates both stressors and (temperamental) vulnerabilities, and examines their interaction: diathesis-stress models. Several diathesis-stress models have been proposed, and we will briefly discuss three of the more influential ones here.

Linehan's and Zanarini & Frankenburg's models

Marsha Linehan (1993a) suggested that emotionally vulnerable individuals growing up in an emotionally "invalidating environment" are at particular risk for developing borderline PD. The emotional vulnerability is a person factor, reflecting individual differences in emotional sensitivity. Individuals high on this dimension have low thresholds for their emotional reactions, tend to experience intense emotional reactions, and have difficulty in downregulating their emotional arousal. The emotionally invalidating environment "refers to an environment in which the patients' behaviour or reports of their thoughts or feelings frequently are met with responses [that] they are invalid, faulty, or inappropriate, or in which the ease of problem solving is oversimplified" (Robins & Chapman, 2004; pp. 74–75). As such, Linehan's biosocial theory holds that borderline PD is a transactional disorder of emotional dysregulation: an ongoing "poorness of fit" between the temperamental qualities of the individual and their social-emotional environment leads to severe maladjustment. Zanarini and Frankenburg (1997) introduced a similar tripartite model of the development of borderline PD that bears similarity to Linehan's model, but adds a third factor: a triggering event that reminds the person of earlier adversity or trauma and sets off the full-blown borderline symptomatology and its comorbid manifestations. These three factors are thought to represent necessary but not necessarily sufficient conditions for the development of borderline PD.

Schema theory of Young

Young's (Young, Klosko, & Weishaar, 2003) more recent theory of the aetiology of borderline PD is highly compatible. The theory describes how various dysfunctional family characteristics, such as deprivation, rejection, or subjugation, lead to frustration of specific core emotional needs of the young child. These frustrations, in turn, give rise to the formation of maladaptive schemata. Subsequent information processing is heavily guided by such schemata, and underlies the borderline PD pathology. Of course, emotionally temperamental children will be more vulnerable to the dysfunctional influences.

However, the dysfunctional schemata are not constantly active in borderline PD patients. Recent insights have led to the view that complex personality disorders are not characterized by one set of pathogenic schemata, but by different sets that can be activated in alternation. The concept of modes has been developed to make sense of the combination of extreme attitudes that are active only under certain conditions. Modes are thought of as states or aspects of the self in which specific schemata are active. They are ways of being, experiences of self, dominated by particular (sets of) schemata. Young distinguishes ten distinctive schema modes, including four child modes, three dysfunctional coping modes, two dysfunctional parent modes, and the healthy adult mode. Five of these are deemed characteristic for borderline PD (see Table 6.2).

Table 6.2 shows these diathesis-stress models as well as those from the psychodynamic formulations of Kernberg (1984) and Bateman and Fonagy (2004a, 2004b), which will be discussed later (see transference-focused therapy and mentalization-based therapy, respectively).

Experimental tests of "splitting" and other information processing biases

Arntz and colleagues have conducted an innovative programme of research on information processing biases in personality disorders that in scope and nature is reminiscent of experimental studies on fundamental processes in anxiety disorders (Arntz, 2005a; Arntz & Veen, 2001; Arntz, Klokman, & Sieswerda, 2005; Giesen-Bloo & Arntz, 2003; Veen & Arntz, 2000). Using creative experiments, several hypotheses have been derived from theories that aim to explain the borderline pathology by postulating specific information processing abnormalities. To the extent that these are elucidated, the development of more effective and efficient interventions may be furthered. To illustrate, we will discuss two examples of this line of research: (a) the tests of the "splitting" hypothesis derived from Kernberg's (1984) theory of borderline pathology, and (b) tests of Young et al.'s (2003) schema theory.

"Splitting" is a central concept in Kernberg's (1984) theory of borderline pathology. Presumably, borderline patients hold separate,

TABLE 6.2

Diathesis-stress models of borderline personality disorder

Model	Diathesis	Stress	D * S
Linehan (1993a) Dialectical Behaviour Therapy	Emotional vulnerability; temperamental predisposition to emotional dysregulation	Invalidating environment; dismissive and disqualifying of private experiences; abuse and neglect as ultimate expressions	The ongoing "poorness of fit" will yield borderline PD, with emotion dysregulation as the core issue
Zanarini & Frankenburg (1997)	Hyperbolic temperament	Traumatic childhood experiences	A triggering event that reminds the person of earlier adversity or trauma will mark the onset of the psychopathology
Young et al. (2003) Schema-focused therapy	Genetics and emotionally intense temperament	Childhood experiences in the family and in the outside world; may involve abuse or neglect	Family environment may be unsafe or unstable, depriving, harshly punitive/ rejecting, or subjugating; this leads to dysfunctional schemata organized in various modes
Kernberg (1984) Transference-focused therapy	Constitutional vulnerability: high on negative emotionality, especially aggression	Environmental factors; e.g., emotional frustration	Unintegrated and undifferentiated affects and representations of self and others results; such "splitting" underlies borderline PD pathology
Bateman & Fonagy (2004a, 2004b) Mentalization-based treatment	Constitutional vulnerabilities	Inadequate mirroring of emotional experience/ traumatic experience in early attachment context	Will result in core deficit in mentalization capacity and fragile self-organization

extreme, all-good, and all-bad representations of self and others. This failure of integration of "good" and bad" aspects of the reality of the self and others is essential given the predominance of severe aggression activated in these patients by early excessive frustration. According to Kernberg, splitting protects the ego from severe annihilation anxiety by means of dissociating or actively keeping apart contradictory experiences of self and others. The dissociation protects the love and goodness of the good from contamination and destruction by overriding hate and badness (the bad). A similar concept in cognitive therapy is called dichotomous thinking. A difference, however, is that dichotomous thinking, in contrast to splitting, does not exclude multidimensional thinking. The same person may be simultaneously evaluated in both positive and negative extremes. The following questions were addressed in an experimental design:

- Is dichotomous thinking characteristic of borderline PD patients?
- Do borderline PD patients, more than control groups, see their social world as "all good" or "all bad?" Do they judge other people as both good and bad?
- Does dichotomous thinking occur only in interpersonal situations specifically related to borderline PD pathology, or does it occur in all interpersonal situations?

Comparing ratings from borderline PD patients with Cluster C patients and nonpatients, movie clips were shown that centred on the emotionally salient themes of abandonment, rejection and abuse, and more neutral clips. Spontaneous reactions were solicited, including trait evaluation of the movie protagonists. Evaluations of the borderline patients appeared not one-dimensional but multidimensional. Patients with borderline PD judged some aspects of their environment and themselves as negative and other aspects as positive, and did not show all-bad or all-good evaluations. In a second experiment, it was shown that in noninterpersonal emotionally negative situations borderline PD patients appear to be characterized by a negativistic thinking style, more than by dichotomous thinking or splitting, that seemed to be unique for interpersonal situations. Some of the findings were in part determined by the response format; in free format borderline PD individuals appear to express extreme one-sided cognitions, but when primed by multidimensional adjectives they expressed both (extreme) positive and negative attitudes about the same person.

Arntz also tested hypotheses based on theories underlying Young et al.'s (2003) schema mode model (discussed later in more detail). Specifically, Arntz and colleagues (2005) addressed the following questions:

- Is there a set of schema modes that characterizes borderline PD patients?

- Do these schemata "behave" as you would expect from the theory, e.g., given the emotionally defensive function of the detached protector mode, is it possible to trigger this mode with salient emotional stimuli?
- Are borderline PD patients characterized by their putative characteristic modes, more so than normal controls or other personality disorders?

Again using movie clips to activate core schema modes, borderline PD patients, Cluster C patients, and nonpatients were compared on a newly constructed schema-mode questionnaire. It was shown that borderline PD patients scored higher than the control groups on the presumed characteristic modes. The stress induction induced negative emotions in all groups, but only the borderline patients reacted with increased activation of the (theory predicted) detached protector mode (see Schema-focused therapy in the next section).

Evidence-based treatments

Until recently, the dominant idea was that borderline PD was essentially untreatable and that clinical management was the best one could do for these "highly dysfunctional and notoriously difficult patients". Accumulating recent evidence, however, points to a considerably more hopeful picture. The APA (2001) has issued a practice guideline for the treatment of borderline PD. With "substantial clinical confidence", it recommends psychotherapy as the primary treatment along with symptom-targeted adjunctive pharmacotherapy. The guideline has drawn criticism that the quality of the evidence supporting the recommendations is inadequate (McGlashan, 2002; Paris, 2002; Tyrer, 2002). Notwithstanding, one has to recognize that several promising psychosocial interventions have been developed, some of which fared rather well in controlled research. To date, four alternative approaches to therapy with borderline PD have been manualized as well as subjected to controlled empirical studies. These are: dialectical behaviour therapy (Linehan, 1993a), schema-focused therapy (Young et al., 2003), transference-focused therapy (Clarkin, Yeomans, & Kernberg, 1999), and mentalization-based therapy (Bateman & Fonagy, 2003, 2004b). The next sections describe each of these approaches in more detail, review the empirical evidence, and draw some overall conclusions.

Cognitive therapy (CT)

Multiple forms of CT for borderline PD exist; there is "classic" CT, dialectical behaviour therapy, and schema-focused therapy. As discussed in the treatment of patients with Cluster C disorders (Chapter 5) CT aims to identify and modify core dysfunctional beliefs that automatically organize biased perceptions of self, others, and the future. Presumably, various disorders can be characterized by their different (sets of) core dysfunctional beliefs. Borderline PD seemed to resist such a formulation, probably because of the diversity and changeability of the clinical picture. Nevertheless, a number of specific core beliefs for borderline PD have been identified (Pretzer, 1990). Borderline PD patients hold highly negative and polarized core beliefs that include extreme helplessness, distrust, and fears of abandonment and rejection. The general CT for borderline PD largely follows the basic principles as described in many other CBT textbooks; we will therefore focus our description on the treatment protocols more specifically designed for borderline pathology. First among equals is dialectical behaviour therapy (DBT), the first fully tested programme and as such the only psychotherapy included in the "probably efficacious" category in the 1995 list of the APA task force for the treatment of borderline PD (Chambless & Ollendick, 2001).

Dialectical behaviour therapy (DBT)

DBT was specifically developed for chronically suicidal and severely dysfunctional borderline individuals (Linehan, 1993a, 1993b). Linehan considers emotional dysregulation at the core of the borderline pathology. Emotional dysregulation leads to a cascade of dysregulation in other domains: interpersonal dysregulation, cognitive dysregulation, and a dysregulated sense of self. The idea is that the patient does not learn to recognize, label, and modulate their (intense) emotional experiences and that they do not develop trust in their private experiences. Accordingly, a stable core sense of self does not evolve, and the borderline PD patient experiences him or herself as a vessel of conflicting, variable, and intense emotions and states. As one might imagine, this in turn complicates the formation of supportive long-term relationships.

In the DBT treatment model, the fundamental "dialectic" of DBT is between acceptance and change. Where (arguably) (C)BT is predominantly a technology of change, DBT emphasizes the importance of providing support and acceptance in alternation with promoting learning and change. DBT assumes that patients are doing the best they can, but they need to do better. A comprehensive DBT treatment package consists of (a) weekly individual outpatient DBT sessions, (b) a weekly DBT group skills training, (c) adjunctive telephone consultation, (d) supported by a consultation team, and (e) auxiliary treatments (e.g., pharmacotherapy). To get a better sense of the actual flow of doing DBT, the reader is referred to Linehan and Kehrer (1993), who provide a detailed and rich case study as well as transcripts illustrating specific therapeutic strategies and techniques.

Prior to embarking on therapy, a specific treatment contract is negotiated that details the respective responsibilities of both patient and therapist. Without a basic agreement on goals and commitment to therapy, treatment does not commence. In DBT, the individual therapy sessions follow a consistent format in that the hierarchy of treatment goals is fixed and that specifically developed diary cards are reviewed to track the patient's functioning and use of behavioural skills over the course of the week. In the first stage of treatment, the primary focus is on stabilizing the patient and achieving behavioural control. Specific targets are to reduce life-threatening or self-damaging behaviours, therapy-interfering behaviours (e.g., being late, not showing up, but also being high or dissociated during sessions), and quality of life-interfering behaviours, while promoting behavioural skills. Irreverently one might say that in order for DBT to be maximally effective it needs the patient to be alive and well (target a), productively collaborating on the tasks of treatment (target b), and on issues that interfere with their effective functioning (target c).

The group skills training is organized in modules that specifically target core features of borderline psychopathology. The training modules are called emotional regulation, interpersonal regulation, distress tolerance, and mindfulness, and these modules map onto the domains of deficit: mindfulness aims at developing a sense of self, an awareness of the present experience, and the other modules address primarily the dysregulation in their respective domains (i.e., emotion, interpersonal, and behavioural/impulsive). The group skills training is very much that of an educational experience in a group format. Borderline PD patients receive a practical training in ways of more effective coping with – and in fact improving upon – their critical functional deficits. As such, each session has a more or less fixed agenda, typically consisting of reviewing the practice of skills used the previous week and an instruction in new skills: it is not a group for processing experiences generally. At face value, the DBT treatment model has a number of distinctive strengths. First, a useful division of labour is maintained between the individual therapy and the group skills training. The group skills training provides cumulative learning irrespective of the client's current situation; the agenda will not be derailed by (usually frequent) momentary crises of individual members. The personal situation is addressed in the individual therapy sessions, where the emphasis is on integrating the skills into their daily functioning; clients are encouraged to use the skills to deal with their idiosyncratic problem behaviours. Another strength is the hierarchy of treatment targets (so-called "house of treatment"). First, the primary focus is on stabilizing the patient and achieving behavioural control. The idea is to "equip" and empower the patient before one starts "digging" into traumatic experiences that patients will not be able to process without the requisite (emotional regulation and distress tolerance) skills.

Also, DBT makes intelligent and systematic use of contingencies and reinforcement throughout its components. For example, the therapist handles crisis calls in a very practical, problem-solving way. The aim is to help the patient use the appropriate skills to manage their current crisis, not to directly manage the crisis itself. If the client executes these skills, an extra session may be scheduled to address the underlying issues. Thus, attention is made contingent upon skills execution, not display of crisis. Likewise, when the weekly diary card indicates episodes of parasuicidal behaviours, an exhaustive behavioural analysis is mandatory. Frequently, patients rather discuss quality of life interfering behaviours but this treatment target is further down the hierarchy. Patients learn by consequences.

Noteworthy is also the specific distress tolerance and crisis intervention module, which tends to be highly appreciated by both patients and inpatient staff. In an integrated programme, nursing staff can ask the client in distress questions like "what skills can you use to get through this difficult time; what would your DBT therapist say?" and expect some productive response. To our knowledge, no similar specific module existed beforehand.

Moreover, DBT explicitly recognizes that therapists treating borderline PD patients need support. Accordingly, it includes an intervision type support team as an integral part of the treatment. During intervision meetings, in addition to receiving emotional support, participating therapists work together to promote adherence to the treatment model.

A final strength worth noting is the "packaging" of DBT. The model takes a nonpejorative stance towards these "notoriously difficult" patients. Patients are not considered "manipulative" but treated with respect. Training materials are well-designed, and make heavy use of acronyms and metaphors to aid patients' retention and mastery of the critical skills. For example, as part of the interpersonal regulation model, patients learn the "dear man" acronym to become more assertive ("Describe the situation"; "Express your feelings/opinion about it"; "Ask for what you want"; "Reinforce" (a positive response); etc.).

That noted, as discussed below the effectiveness of DBT has been more convincingly documented in the realm of curtailing self-damaging externalizing behaviours than in other domains (e.g., quality of life, skills acquired, etc.; see also Scheel, 2000). Indeed, the second and third stages of treatment in DBT are neither as well-articulated nor as distinctive as the first stage (which is primarily aimed at controlling the impulsive, self-destructive behaviours). Trauma processing using exposure techniques and standard cognitive restructuring techniques are central ingredients to the later stages.

Schema-focused therapy (SFT)

SFT is a comprehensive, integrative model. It overlaps with other models of psychotherapy, but has distinctive features in its theoretical approach, technique, and use of the therapeutic relationship. Change is achieved through a range of behavioural, cognitive, and experiential techniques, focusing on the therapeutic relationship, life outside therapy, and past (traumatic) experiences. As such, SFT tends to be inclusive toward techniques as long as their application serves the healing of identified core schemata (Young et al., 2003).

What is a schema? Schemata are complex phenomena, involving memories, physical sensations, emotions, and dysfunctional cognitions; behaviours are not part of a schema. They are broad, deep-seated beliefs and themes about the self and (how) the world (works). They provide a sense of control and predictability, and are part of a person's sense of identity; hence their resistance to change. Old, dysfunctional schemata are rooted in unsatisfied basic emotional needs during childhood. According to Young and Klosko (2005), core emotional needs include (a) the development of secure attachments to others (see Chapter 4), (b) the development of autonomy, competency, and sense of identity, (c) the freedom to express valid needs and emotions, (d) spontaneity and play, and (e) realistic limits and self-control. Young and Klosko also propose four types of early life experience that foster the acquisition of schemata: toxic frustration of needs (leading for example to the schema of deprivation), traumatization (leading to mistrust and abuse schemata), overindulgence (leading to entitlement and dependence schemata), and selective internalization (leading for example to a subjugation schema). For example, a person may hold the defectiveness/shame schema as a result of growing up in an extremely rejecting and withholding environment (and having a sensitive temperament). Such a person would be highly vulnerable to rejection, and be prone to feelings of inferiority, defectiveness, and unlovability.

When, because of similarity to earlier experiences, a basic need is interfered with, a schema is triggered. This in turn elicits strong emotions, which are handled by the person's preferred coping responses. Typically these coping behaviours can be classified into one of three types: (1) overcompensation, (2) avoidance, and (3) surrender. For example, one might respond to the defectiveness/shame schema by exhibiting an arrogant haughty attitude (i.e., thinking, feeling, and behaving as if the opposite of the schema is true – overcompensating); by avoiding intimacy, so people cannot find out how inadequate you really are feeling (i.e., live around the schema, to steer clear of possible triggers – avoidance); or by choosing highly critical friends and partners (accept that what you believe about yourself is true and behave in self-fulfilling ways – surrendering). These three options roughly correspond to the fundamental fight-flight-freeze options organisms have in dealing with danger. The preferred coping responses may have been adaptive at an early age, but are no longer so for adult persons who have more options and higher capacity for cognitive elaboration. According to Young and Klosko (2005), DSM's diagnostic criteria tend to place too much emphasis on these compensatory behaviours instead of on the underlying themes or emotional pain. This is unfortunate, as the same schema can lead to superficially very different coping reactions. To the extent that a schema heals, it is more difficult to trigger. And when it is triggered, it will be less intense, less overwhelming, and easier to recover from.

A complication for the therapy with borderline PD individuals is that they tend to endorse the majority of the (18) schemata (see the handy list of descriptions in Oldham, Skodol, & Bender, 2005). The following vignette illustrates how this can become evident in clinical practice:

Barbara arrived at the ward with her ankle in a cast, a result of jumping out of the car of her (physically abusive) boyfriend in a state of rage. Over 1 year, she presented three times to the inpatient ward because of acute suicidality, each time still in the cast, because she had prematurely broken the plaster, out of anger, frustration, or just impatience. When the Schema questionnaire was administered to her, she had to stop midway – "[she] had them [the dysfunctional schemata] all" and was thoroughly upset by the questions.

Central to SFT for borderline PD is the assumption of five specific schema modes. These are the abandoned/abused child mode and the angry and impulsive mode (both child modes), the detached protector mode, a coping mode aimed at self-numbing, the punitive parent mode, and finally the underdeveloped healthy adult mode. The healthy adult mode, to be internalized after extensive modelling by the therapist, is characterized by emotional stability, goal-directed behaviour, mutually affirming relationships, and general well-being (see Table 6.3).

SFT follows three more or less overlapping phases. First, there is the bonding and emotional regulation phase: the patient and therapist are working towards the shared perception that the therapeutic relationship is a safe place in which the patient is affirmed and the expression of needs, desires, and feelings is encouraged. Once this is more or less established, the schema mode phase follows, during which each of the predominant modes is specifically addressed. For example, the deficits of the abandoned/abused child are addressed by a constancy of affirming messages, which typically is in great contrast to the early messages these patients received. The dynamics of the detached protector mode are explored, including its cost and benefits for the patient. More functional, alternative solutions are tried in the safe context of therapy. Finally, in the third phase, SFT focuses on the development of autonomy and on gaining independence outside sessions; core issues are working on mutually reinforcing (give and take) relationships and solidifying a core sense of self.

Four mechanisms of healing have recently (Kellogg & Young, 2006) been proposed that largely map onto the mix of therapeutic strategies pursued within SFT. First among equals is what Young and Klosko (2005) call *limited reparenting*. While maintaining professional boundaries, the therapist tries to compensate for the deficits accrued by growing up in an emotionally depriving matrix. Key issues in limited reparenting are providing safety, stability and acceptance, as these are thought of as preconditions for growth from functioning emotionally at childlike levels to healthy adult functioning. Second, *emotion-focused* work through imagery and dialogues is thought to

TABLE 6.3

A description of the characteristic borderline personality disorder modes

Abandoned and abused child mode
... embodies the theme of frightened isolation, rooted in the abandonment and abuse the patient experiences as a child. An intensely painful mode, patients report feeling fragile, lost, and helpless when in this mode. Patients believe the pain will never end, that they will be alone forever, with nobody to care for them.

Angry and impulsive child mode
... reflects the part of the child that knows that she did not have her core emotional needs met, that she was mistreated. The mistreatment can refer to abuse, deprivation, abandonment, rejection, neglect, etc. Situations that trigger memories of these various sufferings can elicit intense, and often ultimately self-detrimental, rage in borderline PD patients.

Detached protector mode
... is a coping mode in which the patient "shuts down", and adopts a style of emotional withdrawal, disconnection, or behavioural avoidance through addictive self-soothing, or sensation seeking. Patients tend to feel numb or empty when in this mode. As a child, detachment was effective in protecting/isolating against painful interpersonal attachment experiences and other negative emotional experiences.

Punitive parent mode
... is the patient's identification and internalization of the parent who devalued and rejected the patient in childhood; it perpetuates the abuse internally as patients adopt an extremely harsh, self-punishing attitude. When in this mode, patients experience themselves as fundamentally "bad", defective, and unlovable. These experiences may give rise to self-injurious behaviours.

Healthy adult mode
... is underdeveloped in the borderline PD patient. It is the healthy part that helps the individual in getting her needs met: by nurturing and affirming the vulnerable child, by setting limits to the angry/impulsive child, and by fighting maladaptive coping and self-persecution. First modelled by the therapist, patients can progressively internalize this agency.

produce positive change: empty chair and two chair role-playing techniques, derived from Gestalt therapy, as well as structured letter writing, can help the patient emotionally process childhood scenes and strengthen the more adaptive modes at the expense of the punitive parent or detached protector modes. Other presumed mechanisms involve *cognitive restructuring and education*. Much of this work focuses on teaching the patient what normal emotional needs are, and then validating these needs, emotions, and longings in the patient. Finally, *behaviour pattern breaking* involves developing more adaptive ways to get the emotional needs met than, for example, the typical repertoire of the detached protector mode.

Transference-focused therapy (TFT)

TFT was developed by Kernberg and colleagues (Clarkin et al., 1999, 2001). It is an individual psychotherapy, usually on a twice a week basis, lasting between 2 and 5 years. While it focuses on transference and countertransference and involves free association rules, TFT is quite different from classical psychoanalysis. It requires active therapist involvement and focuses on the here and now transactions in the therapeutic relationship, albeit with the aim of understanding issues that originated in childhood.

The core issue in TFT is to learn to accept and tolerate conflicting feelings and images in one person – both in self and in others. Borderline PD individuals have not developed this capacity: they switch from all-good to all-bad images of self and others, a phenomenon referred to as *splitting*. Why did they not develop this capacity? Psychodynamic theory holds that the split served a defensive function: in order to protect what was good, it had to be completely separated from the extreme bad qualities, as the child would not psychologically survive otherwise. As discussed previously, Arntz and colleagues have called into question the empirical viability of the "splitting" conceptualization, but it remains nevertheless central to TFT.

In TFT, the unfolding therapeutic relationship is used to examine key issues and problems, and to subsequently learn to understand, tolerate, and change them. The assumption is that the important childhood conflicts will surface in the therapeutic relationship, hence the label *transference-focused* therapy. Analyses of transference and countertransference are expected to yield crucial insight. That is, the interpersonal relationship between the therapist and patient is consistently explored for affect-laden themes that may recapitulate dominant object relational patterns. The therapist is also monitoring her personal reactions to the client, noticing what tendencies are evoked in her, which may reflect earlier dynamics. Change is achieved through interpreting the transference and countertransference, focusing primarily on the therapeutic relationship in a here-and-now context. The overall aim is to assist the client in developing the capacity to hold differentiated images of self and others, with both good and bad qualities (see also Clarkin & Levy, 2006).

The therapy follows several, somewhat overlapping and iterative stages. Similar to DBT, substantive issues are addressed in a fixed hierarchy: first, containment of suicidal and self-destructive behaviours, then treatment interfering behaviours, and subsequently the identification of the dominant object relational themes. Before addressing substantive issues, however, and central to TFT, the treatment contract has to be negotiated. Patient and therapist have to agree on the rules and regulations of therapy, including the tasks and responsibilities of each. For example, the therapist commits to specific rules and obligations regarding availability, and is expected to help interpret the ongoing interactions between herself and the client. The client, in turn, is expected to show up for treatment, commit to certain rules regarding self-harm behaviours, and to speak her thoughts as they enter her mind, i.e., to free associate during the sessions. Agreement is necessary before substantive treatment can commence. The second stage focuses on strengthening the control over self-harming and treatment interfering behaviours. As this goal is mastered, increasing emphasis is placed on the analysis of the unfolding transference and countertransference reactions. Patients learn to tolerate and communicate their ongoing feelings more effectively as they practise these behaviours in each session. They learn to recognize, identify, and understand their emotions better, as well as those of others. Over time, they reach a more whole understanding of their own and others' motivations and thus become better able to entertain images of self and others that incorporate both good and bad qualities. This achievement in turn leads to less extreme emotions and behaviours, and better adjustment to reality.

Mentalization-based treatment (MBT)

Bateman and Fonagy (2003, 2004b) have developed an evidence-based treatment programme rooted in attachment theory that integrates research on constitutional factors with environmental influences. Whereas DBT considers emotion deregulation as fundamental to borderline PD, MBT considers borderline PD as a failure to develop a robust self-structure, due to absence of contingent and marked mirroring during development. The key functional deficit involved is called "mentalization" and the focus of MBT is on stabilizing the patient's sense of self by strengthening his or her capacity for mentalization.

Mentalization refers to the capacity to understand and interpret human behaviour in terms of underlying mental states. It involves making sense of the actions of oneself and others on the basis of intentional mental states, such as desires, feelings, and beliefs. The capacity to do this develops through a process of having experienced oneself in the mind of another during childhood within an attachment context, and only matures adequately within the context of a secure attachment. As such, mentalization is seen as a developmental achievement; i.e., in the context of a secure attachment, an intersubjective process can take shape centred around observing, labelling, and communicating feelings, thoughts, and desires, and to link these internal states in a meaningful way to the actions of self and others.

In borderline PD patients, this capacity has not matured, presumably because they did not grow up in a social context conducive to secure attachment and adequate mirroring of their internal states (see Chapter 4). If internal experience is not met by external understanding, it remains unlabelled, confusing, and the uncontained affect generates further dysregulation. Primary experience of affect will not be symbolically represented. Two modes of experiencing predate the mentalizing representation and are critical to understanding the borderline PD reactions: psychic equivalence and the pretend mode. When in psychic equivalence mode, patients fail to distinguish between internal and external experience; reality and subjective experience are perceived as one, leading to overly real, overwhelming experiences. Feelings, fantasies, thoughts, and desires are experienced with considerable force because they can not be symbolized, held in a state of uncertainty, and given secondary representation with meaning. In contrast, in the pretend mode, patients decouple the internal and external worlds, leading to detached, intellectualized experience. It is the integration of psychic equivalent and pretend modes of functioning that give rise to mentalization in which thoughts and feelings can be experienced as representations and inner and outer reality are seen as linked, but separate, and are no longer either equated or dissociated from each other.

Borderline patients cannot easily hold more than one idea, desire, or wish in mind at a time, and they have little access to alternative states or explanations. Moreover, borderline PD patients have difficulty distinguishing between intention and action, or between outcome and intention, or considering more than one possible attribution for events. To illustrate, a female borderline PD patient panicked and became suicidal when her daughter did not show up for the visiting hours. The only possible explanation was "that [the daughter] does not care for me at all, and will never be back". The therapist should promote an examination of the internal experience and the triggering external events, with the aim of bridging the gap between the two.

Treatment strategies target mentalization in order to foster the development of stable internal representations, to aid the formation of a coherent sense of self, and to enable the borderline patient to form more secure relationships in which motivations of self and other are better understood. A precondition for the development of mentalizing faculties is the establishment of a safe secure environment where it is normative to examine internal states, that is, a reliable therapeutic relationship. To enhance mentalization, strategic use of transference is sought, working in the here and now with current mental states, bearing in mind the patient's deficits. The therapeutic task is to assist the patient to link affects to representation and to develop a capacity for symbolic representation (see also Fonagy & Bateman, 2006, for an in-depth description of presumed mechanisms of change). The therapist must help the patient understand and label emotional states and also help the patient place them within a present context with a linking narrative to the recent and remote past. Accordingly, the therapist needs to maintain a mentalizing stance to help a patient develop a capacity to mentalize. As explained by Bateman and Fonagy (2004a), the therapist asks him- or herself: Why is the patient saying this now? Why am I feeling as I do now? Why do you think s/he is feeling as s/he does? What might I have done that explains the patient's stance? Therapists need to retain their own ability to mentalize, maintain mental closeness, focus on current mental states, and avoid excessive use of conflict interpretation and metaphor while paying careful attention to the use of transference and countertransference. Like TFT, MBT is a psychodynamic treatment but even more than SFT it emphasizes working in the "here and now" rather than focusing on the past. To the extent that the past is invoked, it is focused on its role of how it may have influenced the present state.

Treatment outcome

Cognitive therapy

Despite the fact that cognitive therapy has become rather popular among clinicians since the publication of the important volume *Cognitive Therapy of Personality Disorders* by Beck and Freeman (1990), very few controlled studies are available that have demonstrated its effectiveness in the treatment of borderline PD. Brown and colleagues (Brown, Newman, Charlesworth, Crits-Christoph, & Beck, 2004) evaluated the effects of cognitive therapy in 32 borderline PD patients with suicide ideation or self-injurious behaviour. After 1 year of treatment, CT yielded clinically significant changes in depression, hopelessness, number of borderline symptoms, and suicidal ideation, and results were maintained up to 18 months. Further, as predicted by the cognitive theory underlying this treatment, patients improved in measures of dysfunctional beliefs reflecting themes of distrust, helplessness, fears of abandonment and losing emotional control, and dependency. Results were comparable to those of DBT as reported by Koons et al. (2001). At 18 months after base-line 55% of the patients had remitted in terms of borderline PD. Unfortunately, this study was uncontrolled, so that the positive results achieved might be attributed to factors other than the cognitive therapy.

To date, two RCTs have been reported, but both studies involved variants of CT rather than a straight Beckian approach. In the UK, the BOSCOT trial was recently completed, which is the largest RCT into the effectiveness of outpatient psychotherapy for borderline PD so far. In this multicentre study, 106 patients with borderline PD were randomly assigned to either cognitive therapy or treatment as usual. Treatment lasted 12 months and follow-up results were reported up to 24 months after randomization (Davidson, 2006). Patients attended on average 16 of the 30 sessions offered. Cognitive therapy was superior to treatment as usual in terms of a reduction of suicidal acts, state anxiety, and dysfunctional beliefs, but not in depressed mood. The clinically superior outcome was not reflected in the quality of life as assessed with the EuroQol, and not in terms of cost-effectiveness (Palmer, 2006).

Dialectical behaviour therapy

Dialectical behaviour therapy was developed as a comprehensive outpatient treatment programme for individuals meeting criteria for borderline PD. To date, four controlled studies have demonstrated the effectiveness of this approach for borderline patients. In a landmark study in which patients with borderline PD who recently had engaged in parasuicidal behaviour were randomly assigned to 1-year outpatient DBT or treatment as usual, Linehan and colleagues (Linehan, Armstrong, Suarez, Allmon, & Heard, 1991; Linehan, Heard, & Armstrong, 1993) demonstrated efficacy for this form of therapy in reducing the frequency of parasuicidal behaviour, and in retaining patients in therapy: DBT led to less drop-out of treatment (16%). Further, after a year patients receiving DBT spent less time in hospital than patients assigned to treatment as usual. However, DBT was not more effective than the control condition in terms of reduction of hopelessness, depressed mood, and suicidal ideation. At 1-year follow-up differences between DBT and treatment as usual were less pronounced, although patients treated with DBT continued to show superior outcomes on some measures. The first replication study by an independent group, though only a small pilot study, provided further support for the efficacy of the DBT model (Koons et al., 2001). In female borderline patients (US veterans) 6 months of DBT resulted in more improvement than controls in suicidal ideation, hopelessness, depression, and anger expression. How can we explain that in this study DBT resulted in enhanced outcome on depression, hopelessness, and suicidal ideation, when this was not the case in the original Linehan et al. (1991) study? The enhanced outcome in the Koons et al. (2001) study may be attributed to the fact that their patients were less severe in terms of suicidal behaviour. In line with DBT, therapists with more severe parasuicidal patients in the Linehan et al. study would be expected to focus more on life-saving strategies, leaving less time to target quality-of-life issues.

DBT and substance abuse. It should be noted that individuals with substance dependence were excluded from the above investigations. However, individuals meeting criteria for borderline PD are more likely to also meet criteria for substance abuse than individuals with other personality disorders, with the exception of antisocial PD. In addition, individuals with borderline PD and comorbid substance disorders had more severe psychopathology than individuals with borderline PD only (Links, Heslegrave, Mitton, van Reekum, & Patric, 1995). DBT may help substance-abusing patients with borderline PD to learn to cope with some of their personality problems, but is less effective in addressing the substance abuse problems. Verheul et al. (2003) reported that standard DBT could be effectively applied with borderline patients with comorbid substance abuse in terms of lower levels of parasuicidal and impulsive behaviours. However, DBT was not more effective compared to treatment as usual in reducing sub-stance use problems. At 6-month follow-up the benefits of DBT over care as usual persisted. There were still no differences between the treatment conditions for drug abuse, but patients who had received DBT drank less alcohol as compared to patients in the treatment as usual condition (van den Bosch, Verheul, Schippers, & van den Brink, 2003).

Recent years have seen the development of interventions designed specifically to treat patients with borderline PD and substance abuse, the most important being adaptations in the DBT programme

(Linehan et al., 1999). Several modifications were added to standard DBT, including a dialectic stance on drug use that insists on total abstinence. However, in the case of a lapse into substance use, coping strategies from cognitive-behavioural therapy are used to prevent lapses becoming full relapse, followed by a quick return to the original treatment goal of total abstinence. Further, treatment also involved transitional maintenance medication in the perspective of "replacing pills with skills" later on in the programme. In a random-ized controlled trial, patients with borderline PD and drug depen-dence who received this adjusted DBT programme had significantly greater reduction in drug use at 16-month follow-up than control patients who had received treatment as usual. Further, DBT resulted in less attrition from treatment and better social adjustment as com-pared to the controls (Linehan et al., 1999).

DBT as treatment for inpatients. Linehan's DBT was developed as an outpatient treatment to prevent emergency room visits and hospital admissions. Attempts have been made to adapt this treatment to a hospital setting for inpatients with borderline PD (Swenson, Sanderson, Dulit, & Linehan, 2001). Inpatient DBT treatment pro-cedures include contingency management procedures, skills training including mindfulness training and coaching, behavioural analysis, structured response protocols to suicidal behaviours on the unit, and consultation team meetings for DBT staff. Bohus et al. (2004) com-pared DBT (3 months) in a hospital setting with outpatient care as usual. One month after treatment DBT patients improved signifi-cantly more than controls on self-mutilation, depression and anxiety, interpersonal functioning, social adjustment, and global psycho-pathology. However, this study does not demonstrate that hospital-ization enhances DBT effectiveness, since DBT as inpatient treatment was not compared with DBT provided in an outpatient format. Moreover, patients were not randomly assigned to conditions, which further limits the conclusions that can be drawn with respect to the efficacy of inpatient DBT for borderline PD.

Does medication enhance effectiveness of DBT? Many patients with border-line PD are treated with SSRI antidepressive medication. Simpson et al. (2004) investigated whether Fluoxetine (often sold as "Prozac") enhanced the effects of DBT. Adding Fluoxetine to DBT did not yield any additional benefits. On the contrary, patients who had been treated with DBT plus placebo tended to improve more on a number of measures than patients in the DBT plus Fluoxetine condition. The DBT intervention seemed too powerful for Fluoxetine to enhance.

A recent study (Soler et al., 2005) investigated whether Olanzapine, atypical antipsychotic medication, would enhance the effects of DBT. Sixty patients with borderline PD were included in a 12-week, double-blind, placebo-controlled study. All patients received DBT and were randomly assigned to receive Olanzapine or placebo. Thirty per cent of patients dropped out of the treatment study. Combined treatment showed an overall improvement in most symptoms studied in both groups. Olanzapine was associated with a statistically significant improvement over placebo in depression and anxiety. The Olanzapine plus DBT group experienced a significantly greater decrease in the frequency of impulsivity and aggressive behaviours than the placebo plus DBT group. Although self-injury and suicidal gestures decreased slightly more in the combined group, this difference was not significant.

Concluding remarks. Although a number of studies substantively replicated the findings by Linehan et al. (1991), the number of controlled research studies on DBT is still limited. Nevertheless, it is the only treatment for borderline PD that was given the status of "empirically supported therapy" by the Division of Clinical Psychology of the American Psychological Association. Despite this accreditation, there are a number of critical issues that deserve some comment.

First of all, to date all studies have been conducted with relatively small samples, consisting primarily of parasuicidal females. Moreover, in most studies other (Axis-I) disorders were excluded, but in epidemiological and clinical studies comorbid Axis-I disorder and/or Axis-II disorder are the rule rather than the exception in patients with borderline PD (see Chapter 3). As noted before, borderline PD is a heterogeneous condition with significant differences in individual symptom patterns. Some (e.g., Verheul et al., 2003) have suggested that DBT is particularly suited for the impulsive subtype of patients with borderline PD and that DBT is primarily a treatment for parasuicide. It is questionable whether DBT is equally effective for patients who are primarily characterized by chronic feelings of emptiness and boredom, interpersonal instability, or identity disturbance. Another concern relates to the long-term effects of DBT. Few studies have investigated this issue and the observation that after 1 year differences between DBT and treatment as usual tended to disappear (Linehan et al., 1993) does not stem optimism. Further, DBT consists of many elements and research has not yet dismantled the essential elements of this approach. A final issue that deserves further study is whether DBT is easily implemented in routine clinical care. DBT is a highly sophisticated treatment programme that requires intensive training and supervision. In fact, therapists in most studies were either trained by Linehan herself or by (former) collaborators of hers. Whether front-line mental health professionals outside academic research centres can effectively learn this treatment is questionable, although some uncontrolled studies in community mental health centres suggest that this may be feasible (e.g., Turner, 2000).

Schema-focused therapy

Schema-focused therapy (SFT) was recently developed for the treatment of borderline PD (Young et al., 2003) and only few studies have investigated this form of therapy as yet. In a series of controlled case studies of patients with borderline PD, schema-focused therapy was rather effective in five out of six patients (Nordahl & Nysæter, 2005). Three of the six patients no longer fulfilled the criteria for borderline PD by the end of the treatment. By using Cohen's *d* for estimating the size of changes in the group of six patients as a whole, the results show that the pretreatment to follow-up effects were large, with effect sizes ranging from 1.8 to 2.9. Based on the self-report scores, five of the six patients had greatly improved on general symptomatic and interpersonal distress 12–16 months after treatment. Recently, Giessen-Bloo et al. (2006) reported on a randomized controlled trial (RCT) into the effects of SFT with patients with borderline PD. In this study the effects of SFT were compared with those of transference-focused therapy, a psychodynamically oriented individual psychotherapy. Patients were treated for a maximum of 3 years. Effectiveness of treatment became apparent at 12 months and steadily increased. SFT was superior to transference-focused therapy on changes in borderline criteria, including parasuicide, general psychopathology, and change in pathogenic personality features. Additional advantages of SFT over transference-focused therapy were lower attrition and better cost-effectiveness.

Psychodynamic therapeutic community treatments

A long-term psychodynamically oriented therapeutic community is a treatment approach that is widely used in the care of patients with borderline PD. In such therapeutic communities intense individual and group psychodynamic psychotherapy are offered. Unfortunately, the effectiveness of this long-term hospital-based approach has rarely been tested. Chiesa, Fonagy, Holmes, and Drahorad (2004) contrasted a long-term (12-month) psychodynamic hospital-based treatment with a phased "stepped-down" programme, in which patients were admitted for only 6 months and a follow-up of 12 months' outpatient therapy with community support. Both hospital-based treatments were compared with routine psychiatric care. Patients had to fulfil criteria for at least one diagnosis of PD. Two-thirds of the included patients received a diagnosis of borderline PD, most patients having two to three personality disorder diagnoses, most often of Cluster B. Results did not support the effectiveness of this intensive form of long-term psychodynamic treatment. The stepped-down approach was the most effective, followed by the routine psychiatric care group. Patients in the long-term residential model showed no improvements in self-harm, attempted suicide, or number of readmissions. Hospital readmissions in the year following treatment were 49% for the inpatient group compared to 11% for the step-down programme and 33% for the general psychiatric care group.

Given the rather disappointing results of the long-term psychodynamic treatment for severe personality disorder, one may wonder how effective partial hospitalization and outpatient programmes based on psychodynamic approaches are. In the case of borderline PD, research efforts have concentrated on two psychodynamic treatment approaches: mentalization-based treatment (Bateman & Fonagy, 1999) and transference-focused therapy (Clarkin, Levy, Lenzenweger, & Kernberg, 2004).

Transference-focused therapy. A few investigations have examined the effectiveness of transference-focused therapy in borderline patients, but only two RCTs have been reported (Clarkin et al., 2004; Giessen-Bloo et al., 2006). In an initial uncontrolled open study (Clarkin et al., 2001), women between the ages of 18 and 50 who met criteria for borderline PD with at least two incidents of suicidal or self-injurious behaviour in the last 5 years were admitted to the study. Of the 23 patients that entered the study, 17 completed the planned 1 year of treatment. The 1-year attrition rate was 26%, which is slightly higher than reported in DBT (16%: Linehan et al., 1991). Half of the patients no longer met criteria for borderline PD after 1 year of twice-weekly outpatient treatment. TFT showed marked reductions in the severity of parasuicidal behaviours, and resulted in fewer emergency room visits, hospitalizations, and days hospitalized. The effect sizes were large and comparable to those reported for DBT (Linehan et al., 1991) and mentalization-based treatment (Bateman & Fonagy, 1999). Results were compared with treatment as usual, but the comparison was not randomized.

A recent RCT compared transference-focused therapy with DBT (Clarkin et al., 2004). A third treatment condition, supportive treatment, was used as a control for attention and support. Male and female borderline PD patients were randomly assigned to one of these three treatment conditions for 1-year outpatient treatment. Results have been reported to 12 months. Suicidality and anger reduced in patients treated with TFP and DBT, but not in those treated with SPT; all three treatments were effective in reducing depression and in improving global functioning and social adjustment (see Fonagy, Roth, & Higgitt, 2005; Levy et al., 2006).

Mentalization-based treatment. Bateman and Fonagy (1999, 2004a) have developed and tested an intervention specifically targeting severe borderline PD, that integrates individual and group psychoanalytic psychotherapy within a structured partial hospitalization programme. In an RCT study by Bateman and Fonagy (1999), 38 patients with borderline PD were allocated randomly to a partial hospitalization programme or to a standard psychiatric care (control) group. Results revealed that the psychoanalytically oriented partial hospitalization programme was superior to the standard psychiatric care. Patients who were partially hospitalized showed a statistically significant decrease on depressive symptoms, a decrease in suicidal and self-mutilatory acts, a reduction in inpatient days, and gains in social and interpersonal function. In contrast, the control group showed limited change or deterioration over the same period. Improvement started at 6 months and continued until the end of treatment at 18 months. In another report Bateman and Fonagy (2001) published the results of follow-up treatment. The treatment consisted of 18 months of outpatient psychoanalytically oriented group therapy. Results indicated further significant improvement with continued treatment. Of note, although the results achieved are clinically interesting and comparable to those achieved with DBT, it is questionable whether the effects should be attributed to the specific psychodynamic content of the treatment or to the intensive, structured format. As noted by Tyrer (2002), it may not be the specific elements of DBT and mentalization-based treatment respectively that moderate treatment effects, but instead the ability to structure treatment and to create a common team approach with borderline patients is the necessary condition for treatment to be effective.

Concluding remarks

From the presentation above, it apparent that evidence-based treatments for borderline PD have a number of features in common. First, extended time and effort is invested in developing a positive, safe, collaborative therapy relationship, with clear rules (e.g., limit setting) and expectations regarding the roles of both therapist and patient. Second, each treatment has a specific, coherent (but different) theory of the aetiology and mechanisms of change regarding borderline PD. This theory is shared with the clients, and guides the flow of therapy. All evidence-based therapies follow to some extent an explicit or implicit hierarchy of treatment goals/priorities; work alliance and safety come first, more substantive issues later. Regarding procedural aspects, the treatments tend to be structured, long term (i.e., measured in years), and often involve several planned or unplanned auxiliary services (including for example telephone consultation, group skills training, occasional inpatient services, medication management, etc.). The therapists tend to be active rather than passive, but pay greater attention to validation and support than in regular therapies for clinical syndromes. Another common feature is the recognition of the need for supervision and emotional support for the therapists treating patients with such a challenging mix of psychopathology.

The treatment outcome review also shows that CBT and structured psychodynamic therapy have something to offer in the treatment of borderline PD. As noted by Fonagy et al. (2005), psychodynamic therapy as a generic treatment is very unlikely to be effective. Indeed, when psychodynamic therapy was found as effective as CBT, special efforts had been made to modify the generic psychodynamic approach for the particular PD, using manualized treatment protocols. Moreover, each school of therapy emphasizes its own putative mechanisms of change, but it is unclear to what extent the diverse theoretical positions translate to recognizably different therapist behaviours, and, at present, we have only speculations on the specific effective components of each (multicomponent) treatment.

Pharmacotherapy

Accumulating evidence suggests that neurochemical imbalances are involved in personality pathology (Markovitz, 2001; and Chapter 4). This is not surprising: numerous studies have documented that impulsivity, aggression, and more broadly negative emotionality are based in dysregulated neural circuitry, and these traits are likely candidates for a dimensional representation of personality disorders. Psychotropic medication may help alleviate these imbalances, and the APA recommends pharmacotherapy as one of the modes of treatment in borderline PD in their practice guidelines (2001). Most often, medication is used as an auxiliary treatment, in support of psychotherapy. Typically, pharmacotherapy targets key symptoms that are particularly troublesome for the individual borderline PD patient, such as depressive symptoms, mood swings, or distorted thinking processes. Generally, the effects of pharmacotherapy last for the duration of their active use. Therefore, given the chronicity of most borderline PD symptoms, patients are likely to be on their medication for extended time. The quality of life enhancing effects of short-term symptom relief should not be underestimated. Such changes may help patients function more effectively in social and work situations. Moreover, symptom relief may benefit the patient's ability to work on the task of therapy. For example, improved motivation, energy, and concentration can boost the active involvement in homework assignments (e.g., in DBT). On the other hand, given the side effects and the chronicity and multifaceted nature of the disorder, restraint in prescriptions seems warranted.

Most of the diverse pharmacological agents used in the clinical care of borderline PD patients can be grouped into three clusters: antidepressants, anticonvulsants, and antipsychotics. More rarely, lithium, benzodiazepines, and opioid antagonists have been used. A number of issues are particularly salient in planning pharmacotherapy with borderline PD patients. First, this population is characterized by chronic suicidality. Medication that is highly toxic in higher dosages is therefore contraindicated. Second, compliance tends to be especially problematic in this generally dysregulated group. This means that medication that depends on close observation of blood serum levels (e.g., lithium) will probably not work out. Yet another consideration is the heightened potential for addiction, a highly frequent comorbid disorder among borderline PD individuals. This complicates the prescription of benzodiazepines. Benzodiazepines may be effective in downregulating state anxiety or even psychotic phenomena, but they also have substantial addictive potential. These and other considerations have led Dimeff, McDavid, and Linehan (1999) to formulate a number of practical integrated guidelines when prescribing psychotropic medications for borderline PD individuals. Among others, these include: (a) combine pharmacotherapy with an active psychosocial treatment, (b) do not give lethal drugs to lethal people, (c) consult with the patient about how to interact effectively with his or her pharmacotherapist, and (d) treat medication noncompliance as treatment-interfering behaviour.

Summary

Instability is the hallmark of borderline PD. The prototypical borderline PD patient shows a pervasive pattern of instability across the domains of mood, cognition, interpersonal relationships, self-image, and impulse control. The construct validity of the disorder is subject to much debate and quite diverse conceptualizations of the core nature of the disorder are proposed. This state of affairs may in part be due to the great heterogeneity allowed by the polythetic definition of borderline PD in the DSM. Current theoretical models of borderline PD generally follow a diathesis-stress format: temperamentally vulnerable individuals growing up in unfavourable environmental contexts. The chapter closes with a description and empirical review of the current evidence-based psychological treatments for borderline PD, and a brief review of psychopharmacology.

The narcissistic and histrionic personality disorders

7

> Whoever loves becomes humble. Those who love have, so to speak, pawned a part of their narcissism.
>
> (Freud, 1914, p. 218)

Narcissistic personality disorder

Narcissism owes its name to the Greek myth of Narcissus. Narcissus fell in love with his own reflection in a pool of still water. Consumed by his own desire, he was transformed into a flower. Narcissism, then, has to do with excessive self-love; or as psychodynamic thinkers would have it, a withdrawal of object love and reinvestment in (pathological) self-love. Narcissism has many, somewhat diverse connotations in psychology: it can refer to normal range mechanisms of maintenance and regulation of self-esteem, to a normal range personality trait, to an extreme amount of self-esteem, or be a descriptor term for a DSM-IV syndrome.

Central to patients who meet criteria for a DSM-IV narcissistic PD is their overt grandiose sense of self-importance and uniqueness. They harbour fantasies of unlimited success, power, brilliance, beauty, or ideal love (APA, 2000). Requiring constant attention and admiration, they can react with intense anger to criticism and to (readily perceived) humiliation and rejection, or other situations that threaten their grandiose self-image. Towards others, they tend to be exploitative and lacking in empathy. Individuals with narcissistic PD believe they are entitled to special, preferential treatment based on their uniqueness. In thinking about narcissistic PD, perhaps more so than with other personality disorders, it is important to understand the dynamics between such diverse and seemingly inconsistent descriptors as grandiosity, entitlement, hypersensitivity to humiliation, proneness to shame, and rage. Underlying the demanding and entitled presentation is the preoccupation with a fragile sense of self and self-esteem; grandiosity may be seen as the core trait, but self-esteem regulation is likely to be the core defect in narcissistic PD. The "narcissistic paradox" (Emmons, 1984) seems to be that persons hold inflated self-concepts but also need an inordinate tribute from others, expressed in money, status, and admiration. Narcissism, like most personality traits, can lead to positive and negative adaptations; versions of it are observable in various influential people, including (political) leaders, terrorists (Meloy, 2004), and even scientists.

Widespread usage of the term by clinicians and an extended history of psychodynamic theorizing culminated in the introduction of narcissistic PD in the DSM. As of yet, it has not been formally adopted into the ICD-10 (WHO, 1992). While there is extensive psychodynamic theorizing on the developmental pathway towards the narcissistic disorders, salient dynamic themes, etc., the empirical evaluation of the concept has been amazingly scarce. In 1988, Raskin and Terry noted that close to 1000 books and articles had appeared on narcissistic PD, but only 50 of those were empirical in nature, and these were essentially all devoted to scale development or scale validation. We will heavily emphasize our discussion towards the empirical literature.

Given the paucity of empirical research on narcissistic PD (Gunderson, Ronningstam, & Smith, 1995; Paris, 1995), definite statements about its specific aetiology and course are suspect. Nevertheless, it is a diagnosis regularly encountered in clinical practice. Self-referrals more often than not focus on the secondary consequences (e.g., frustration or depression about unrealized self-perceived potential; constantly disappointing relationships) of the disorder, rather than the disorder itself. Several psychotherapy models have been specifically developed to address the narcissistic PD pathology (e.g., Kernberg, 1984; Kohut, 1971, 1974; Masterson, 1993; Young, Klosko, & Weishaar, 2003), but no controlled studies have yet been conducted to document their efficacy (see also Chapter 4). Best practice probably involves psychodynamic therapy, along the lines of Kohut or Kernberg, or cognitive/schema-based therapy, along the lines of Beck, Freeman, and Davis (2003) or Young et al. (2003).

In the DSM, narcissistic PD has overlap with other Cluster B diagnoses, particularly antisocial PD and borderline PD. To enhance discrimination with borderline PD, DSM-IV dropped the DSM-III-R subcriterion of "relationships that alternate between the extremes of overidealization and devaluation". With antisocial PD, it has in common what has been referred to as "interpersonal disesteem": an exploitative, selfish interpersonal orientation. In 1990, Ronningstam and Gunderson tried to empirically identify criteria for narcissistic PD, aiming to contribute to subsequent fine-tuning of the diagnostic criterion set. They compared 24 narcissistic PD patients to 36 near neighbour diagnoses from Cluster B and 22 other, mainly Axis-I type, patients on putative indicators of pathological narcissism. Discriminating features included (a) a sense of superiority, (b) exaggeration of talents, (c) boastful and pretentious behaviour, (d) grandiose fantasies, (e) self-centred and self-referential behaviour, (f) need for attention and admiration, (g) arrogant and haughty behaviour, and (h) high achievement. However, to set it apart, grandiose fantasies and a sense of personal uniqueness and superiority are much more descriptive of narcissistic PD than of antisocial PD individuals (Gunderson & Ronningstam, 2001). Similar findings were obtained by another group of researchers. Blais, Hilsenroth, and Castlebury (1997) identified three primary features of narcissistic PD, i.e., grandiose self-image, lack of empathy, and excessive reliance on external factors to regulate self-esteem. Again, it was particularly the first factor, grandiosity, that sets narcissistic PD apart from the near neighbour diagnoses of Cluster B (Holdwick, Hilsenroth, Castlebury, & Blais, 1998).

Do narcissistic patients improve? Interesting findings on this issue were reported by Ronningstam, Gunderson, and Lyons (1995). These researchers not only found that pathological narcissism decreased over the course of 3 years, but also obtained evidence that these gains in functioning were associated with three specific kinds of corrective experiences: achievements, new durable relationships, or disillusionments. As noted by the authors, these types of corrective experience seem to be incorporated in the therapeutic strategies as expounded by Kohut (1971, 1974): establishment of a corrective relationship in which the "mirroring" of archaic grandiosity needs takes place through empathic immersion, and subsequently is replaced by more mature and appropriate self-appraisals (see later in this chapter).

Frances noted in 1980 that the DSM rendering of narcissistic PD does not fully reflect the intrapsychic dynamics essential to narcissistic PD. Available evidence also suggests a mismatch between the use of the narcissistic PD label in clinical practice and the formal definition stated in the DSM, with clinicians assigning the label to persons not meeting the formal criteria but also not assigning the diagnosis to those who formally do. Indeed, there is quite a bit of tension between the DSM-IV narcissistic PD and the predominant psychodynamic conceptualizations, and the same might be said of Young et al.'s cognitive theorizing regarding narcissistic PD. Let us review these ideas briefly.

Theories on narcissistic personality disorder

Most of the literature about narcissistic PD is of psychodynamic origin, most notably the writings by and inspired by Kohut (1971, 1974) and Kernberg (1984, 1996). Central to Kohut's thinking is the concept of self-objects. Self-objects are representations in one's mind of close, sustaining relationships that fuel a sense of personal strength and confidence. When these intrapsychic supports fail to develop adequately, a feeble self-structure with compromised affect regulatory capacity will emerge. As such, Kohut sees narcissistic PD as a developmental arrest. Archaic grandiosity remains if the mother's confirming responses are deficient and if the empathic attunement between mother and child is severely lacking. Kohut finds the descriptive symptom presentation of the narcissistic PD inadequate for diagnosis. Diagnostically more valid, according to Kohut, are the characteristic unfolding transference patterns of the narcissistic PD patient. Kohut places the narcissistic personality in the neurotic spectrum of psychopathology, implying important distinctions with borderline PD. In treatment, according to Kohut, narcissistic PD patients should be allowed to exhibit their grandiosity and be given the opportunity to idealize the therapist. Through sustained empathic immersion, a corrective relationship experience is created that provides the circumstances for a gradual reappraisal of self and internalized others. Patients learn to appreciate their own and their therapist's limitations, thus lifting the developmental arrest.

Kernberg (1984, 1996) places the narcissistic personality at the borderline level of organization. According to Kernberg, the structural damage seen in the narcissistic patient is rooted in growing up in an emotionally depriving environment, e.g., a chronically cold, unempathic mother. Feeling unloved and "bad", the child projected his rage onto his parents, who then were perceived as even more sadistic and depriving. The child's defence was to take refuge in some aspect of himself that his parents valued. Thus, the grandiose self developed. According to Kernberg, the therapist needs to interpret the defensive function of the grandiosity to the patient, i.e., it protects them from feeling unlovable and inferior. The interpretations aim to connect the extreme positive (grandiose) and negative (inferior, unlovable) self-representations.

A social learning account of the narcissistic personality disorder has been proposed by Millon (1981), who posited that it was parental overvaluation rather than devaluation that is at the root of narcissistic PD. Children are led to believe they are special and perfect through a constant showering of attention and admiration. When disappointment occurs, the overinflated sense of self-worth fuels rage. This overinflated self-image is intermittently reinforced, thus making it highly resistant to extinction. Millon's review of the literature was important in the formulation of the first DSM criterion set of the narcissistic PD.

The link between inflated self-image and hostility and aggression has received some experimental support. Morf and Rhodewalt (2001) introduced a dynamic self-regulatory processing model of narcissism. The model addresses the "paradox" of narcissism, which is the simultaneous coexistence of vulnerablity and grandiosity in these individuals. The basic argument is that narcissists are high in explicit but low in implicit self-esteem. The latter, however, does not require effort and is quicker to respond to critical situations, whereas the former requires effortful reasoning; implicit self-esteem refers to "hot" cognitions and is associated with strong affective reactions including shame and public anxiety, and explicit high self-esteem is subsequently maintained and defended by self-regulatory and interpersonal strategies that include displays of anger and hostility. The link between vulnerable high self-esteem and aggression has been noted before (Baumeister, Smart, & Boden, 1996). Perceived threat to the explicit, elevated self-concept invites intense affective reactions, including rage, to safeguard and defend the self-concept. These proposed dynamics are quite compatible with Kohut's concept of narcissistic rage, and future experimentation using clinical subjects may be of potentially great heuristic value.

More recently, cognitive therapists have provided theoretical conceptualisations of narcissistic PD (e.g., Beck et al., 2004). Young et al. (2003) consider the *lonely child*, the *self-aggrandizer*, and the *detached protector modes* preeminent in narcissistic PD. As a young child, the narcissistic PD patient feels unloved and unlovable, and develops the emotional deprivation schema. When, for example because of interpersonal or status loss, this schema is triggered, narcissistic PD individuals try to switch to the compensatory coping modes of the self-aggrandizer or detached protector. In fact, the self-aggrandizer is the typical social face of the narcissistic PD patient: demanding, competitive, and superior. When alone, the patient may soothe or excite himself to avoid feeling the pain of the lonely child (detached protector). Conceptually, schema-focused therapy aims to teach the patient to love and be loved to repair the emotional deprivation schema of the lonely child, and to develop more adaptive options of coping with emotional pain by strengthening the healthy adult mode at the expense of the *self-aggrandizer* and the detached protector modes.

Despite the unifying force of the DSM, it is hard to avoid the conclusion that various theorists refer to different things when they describe their version of the narcissistic patient. On the other hand, growing up in an emotionally cold environment seems a shared feature of these diverse lines of theorizing. Compared to borderline PD, aetiological accounts pay much less attention to physical or sexual abuse experiences in childhood; it is the emotionally unattuned, unresponsive, and cold attachment context that is deemed pathogenic for some, perhaps temperamentally more vulnerable, individuals.

Assessment of narcissistic personality disorder

While narcissistic PD may be a disorder for which there is little empirical evidence supporting its construct validity or clinical utility, there is no lack of assessment instruments to measure it. The most widely used instrument is the 40-item Narcissistic Personality Inventory (NPI; Emmons, 1984; Raskin & Hall, 1981; Raskin & Terry, 1988), a self-report trait measure of narcissism. Four subscales can be derived that measure leadership/autonomy, superiority/arrogance, self-absorption/self-admiration, and entitlement/exploitation, respectively. Interestingly, only the entitlement/exploitation scale has consistently been related to dysfunction; the other factors apparently can serve adaptive functions in certain environments. Its interview counterpart is the Diagnostic Interview for Narcissism (DIN; Gunderson et al., 1990). The usual relative strengths and weaknesses also apply for the assessment instruments for narcissistic PD. Assessment by self-report is quick and cheap, and particularly well suited for screening purposes. Assessment by interview requires more time and resources, but allows for flexibility, observations, and the use of more indirect, inferential assessment, which may be especially important in an ego-syntonic disorder involving such traits as egocentrism, self-indulgence, and an exaggerated sense of entitlement. Concurrent use of the Rorschach inkblot method and Thematic Apperception Test (TAT) is advocated by some authors to arrive at a multimethod assessment of narcissistic PD (Hilsenroth, Handler, & Blais, 1996). Blais (1997) explored the associations among the domains of the Five-Factor Model (FFM) of personality and the DSM-IV personality disorders using clinician ratings for 100 PD patients. The narcissistic PD was positively correlated with extraversion and negatively with agreeableness, indicating that "NPD patients are seen as socially outgoing, active, and inter-personally antagonistic" (p. 35). On the facet level, evidence was found that narcissistic individuals endorse high achievement striving and fantasy, and low modesty, traits that were indeed theoretically predicted (Trull, Widiger, & Burr, 2001). Many other scales are available, which often do not intercorrelate (Wink, 1991). One expla-nation that has been offered for this lack of convergence is that narcissism, in fact, has "two faces": the DSM grandiose, overt version, versus a subtler covert version, each with a set of associated scales.

On the covert, closet, vulnerable, hypersensitive narcissist. Several authors have proposed a distinction between the grandiose, exhibitionistic, or "oblivious" narcissistic PD as presented in the DSM, and a more subtle, hidden narcissistic PD, alternatively referred to as the hypervigilant (Gabbard, 1989), covert (Akhtar & Thompson, 1982), closet (Masterson, 1993), vulnerable (Dickinson & Pincus, 2003), or hypersensitive (Hendin & Cheek, 1997) narcissist. This latter more avoidant subtype does not overtly exhibit the haughtiness and arrogance characteristics of narcissistic PD, but secretly holds a similar sense of entitlement and grandiose expectations. Whereas the overt narcissistic PD patient manages his self-esteem by overt self-enhancement and aggressively asserting himself for his entitled expectations, the covert narcissistic PD patient is conflicted between asserting her demands, and being ashamed about them and stifling them. Covert narcissists may impress like avoidant PD patients initially, as their narcissistic grandiosity is still hidden, but as treatment progresses the sense of entitlement and superiority will emerge. Indeed, covert narcissistic PD has phenom-enological similarities with avoidant PD: by virtue of their shared fear of humiliation, embarrassment, and rejection, both closet narcissistic PD patients and avoidant PD patients may avoid close connections. However, the motivation is somewhat different: narcissistic PD patients do not wish to expose themselves to the disappointment and shame of unmet expectations, while the avoidant PD patients fear social rejection because of being inadequate. At present, the shy narcissist is not part of the DSM and its construct validity is an open question much deserving further empirical research.

Histrionic personality disorder

Histrionic PD has a long history of theorizing (Merskey, 1995; Pfohl, 1995), but very few empirical studies have focused on histrionic PD specifically. To illustrate, Pfohl (1995) had to base his appraisal of the DSM-III-R criteria set on four published data sets, and a current literature search in Scopus (www.scopus.com) using histrionic PD in the title yielded less than 30 articles. Moreover, a good part of this literature is on evaluating the potential gender bias in the criteria set of the DSM (see Chapter 3 and, for example, Ford & Widiger, 1989, or Sprock, 2000).

Brief history of histrionic personality disorder and its current DSM rendering

Histrionic PD was formerly known as hysteria, as hysterical neurosis, and as hysterical PD. In 1973, Slavney and McHugh compared psychiatric charts of psychiatric inpatients with the DSM-II diagnosis of hysterical PD to a control group of inpatients. The following portrait emerged: "a young woman, hospitalized after a suicide attempt or with symptoms of depression. The product of an unhappy early environment, she has had previous suicide attempts and, if married, views her union as unsatisfactory. She is described as a dramatic person, and her treatment requires several months in the hospital" (p. 329). The DSM-II (APA, 1968) stated: "these behaviour patterns are characterized by excitability, emotional instability, over-reactivity, and self-dramatization. This self-dramatization is always attention seeking and often seductive, whether or not the patient is aware of its purpose. These personalities are also immature, self-centred, often vain, and usually dependent on others" (p. 43). From these descriptions, one can appreciate the evolution the construct of histrionic PD has made over time and DSM versions. Clearly, it has "lost" some of its features to borderline PD, a PD not yet present in the earlier versions of the DSM. This conclusion implies another: histrionic PD is rather like a "moving target", and evidence from earlier studies may refer to different patients than those of later studies. The DSM-IV-TR (APA, 2000) describes histrionic PD as marked by long-standing proclivity towards attention seeking and excessive emotionality, as manifested in seductive and dramatic behavioural patterns.

Histrionic personality disorder and gender

Is there a sex bias inherent to the diagnosis of histrionic PD? The evidence suggests that histrionic PD is indeed a predominantly female disorder, but that is quite something else than demonstrating a sex bias (see Chapter 3). First, an obvious reminder is that sex differentiated prevalence numbers always have to be compared to the base rate of the sexes in the sample. Second, it is entirely conceivable that the higher prevalence among women is related to sex-related differences in underlying psychopathology. Our review of the evidence (see also Chapter 3) concurs with Pfohl (1995, p. 182), who concluded that "it appears that although the criteria for diagnosis may not be sex-biased, the application of the diagnosis may indeed be".

Another gender-related issue that has received empirical testing is the hypothesis that histrionic PD is expressed in gender specific ways. Specifically, from a review of the diagnostic and family records among 250 diverse patients, Lilienfeld, van Valkenburgh, Larntz, and Akiskal (1986) concluded that histrionic PD, antisocial PD, and somatization disorder share an underlying diathesis. Perhaps, it was reasoned, the disorders are not discrete entities, but histrionic individuals develop antisocial PD when male, and somatization disorder when female. Or, as Lilienfeld et al. (p. 721) put it: "Antisocial PD and somatization disorder may ... constitute sex-typed alternative pathways for the expression of histrionic PD." Follow-up experimental research and review (Cale & Lilienfeld, 2002a, 2002b), however, did not confirm these conjectures, and the observed comorbidity remains an interesting, yet open question.

Histrionic personality disorder as seen through assessment instruments

Findings from several different assessment instruments underscore the key features of histrionic PD. The MMPI scores of histrionic PD patients show a meaningful elevation for the clinical scale 9–Mania, and a lower score for 0–Social Introversion (Schotte, de Doncker, Maes, Cluydts, & Cosyns, 1993), as compared to patients with other personality disorders. These findings are characteristic of more energetic, expansive individuals who are not bothered by uneasiness or shyness in social situations. On an interview measure tapping the Five-Factor Model (Structured Interview for the Five-Factor Model or SIFFM; Trull & Widiger, 1997), histrionic PD was characterized by a lower trait level of altruism, and on the facet level, elevated scores on gregariousness, feelings, warmth, and tendermindedness were observed. This pattern again suggests an emotionally expressive, outgoing person who is also self-centred and rather superficially engaged in relationships. Rorschach protocols showed a relative preponderance of emotional (i.e., colour determined) responses, and responses suggesting intense dependency needs (i.e., texture responses) among patients endorsing more histrionic symptoms (Blais, Hilsenroth, & Fowler, 1998).

Treatment issues

"Pure" histrionic PD is very rarely seen in clinical practice, although it is rather common in community studies (see Chapter 3). While Beck et al. (2003) as well as Sperry (2006) provided specific suggestions for the treatment of histrionic PD, to our knowledge, no structured histrionic PD-specific treatment protocols have been tested in controlled treatment outcome studies. To form an impression of treatment response, one therefore has to rely on outcome data of near neighbour conditions that have histrionic PD as a comorbid condition, and on expert opinion. As suggested by Stone (2003), more than likely, the course and prognosis of histrionic PD will largely depend on its severity and comorbidity. More specifically, more extreme versions will be harder to treat than the milder versions and when concurrent features of antisocial PD and narcissistic PD are present one should not be optimistic about treatment gains or, for that matter, motivation for treatment.

Cluster B and interpersonal violence

Narcissistic PD and histrionic PD more often than not occur in combination with other Axis-II diagnoses, especially with the other Cluster B diagnoses and dependent PD. For example, estimates of co-occurrence of histrionic and narcissistic PD range from 8% to 44%, and for histrionic PD and borderline PD from 44% to 95% (Pfohl, 1995)! This raises the question as to whether these disorders are in fact distinguishable categories. Given the overlap, it seems highly questionable that borderline PD and histrionic PD constitute separate syndromes, even more so when considering the lack of evidence supporting a separate aetiological pathway, course, or treatment response. Or, as Tyrer provocatively titled his 1992 article: "Flamboyant, erratic, dramatic, borderline, antisocial, sadistic, narcissistic, histrionic and impulsive personality disorders: Who cares which?" Accordingly, many researchers have focused on correlates of Cluster B characteristics, rather than on correlates of any separate PD. The underlying impulsive and emotionally volatile features are associated with various behavioural patterns. Of great societal importance is that Cluster B pathology has emerged as a risk factor for various forms of violence. For example, the narcissistic PD patient is particularly sensitive to humiliation, and may react to challenges to his self-esteem with what has been called "narcissistic rage" (Kohut, 1971). In more impulsive, less inhibited subtypes, these intense emotional experiences may be acted upon. Stone (2006) recently provided highly readable descriptions of famous cases that involved severe Cluster B pathology (see the chapter on untreatable personality disorders) and extreme violence. Of note, one might also conceptualize some of the self-injurious behaviours and even suicidal behaviours as inwardly displaced violent behaviours.

Cluster B personality disorders and stalking as interpersonal violence

Stalking can be defined as the "wilful, malicious, and repeated following or harassing of another person that threatens his or her safety" (Meloy & Gothard, 1995, p. 258). Stalking behaviours typically consist of a mix of intrusive following, persecutory unwelcome communications, and (threats of) violence. Stalkers make unexpected and unwelcome appearances in the target's private domain, and push themselves into the awareness of the victim by frequent (often nightly) telephone calls, letters, email, and by leaving notes, packages, etc. The variety of stalking behaviours is endless, but it deserves mentioning that both threats of violence and actual violence are common, and it is not unusual that third parties, such as family members or friends, become secondary targets (Kamphuis & Emmelkamp, 2000). The psychological consequences for the victims are often severe, and may involve PTSD-like symptomatology.

By its very nature, stalking represents an abnormal enduring pattern of interpersonal behaviour. Prima facie, then, there is reason to suspect that personality pathology may be involved in stalking. To date, no systematic research has investigated the motivations and personality of stalkers. Reflections on personality and intrapsychic functioning of stalkers are predominantly psychodynamic in nature and are focused on the postintimate stalkers, i.e., the stalking after "the romance has gone sour". A central feature in these theories is an intense narcissistic reaction to rejection and loss, in combination with borderline defence mechanisms such as splitting, initial idealization, and subsequent devaluation, projection, and projective identification. The stalker's rage is thought of as a defence against the intense feelings of humiliation, shame, and sadness. Such motivations, vulnerabilities, and dynamics would jive well with narcissistic PD and borderline PD pathology.

Most data on stalkers are from extreme, forensic cases as those who are not in jail are rarely willing to be interviewed. One way to bypass this problem is to use an informant assessment paradigm. Using 112 female stalking victims as informants, Kamphuis et al. (2004) obtained Five-Factor personality descriptions as well as ratings of prototypical attachment and psychopathology vignettes. The psychopathology vignettes thus obtained showed that four out of five stalkers were described as "reasonably functional people but who were extraordinarily sensitive to rejection, abandonment or loss" (p. 176). Ex-partners' answers revealed that 86% of stalkers displayed an insecure attachment style. In terms of the object relations, stalkers were reported as seeing themselves in a negative way while having neutral or negative views on others. Compared to the normal population, postintimate stalkers scored extremely low on agreeableness. Individuals with low agreeableness scores are characterized as domineering, authoritarian, egocentric, and exploitative. In addition, stalkers were described as substantially less disciplined and organized than normal, as well as substantially less emotionally stable. These findings were strikingly similar to those observed by Dutton, Saunders, Starzomski, and Bartholomew (1994) among 120 men undergoing treatment for battering their female partners.

It is interesting to speculate on what these findings mean in terms of proposed theories of stalking. The findings seem to support Meloy's (1998) conceptualization of stalking as a reflection of attachment pathology. Attachment theory may help explain the lengths that wife batterers and postintimate stalkers will go to in order to regain the attention and affection of their targets. Perceived rejection or abandonment activates the stalker's maladaptive attachment system and leads him to seek proximity to an attachment figure, even if that figure is the source of the threat. The intrusive behaviour and violent efforts to regain the partner can best be seen as a protest triggered by a lack of attachment competence. From a self-psychological perspective, one might say that the stalker, motivated by the disintegration anxiety of a vulnerable self-system, is unable to let go of the person who holds the key to his fragile psychic equilibrium.

Summary

While frequently the topic of psychodynamic theorizing, the empirical research literature on the narcissistic and histrionic PDs remains scarce. Accordingly, definite statements about their specific aetiology, course, and treatment response are currently suspect. For the narcissistic PD, the official DSM criteria are discussed, along with the influential theoretical accounts of Kohut, Kernberg, Millon, and Young. A distinction is introduced between the overt and the covert narcissist. For histrionic PD, the evidence is even more limited. Gender issues and diagnostic and treatment relevant issues are briefly reviewed. Finally, recognizing the extensive comorbidity characterizing Cluster B personality disorders, several researchers have lumped the disorders together and examined key correlates (such as interpersonal violence) at the cluster level rather than at the level of the comprising separate disorders.

Antisocial personality disorder and psychopathy 8

> We believe that ... psychopaths are fundamentally different from other offenders and that there is nothing "wrong" with them in the manner of a deficit or impairment that therapy can "fix". Instead they exhibit an evolutionary viable life strategy that involves lying, cheating, and manipulating others.
>
> (Harris & Rice, 2005, p. 568)

Antisocial behaviour is worldwide a large problem leading to victimization in a substantial number of persons, mortality in victims and perpetrator, and diseases related to violence and substance abuse (WHO, 2002). It is already known for more than three decades that fewer than 10% of individuals perpetrate more than half of violent and nonviolent crimes (Wolfgang, Figlio, & Sellin, 1972). Many of these perpetrators meet the criteria for antisocial PD.

In this chapter a number of issues will be addressed. Given the close link between aggressive behaviour and conduct disorder in childhood and adult antisocial behaviour, research on aggressive behaviour and conduct disorder pertinent to antisocial personality disorder will be discussed. Further, the similarities and differences between psychopathy and antisocial PD will be addressed. Finally, we will discuss psychological treatment of antisocial behaviour.

Aggressive behaviour

Cognitive deficits and distortions

Over the past decade, cognitive deficits and cognitive distortions of aggressive children have been extensively studied from the perspective of Dodge's model of social information processing (Crick & Dodge, 1994). In Dodge's view, "reactive" and "proactive" anti-social behaviour should be differentiated. Reactive acts occur in response to actual or perceived threat from others, whereas proactive behaviours are initiated by the individual him- or herself. Dodge posits that multiple processing operations are involved in aggressive behaviour. A central idea in Dodge's model is that reactive aggression is mediated by a readiness to perceive hostile intent in the actions of others. When an individual is primed with an aggressive cue, an immediate response occurs as a sequential set of emotional and mental processes followed by behaviour. Further, Dodge distinguishes four different phases: aggressive children (a) selectively attend to hostile cues, (b) display hostile attributional biases, (c) readily access aggressive responses and fail to access many competent responses, and (d) are inclined to give positive evaluations of aggressive responses (Dodge & Pettit, 2003).

There is now considerable evidence that priming, including subliminal priming, of mental constructs related to aggression leads individuals to perceive ambiguous behaviours as more aggressive (Todorov & Bargh, 2002). Studies using priming techniques found that aggressive children were highly likely to use aggressive constructs to describe peers (e.g., Stromquist & Strauman, 1992). A study by Graham and Hudley (1994) revealed that the priming of hostile constructs in aggressive children led to a heightened tendency to make hostile attributions about peers' behaviour. Zelli, Huesmann, and Cervone (1995) used priming in participants having either high self-reported aggression or low self-reported aggression. Participants high on self-reported aggression showed a clear recall advantage for sentences for which the cues were aggressive traits as compared to participants low on self-reported aggression. Finally, implicit, automatic cognitive processes may also be involved in sexual aggression. In a study by Kamphuis, de Ruiter, Janssen, and Spiering (2005), subliminally presented sex words elicited a facilitation effect for power words among child molesters, but not among forensic or normal controls. These results provide preliminary evidence for an automatic sex–power association in child molesters and may point to a crucial pathological link in the cognitive schemata of sex offenders.

A meta-analysis by Yoon, Hughes, Gaur, and Thompson (1999) compared the effect sizes for the four different stages of Dodge's model of social information processing between aggressive and nonaggressive children (Crick & Dodge, 1994). The results of this study confirmed that aggressive children show a broad pattern of deficits and biases in social information processing. Medium effect sizes were found for each of the four processes.

These processing patterns (failure to encode relevant cues, hostile attributional biases, aggressive response generation, and positive evaluation of aggressive responses) were associated with negative early life experiences of physical abuse (Dodge, Bates, & Pettit, 1990). Further, Dodge, Pettit, Bates, and Valente (1995) found that abused children are hypervigilant for hostile cues from peers and present a bias towards the attribution of hostile intent, when other children would be more likely to attribute more neutral intent. Finally, these four processing patterns predicted later chronic conduct problems (Dodge & Pettit, 2003).

Physiological arousal and aggressive behaviour

Low physiological arousal (e.g., low resting heart rate) in children has been found to be associated with violent offending in adulthood. The fearlessness interpretation of these findings holds that lack of fear of punishment interferes with normal socialization and parental rearing and would predispose such youngsters to antisocial behaviour. An alternative account to explain the association of low physiological reactivity and antisocial behaviour can be found in the stimulation-seeking theory (Quay, 1965; Raine, 2002). According to this theory, low arousal represents an unpleasant physiological state, and antisocial individuals will seek stimulation in order to increase their arousal level. According to Raine (2002), antisocial behaviour is "viewed as a form of stimulation-seeking in that committing a burglary, assault, or robbery could be stimulating for some individuals" (p. 315).

Conversely, it has been suggested that *heightened* autonomic arousal may have a protective function against the development of antisocial PD (Raine, 2002). Adolescent antisocial behaviour and having a criminal father are both risk factors for later criminal behaviour, but some antisocial youngsters do not develop a criminal career. Interestingly, these youngsters show increased electrodermal and cardiovascular arousal compared to antisocial controls who persist in conducting antisocial behaviour (Raine, Venables, & Williams, 1996) and to criminal offspring with criminal fathers (Brennan et al., 1997). The fearlessness and stimulation-seeking interpretations of low physiological arousal are not mutually exclusive but may complement each other. As shown in a study of Rayne et al. (1998) the combined effects of stimulation-seeking and fearlessness assessed in children at age 3 were found to predict aggressive behaviour 8 years later.

Antisocial personality disorder versus psychopathy

The central characteristic of antisocial PD is a long-standing pattern of socially irresponsible behaviours that reflects a disregard of the rights of others. Antisocial PD is associated with violence and crime and has its precursors in youth. Although a diagnosis of antisocial PD is not given before the age of 18, a history of repeated conduct disorder before the age of 15 is required for the formal diagnosis. According to DSM-IV-TR, for a person to be diagnosed as antisocial PD he/she should have at least three symptoms of conduct disorder (such as destruction of property, aggression to animals or people, or theft). Further, there should be at least three behavioural problems occurring after the age of 15. Although many delinquents fulfil the criteria of antisocial PD, there are also a number of individuals with criminal records who do not fulfil these criteria. On the other hand, many individuals with antisocial PD do not have criminal records (e.g., Robins & Regier, 1991).

The diagnosis of antisocial PD has been criticized since its inclusion in DSM-III in 1980, the main criticism being that it emphasizes behavioural characteristics over personality-based characteristics. According to DSM-III, antisocial PD was defined by a pattern of conduct disorder in childhood as well as by a series of antisocial behaviours in adulthood. Although many workers in the field found the emphasis in DSM-III on behavioural characteristics of psychopathology an important step forward that enhanced the reliability of the diagnoses, in the case of antisocial PD it was felt that validity was being sacrificed for reliability (e.g., Alterman et al., 1998).

In the current DSM-IV-TR diagnostic criteria of antisocial PD, many of the typical characteristics of "psychopathy" are missing. As early as 1835 Pritchard introduced the term "moral insanity" to characterize individuals with a pattern of repeated immoral behaviour for which they could not be fully responsible. Cleckley (1941) defined "psychopathy" as a syndrome characterized by a constellation of affective, interpersonal, and behavioural characteristics. Psychopaths are characterized as manipulative, impulsive, showing superficial charm, and having shallow affect. Further, they lack insight and empathy for the effect of their antisocial and offensive behaviour on others and show a lack of remorse or guilt. In comparison with antisocial PD, psychopathy places a greater emphasis on interpersonal and affective traits. Psychopathy may be associated with a socially deviant lifestyle. However, while most psychopaths can be diagnosed with antisocial PD, most adults who fulfil the criteria of antisocial PD are not psychopaths. Also in forensic settings, most individuals who meet the diagnostic criteria for antisocial PD are not psychopaths (Hare, 2003). In a sample of 119 prisoners only 30% with antisocial PD received diagnoses of psychopathy (Hart & Hare, 1997).

The construct of psychopathy

The last two decades have seen an increasing interest in the construct of psychopathy, spurred by considerable evidence that psychopathy is related to violent offending and recidivism (Hart, Kropp, & Hare, 1988; Hildebrand, 2004). Based on Cleckley's (1941) definition of psychopathy, the Hare Psychopathy Checklist (Hare, 1980) was developed, more recently revised in the Hare Psychopathy Checklist– Revised (PCL-R; Hare, 1991, 2003). Given that the PCL-R is currently the most widely used instrument to assess psychopathy and con- sidered by many to be the gold standard, the items on the PCL-R are shown in Table 8.1.

The PCL-R assessment is performed by reviewing the individual's institutional file, complemented by a semistructured interview covering school adjustment, employment history, intimate relation- ships, family, friends, and criminal activity. The PCL-R has to be coded on a three-point scale, ranging from 0 "item does not apply", 1 "item probably or partially applies", to 2 "item definitely applies". The total score ranges from 0 to 30. The cut-off score for the diagnosis of psychopathy in the USA is 30, but in a number of European Countries (e.g., the Netherlands, Sweden, and the UK) a score of 25 or 26 is currently used (Cooke et al., 2005; Hildebrand, 2004). Scores on the PCL-R obtained in these countries are not directly comparable with those obtained in North America: the same level of psychopathy was associated with lower PCL-R scores in Europe. There is a substantial literature attesting to the reliability and validity of the PCL-R as a measure of psychopathy (Hare, 2003; Hildebrand, 2004).

Currently, psychopathy is conceived of as consisting of two dis- tinct, but interrelated facets (Brinkley, Newman, Widiger, & Lynam, 2004). The first of these dimensions, primary psychopathy or core psychopathy, consists of emotional-interpersonal traits emphasizing narcissism and social dominance (grandiosity, entitlement, shallow- ness, manipulativeness, lack of remorse, low anxiety, etc.), whereas the second dimension, secondary psychopathy, refers primarily to

TABLE 8.1
The Psychopathy Checklist – Revised (Hare, 1991)

Glibness/superficial charm*
Grandiose sense of self-worth*
Need for stimulation/prone to boredom***
Pathological lying*
Cunning/manipulative*
Lack of remorse or guilt**
Shallow affect**
Callous/lack of empathy**
Parasitic lifestyle***
Poor behavioural controls****
Promiscuous sexual behaviour
Early behavioural problems****
Lack of realistic, long-term goals***
Impulsivity***
Irresponsibility***
Failure to accept responsibility**
Many short-term marital relationships
Juvenile delinquency****
Revocation of conditional release****
Criminal versatility****

Note: *Interpersonal factor; **affective factor; ***lifestyle factor; ****antisocial factor.

social deviance (impulsiveness, aggressiveness, low tolerance to frustration, anxiety, irresponsibility, antisocial behaviors, etc.). The latter factor is more or less similar to the DSM-IV classification of antisocial PD. Hare (2003) has proposed a four-factor solution to the PCL-R in which the original two factors are split into narrower facets. Indeed, more recent studies of the PCL-R found support for a two-factor four-facet model including *interpersonal* (e.g., glibness, pathological lying), *affective* (callousness, shallow affect), *lifestyle* (e.g., impulsivity, parasitic lifestyle), and *antisocial* factors (e.g., juvenile delinquency, criminal versatility) (for review see Hare, 2003; Hildebrand, 2004; for items belonging to specific factors: see asterisks in Table 8.1). Two items do not fit in any of these factors: "many short-term marital relationships", and "promiscuous sexual behaviour", which may come as a relief to some of our readers.

Hare's (2003) decision to include the antisocial factor was based on his conceptualization of psychopathy as consisting of both personality traits and antisocial behaviour, both being considered core features of psychopathy. Not all scholars in the field, however, agree with this (e.g., Widiger & Lynam, 1998). In their view psychopathy should not be regarded as a distinct clinical syndrome, but rather as a constellation of malignant personality traits. In a number of studies psychopathy and violent behaviour have been found to be associated with narcissistic PD. Given this relationship, it has been argued that psychopathy begins with a basic antisocial personality orientation that is made more malignant by its combination with the grandiosity and lack of concern for others intrinsic to narcissistic states (Warren et al., 2003). Others, however, have suggested that antisocial behaviour may be better conceptualized as a consequence of psychopathy, rather than being itself part of it, thus being a product of the underlying personality trait (Jones et al., 2006).

Psychopathy in children and adolescents

It has been questioned whether the construct of psychopathy is also applicable in children and adolescents (Edens, Skeem, Cruise, & Cauffman, 2001; Seagrave & Grisso, 2002). Jones et al. (2006) investigated whether the Psychopathy Checklist: Youth Version (PCL:YV) has a comparable factor structure to its adult version, the PCL-R. In a study on a large sample of serious adolescent offenders, Hare's (2003) four-factor model discussed above demonstrated a good fit, thus suggesting that the structure of psychopathy is comparable across adolescents and adults. However, this does not necessarily mean that the results of studies conducted with adults can be generalized to adolescents. To give an example, although it is widely found that psychopathy predicts future violence in female adults (Nichols, Ogloff, Brink, & Spidel, 2005), in female adolescents the data are far from conclusive. In a study by Odger, Reppucci, and Moretti (2005) on female juvenile offenders, it was found that PCL-YV scores were not predictive of future offending, while victimization experiences significantly increased the odds of reoffending.

Psychopathy: Categorical or dimensional?

There has been some debate whether psychopathy should be considered categorical or dimensional in nature. Harris, Skilling, and Rice (2001) hold that psychopathy should be considered as a categorical variable that would justify research into qualitative differences between psychopaths and nonpsychopaths. In their view, psychopaths represent a distinct class of individuals. Others, however, have argued that psychopathy is a configuration of extreme scores on normal personality traits. In terms of the personality traits of the Five-Factor Model it has been argued that psychopathy is a constellation of low conscientiousness and low agreeableness (Benning, Patrick, Blonigen, Hicks, & Iacono, 2005; Edens, Marcus, Lilienfeld, & Poythress, 2006; Miller, Lynam, Widiger, & Leukefeld, 2001). As noted by Edens et al. (2006), the dimension versus category discussion is relevant to the study of the aetiology of psychopathy. If psychopathy were shown to be dimensional, rather than categorical: "it would be unlikely to result from a dichotomous causal agent, such as the presence-absence of frontal lobe damage, a threshold level of an environmental stressor (e.g., severe child abuse), or a dominant gene" (p. 132). Using multiple taxometric procedures Edens et al. did not find any support for the contention that psychopathy, as assessed by the PCL-R, is underpinned by a latent taxon or a dichotomous causal agent. Thus, these results cast serious doubts on the validity of the categorical rather than dimensional approach of psychopathy. The results of this study may have important implications for the justice system. In many countries, identification of psychopaths is based on a categorical rather than a dimensional perspective. The diagnosis of "psychopath" is often used to justify the lengthening of incarceration and of prescribing other constraints. Results of the Edens et al. study show that it is highly arbitrary to draw exact categorical boundaries between psychopathic and nonpsychopathic criminals. At present, research does not justify a natural break point to identify someone as a "psychopath".

Sequelae of psychopathy

Psychopathic traits have already been established in early childhood and may make children vulnerable to persistent very serious anti-social behaviour. Compared to individuals who are characterized by overt antisocial behaviour only, antisocial individuals who are also characterized with the affective personality core of callous-unemotional traits (psychopathy) start offending at an early age. Children with psychopathic tendencies have a greater number and range of conduct problems and are less distressed about their antisocial behaviour than children with antisocial behaviour who do not display core psychopathic features (Christian, Frick, Hill, Tyler, & Frazer, 1997). The fact that the conduct problems do not lead to distress in children with psychopathic tendencies may explain why these children persist in the severe antisocial behaviour (Barry et al., 2000). Such youngsters with core psychopathy offend with acts that are often predatory in nature across the life-span.

Recent research efforts have shown that there is a relationship between psychopathy and both general and violent crimes (e.g., Salekin, 2002). A number of studies have revealed relations between (specific factors of) psychopathy and type of offending behaviour, community violence, and recidivism (Dolan & Anderson, 2003; Hemphill, Hare, & Wong, 1998; Jones et al., 2006; Skeem & Mulvey, 2001). In addition, psychopathy has been found to predict misconduct in a variety of forensic residential settings (e.g., Buffington-Vollum, Edens, Johnson, & Johnson, 2002; Edens, Buffington-Vollum, Colwell, Johnson, & Johnson, 2002; Hildebrand, de Ruiter, & Nijman, 2004; Kroner & Mills, 2001). Psychopathy is generally weakly related to sexual offences, but more so to rape than to child molesting (Coid, 2005). Psychopaths appear to be more likely than nonpsychopath criminals to commit rape (Knight & Guay, 2005).

The predatory character of the offences of psychopaths is shown by a study of Woodworth and Porter (2002). These investigators studied the association between psychopathy and the most serious form of crime: murder. In this study murderers with core psychopathic features were highly likely to have committed ruthless pre-meditated murder ("cold-blooded" homicides), whereas this was not the case for nonpsychopathic murderers, whose offence was often a "crime passionel", or occurred impulsively in response to a provocation, or in the context of an emotion-laden dispute. To give a few examples of "cold-blooded" homicides: in the psychopathic group, one subject carefully planned the murder of his wife because he stood to gain financially from her insurance; another psychopathic murderer decided to murder his girlfriend in order to enable him to start a new relationship (Woodworth & Porter, 2002, p. 442).

The consequences of psychopathy are not limited to delinquency and crime, but also affect interpersonal relationships. For example, psychopaths view their interpersonal functioning as much more adequate than others do. Milton et al. (2005) found that psychopaths underestimated their worst qualities, such as dominance or coerciveness, and overestimated their best qualities, such as nurturance, a finding that does not come as a surprise. Further, it has been shown that psychopathic features are associated with couple distress and divorce (Han, Weed, & Buttcher, 2003; Savard, Sabourin, & Lussier, 2006). In particular, impulsivity and aggressiveness in the male partner were associated with couple distress 1 year later. Further, marital dissatisfaction may provide a stressful event enhancing psychopathic traits. Marital distress experienced by men predicted an aggravation of primary psychopathy (Savard et al., 2006). According to the authors, an increase in narcissism and dominance can be conceptualized as a plausible repercussion of marital disharmony for men.

Aetiological theories of psychopathy

Over the years, many theories have been proposed to explain the aetiology of psychopathy, but most of these theories have not been empirically tested. Kohut (1982) made an important contribution to the psychodynamic conceptualization of psychopathy by emphasizing stagnations in the development of the self-structure. In his view, the self-system is compiled of self and internal representations of significant others (see also attachment theory). In Kohut's theory, the symptoms of psychopathy are accounted for by poor superego development (e.g., criminal activity, disregard for others) and defence mechanisms (e.g., grandiosity, superficial charm) (see Salekin, 2002). More recent theorizing stresses the borderline personality organization and the relationship between defensive process and cognitive style in the psychopath's inability to feel (Helfgott, 2004).

Earlier social learning theories of psychopathy (called sociopathy at that time, given the assumed role of environmental factors) relied heavily on the notion that psychopathy may be accounted for by classical and operant conditioning and modelling experiences (e.g., Bandura, 1973; Ullman & Krasner, 1969). More recently, the emphasis has switched to cognitive learning processes (e.g., Dodge & Pettit, 2003), which have already been discussed.

In contrast to psychodynamic and cognitive-behavioural accounts of the aetiology of psychopathy, more recent theories stress that there is a predisposition for psychopathy consisting of small neurological deficits (Hare & Jutai, 1988) and low fearfulness (Lykken, 1995). A number of studies have shown that psychopaths are characterized by a lower resting electrodermal activity than nonpsychopathic control (Lorber, 2004). Further, psychopaths tended to show relatively small skin conductance changes to loud tones, pictures of mutilated faces, insertion of a hypodermic needle, and during anticipation of receiving painful stimuli (see Kiehl, 2006). Studies examining the two main dimensions of psychopathy found that anxiety level is inversely associated with the interpersonal-affective dimension of psychopathy, but positively associated with the antisocial behaviour dimension. Increases in anxiety enhance the risk of antisocial behaviour, particularly reactive aggression (Blair et al., 2006).

Finally, a series of studies demonstrated that children with anti-social problems who exhibited core psychopathic features (callous and unemotional traits) differ from other children with antisocial problems in having fewer language deficits and in coming from families with normal rearing practices as compared to the bad parenting characteristic of parents of children with conduct disorders (Barry et al., 2000; Loney, Frick, Ellis, & McCoy, 1998; Wooton, Frick, Shelton, & Silverthorn, 1997). Further, adolescents characterized by these psychopathic core features have a reduced ability to recognize fear and sadness (Stevens, Charman, & Blair, 2001).

Emotion recognition and processing

Reduced responsiveness to the expressions of sadness and fear is not only characteristic of adolescents with psychopathic primary features, but has also been found in adults with psychopathy (Blair et al., 2004; Montagne et al., 2005). In a study of Blair, Sellars, Strickland, and Clark (1995) psychopaths and nonpsychopath controls were asked to attribute emotions to a protagonist in a vignette. The psychopaths and controls did not differ in their emotion attributions to protagonists in the happiness, sadness, and embarrassment stories. However, the psychopaths and controls did differ in their emotion attributions to the guilt stories, the primary attribution of the psychopaths being happiness or indifference, in contrast to guilt in controls.

There are a substantial number of studies that have shown that psychopathy is related to dysfunctional processing of emotional stimuli. Psychopathy is associated with difficulties in processing some face stimuli, particularly distress and disgust cues (Blair, Jones, Clark, & Smith, 1997; Kosson, Suchy, Mayer, & Libby, 2002). Further, individuals with psychopathic tendencies show reduced facilitation for processing emotional words during affective lexical decision tasks (Loney, Frick, Clements, Ellis, & Kerlin, 2003). In experiments studying fear-potentiated startle, individuals characterized as psychopaths show other emotional processing of fear cues than nonpsychopaths (Levenston, Patrick, Bradley, & Lang, 2000; Sutton, Vitale, & Newman, 2002). In a study investigating the ability of adult psychopathic individuals to process vocal affect subjects were presented with neutral words spoken with intonations conveying happiness, disgust, anger, sadness, and fear. The results indicated that psychopathic individuals were particularly impaired in the recognition of fearful vocal affect as compared to nonpsychopathic controls (Blair et al., 2002).

Precursors of antisocial personality disorder

More or less by definition, antisocial PD is preceded by a number of conduct problems before the age of 15. Antisocial behaviour problems in childhood are very similar for boys and girls, but there may be a few exceptions. First, conduct problems of girls are more often characterized by lying and running away than by severe physical violence. Further, interpersonal relationships may account for some important gender differences in the expression of conduct problems. For girls more than for boys, antisocial behaviours are more likely to be a consequence of the quality of interpersonal relationships with others, particularly opposite-sex peers and partners. A review by Ehrensaft (2005) revealed that girls' antisocial behaviour is more likely to be motivated by interpersonal conflict than boys' conduct problems. Further, girls with antisocial behaviour are more likely to come to the attention of the authorities because of chaotic, unstable family relationships, and to express antisocial behaviour in the context of close relationships.

Child abuse and maltreatment

One of the best-known textbook cases of antisocial personality disorder is the case of Gary Gilmore, who was sentenced to death after being convicted of two murders. He started drinking as early as age 10, and started to use all kinds of illegal drugs in early adolescence. When he was 14 he was convicted for stealing a car, shortly followed by other convictions for burglaries and robberies. He never had a relationship or steady employment. Given that his brother published a book on the family situation in childhood (Gilmore, 1994), we have collateral information on potential precursors of his antisocial behaviour. His early years are characterized by living in fear of severe maltreatment by his harsh and cruel father.

Although it is tempting to assume that this severe maltreatment as a child from the hand of his cruel father was causal in "the making of an antisocial personality" of Gary Gilmore, there are also other explanations possible. For example, how did it happen that his brother Mikal eventually became a successful writer, rather than ending up as an antisocial person himself? Although it is likely that Mikal had been treated less harshly than Gary (Gillmore, 1994, p. 173), other factors may be involved as well, including individual differences mapping on to biological/genetic influences, attachment style, social support, and peer group influences.

What evidence is there for a causal relationship between that bad parenting and antisocial behaviour in the offspring? There is consistent evidence that bad parenting, including lack of discipline, child neglect, and (sexual) abuse, is associated with children's physical aggression and antisocial behaviour (see Ehrensaft, 2005; Farrington, 2005; Lahey, Moffitt, & Caspi, 2003). A number of studies suggest that the quality of early parental care, such as unresponsiveness and rejection, plays a significant role in the development of *early-onset* antisocial behaviour (Shaw, Ingoldsby, Gilliom, & Nagin, 2003). Further, a lack of parental responsiveness and sensitivity to social cues during infancy (Shaw et al., 1998; Wakschlag & Hans, 1999) and parental rejection (Campbell, Pierce, Moore, & Markovitz, 1996; Young, Oetting, & Deffenbacher, 1996) have both been associated with antisocial behaviour later in childhood and adulthood.

It should be noted, however, that there are race differences in long-term effects of physical discipline on antisocial behaviour. Antisocial behaviour in European American adolescents was associated with harsh physical discipline, but not in African American adolescents, probably due to the different meanings that children attach to the experience of physical discipline (Lansford, Deater-Deckard, Dodge, Bates, & Pettit, 2004).

Prenatal and perinatal precursors

Maltreatment may occur already before the child is born. There is substantial evidence that irresponsible mothers who expose their foetuses to alcohol (Olson, Bookstein, & Theide, 1997), marijuana (Goldschmidt, Day, & Richardson, 2000), and opiates (de Cubas & Field, 1993) increase the risk for conduct problems in the offspring 10–13 years later. Further, smoking during pregnancy may be an important contributory factor to the brain deficits that have been found in adult offenders. Both Brennan, Grekin, and Mednick (1999) and Rasanen et al. (1999) found a twofold increase in violent criminal offending in adulthood in the offspring of women who smoked during pregnancy.

Other studies have shown that birth complications are associated with an enhanced risk of conduct disorder, delinquency, and violence in adulthood. Interestingly, there is some evidence for an interaction between biological factors and parental rearing style in predicting antisocial behaviour. In a large prospective study in Denmark, Raine,

Brennan, and Mednick (1994, 1997) found that birth complications significantly interacted with maternal rejection of the child in predicting violent offending at age 18 and 34 years, but this was unrelated to nonviolent offending. These results have been replicated in a large Swedish study (Hodgins, Kratzer, & McNeil, 2001).

Risk factors for antisocial behaviour in adolescence

Additional childhood predictors of persisting antisocial behaviour include hyperactivity and high levels of aggression. In a large prospective study in Australia by Bor, McGee, and Fagan (2004), a range of significant risk factors for adolescent antisocial behaviour were identified. High levels of aggression and attention problems/restlessness (attention deficit hyperactivity disorder; ADHD) at age 5 increased the risk of antisocial behaviour at age 14 by a factor of two. Other important predictors included marital disruption and poor language development. The latter finding corroborates earlier research into poor language development (Humber & Snow, 2001) which suggests that overcoming early language deficits may enhance coping skills and decrease the risk for adolescent antisocial behaviour (Moffitt & Farrington, 1996; Snowling, Adams, Bowyer-Crane, & Tobin, 2000).

In addition to early conduct disorders, ADHD, marital disruption, poor language development, and bad parenting, behavioural problems of the mother during her childhood have also been implicated. Ehrensaft et al. (2003) investigated the independent contributions of maternal history of antisocial behaviour and parenting practices to the worsening course of sons' behaviour problems in a sample of young urban boys at risk for antisocial behaviour. Maternal conduct disorder before age 15 contributed to the worsening of boys' behaviour problems 1 year later, but the effect of parenting was more substantial. Worsening of delinquency was predicted by mothers' lower monitoring of sons' activities and companionships. Lower involvement, lower monitoring, and higher levels of parent–child conflict accounted for 17% of the worsening of behavioural problems, whereas a maternal history of conduct disorder accounted for only 6%.

Risk factors for antisocial behaviour in adulthood

Children who show antisocial behaviour from early childhood are at great risk for showing antisocial and criminal behaviour in adulthood. Factors influencing antisocial behaviour in adolescence have also been involved in predicting antisocial behaviour in adulthood. For example, in a study of Simonoff et al. (2004) both childhood hyper-activity and conduct disorder were independently strongly predictive of adult antisocial personality disorder. Within their sample, two-thirds of the individuals who qualified for both hyperactivity and conduct disorder in childhood had adult antisocial personality disorder. Of participants with neither hyperactivity nor conduct disorder, only 2% had current antisocial personality disorder.

Several studies have examined the relationship between crime/delinquency in adulthood and parental rearing styles. In a study of Norden, Klein, Donaldson, Pepper, and Klein (1995), antisocial personality disorder traits were found to correlate negatively with maternal and paternal care. In adult criminals, antisocial personality pathology, measured dimensionally, was associated with less mater-nal and paternal care (Timmerman & Emmelkamp, 2005b). Similar results with respect to lack of maternal and paternal care were reported for child molesters, who were primarily characterized as having either an antisocial or a schizoid PD (Bogaerts et al., 2005).

It has been suggested that (repeated) trauma in adolescence and adulthood may be a precursor of antisocial PD. Most studies investi-gating this issue have been based on war veterans. A number of studies of the postwar adjustment of Vietnam veterans have examined the relationship of postmilitary antisocial behaviour to premilitary antisocial behaviour, atrocities and intensity of combat exposure, traumatic exposure during the military, and posttraumatic stress disorder. Although a number of studies found that both atrocities and intensive combat exposure were associated significantly with post-military antisocial behaviour (e.g., Collins & Bailey, 1990; McFall, Fontana, Raskind, & Rosenheck, 1999; Resnick, Foy, Donahoe, & Miller, 1989), a more recent study indicated that antisocial premilitary behaviour exerted the largest influence on postmilitary antisocial behaviour. In this study (Fontana & Rosenbeck, 2005) on a large sample of war veterans, postmilitary antisocial behaviour was found to represent the current manifestation of a lifetime history of antisocial behaviour far more than it reflected the after-effect of war zone stress and trauma.

Genetic factors

Research has revealed that there is a concentration of perpetrators of crime in families: half of the crimes are committed by fewer than 10% of the families (e.g., Farrington, Jolliffe, Loeber, Stouthamer-Loeber, & Kalb, 2001). In the Farrington et al. (2001) study in about 1400 boys aged 8–14, offenders were highly concentrated in families; if one relative had been arrested, there was a very high likelihood that another relative had also been arrested, including brothers, sisters, fathers, mothers, uncles, aunts, grandfathers, and grandmothers. But should this family concentration be attributed to environmental or genetic factors? Although it could be explained by social transmission and modelling of antisocial behaviour in families, it may just as easily be explained by genetic influences. Unfortunately, few studies have tried to disentangle environmental and genetic influences in individuals with antisocial PD.

There is considerable evidence that up to 50% of the variation in aggression and antisocial behaviour may be accounted for by genetic factors, leaving 50% of variation still to be explained (see the meta-analysis by Rhee & Waldman, 2002). It is likely that an additional 15–20% of this behaviour can be explained by environmental factors shared by family members (shared-environment), leaving 30–35% for unique environmental influences not shared by other family members (e.g., being the only child abused) (Moffitt, 2005).

There is some evidence that genes may play a protective role in the development of antisocial behaviour. Adoption and twin studies found that bad parenting had relatively little effect on antisocial behaviour in children who were at low genetic risk. In a recent UK cohort study of 5-year-olds (Jaffee et al., 2005), antisocial behaviour in childhood was most likely to emerge when genetically vulnerable children were physically maltreated. Maltreatment was only weakly related to antisocial behaviour among children who were at low genetic risk for conduct disorder, suggesting the protective role of genotype on children's risk for antisocial problems. In two other studies, child maltreatment predicted antisocial behaviour, but within the high-MAO-A-activity genotype group its effects were reduced by more than half (Caspi et al., 2002; Foley et al., 2004), suggesting a protective role of MAO-A.

Treatment for antisocial personality disorder

In contrast to conduct disorder for which a few evidence-based interventions exist, there are no evidence-based interventions available for individuals with antisocial PD. Generally, clinicians are highly pessimistic about the results of psychological treatment of antisocial PD and psychopathy. Although this pessimism may be understandable for the treatment of true "psychopaths" (e.g., Ogloff, Wong, & Grennwood, 1990; Rice, Harris, & Cormier, 1992), a negative attitude with respect to possible outcome of psychological treatment of antisocial PD may not be totally justified. There is a clear need of effective treatment for antisocial PD and some potential gains may be achieved in nonpsychopathic antisocial PD patients.

Motivation enhancement

Usually, individuals with antisocial PD are referred to treatment (e.g., by family members or court order) or they apply for treatment of some other Axis-I disorder (e.g., gambling, marital discord, substance abuse). Most patients with antisocial PD do not suffer themselves from the personality disorder, which limits their motivation to seek treatment, or – when referred – limits motivation to comply with treatment recommendations and to stay in treatment when difficult problems have to be discussed or dealt with. Motivational interviewing (Miller & Rollnick, 2002) has some promise as a start to treatment of patients with antisocial PD. Motivational interviewing, designed to prepare individuals to engage them in treatment, has not yet been evaluated with individuals with primary antisocial PD, but has been found to be effective in the treatment of substance abuse, especially with individuals who are characterized as highly hostile (Emmelkamp & Vedel, 2006). The clinical method of motivational interviewing was developed specifically to enhance intrinsic motivation for change. This treatment does not attempt to train the patient through recovery, but instead employs motivational strategies to mobilize the patient's own resources. Motivational interviewing aims to elicit concerns about the problems the patient encounters as a result of his antisocial behaviour (e.g., debts, arrests, violence, marital disruption) and reasons for change from the patient, rather than directly confronting the patient as having to change. Thus, the therapist seeks to evoke the individual's own motivation to change his antisocial behaviour. Although inspired by the humanistic movement in psychotherapy, motivational interviewing is more directive than Rogerian nondirective therapy and has been defined as a person-centred, directive communication style (Miller & Rollnick, 2002).

Effects of psychological treatment

Research into treatment of antisocial PD has been conducted in the context of the criminal justice system. Several studies have examined the effects of treatment for offenders and forensic psychiatric patients. Although it is likely that many of these patients met the criteria of antisocial PD, this was not formally established in most studies. The conclusions drawn from several meta-analytic studies on the effectiveness of treatment outcome studies in general were that treatment reduces recidivism rates (roughly estimated at about 10%) and that (cognitive) behavioural treatment is more effective in reducing recidivism (Allen, Mackenzie, & Hickman, 2001; Andrews et al., 1990; Hollin, 1999) than psychodynamic and nondirective interventions. In general, there is some consensus that structured treatment, aimed at the alteration of cognitions and behaviours, is more effective in offender populations than less structured treatment.

There is some evidence that offenders with Cluster B personality pathology benefit less from treatment. In studies on the outcome of treatment programmes in a high security setting, psychopathy was negatively associated with therapy outcome in terms of clinical improvement (Hughes, Hoque, Hollin, & Champion, 1997) and in terms of reoffending (Rice et al., 1992). Another study found a relapse prevention programme to be less suited for younger patients with Cluster B personality pathology who had committed a nonsexual offence than for older child molesters with Cluster C pathology (Derks, 1996).

Effects of treatment in psychopaths

Although most workers in the field agree that true psychopaths are difficult to treat and that some therapies are contraindicated (e.g., psychodynamic therapy; Gabbard, 2005), a meta-analysis on the effectiveness of treatment of psychopathy (Salekin, 2002) suggests that intensive individual cognitive-behavioural, psychodynamic, and eclectic therapy for psychopathy were effective, not only in terms of a reduction in recidivism, but also in terms of a reduction of core psychopathic features (e.g., a decrease in lying, an increase in remorse and empathy), and improved relations with others. Treatment in the context of therapeutic communities where mental health professionals had little or no contact with patients was generally ineffective. Most studies reviewed, however, were of poor methodological quality, often including case studies, and lacking objective measures of criminal recidivism, which render the conclusions to be drawn from this meta-analysis inconclusive. Further, psychopathy was often loosely defined. Studies that used the more stringent criteria of Hare

(2003) resulted in less positive outcome than studies using more lenient criteria.

Recently, effects were reported of a behavioural programme in a high security hospital in the Netherlands. Most patients met the criteria for antisocial PD and/or other Cluster B disorders, including psychopathy. The behavioural programme focused on (a) improving coping skills and social skills; (b) reducing distrust, hostility, anger, and aggression; (c) improving social awareness and self-confidence; and (d) improving well-being. At the patients' wards, a supportive milieu was created in which behavioural treatment principles were integrated. The staff members were all trained in cognitive-behavioural treatment principles, and the focus of attention was on behaviour modification (i.e., reinforcement, shaping, modelling, and giving time out) with cognitive elements (challenging irrational thoughts) if needed. Also, patients and therapists made analyses of the offences (i.e., offence scenarios), resulting in a relapse-prevention plan.

The results of this study (Timmerman & Emmelkamp, 2005a) suggest that such a multidisciplinary cognitive-behavioural intra-mural treatment is effective in improving coping skills, interpersonal functioning, and well-being of offenders with serious personality disorders. After 2½ years of treatment, patients were less likely to react with anxiety, fear, anger, or aggression in stressful situations. Improvement on the self-report measures varied from small to moderate. As for personality characteristics, significant changes were found with respect to egoism, indicating that patients were less concerned about their own needs and showed more interest in other people and their problems, which might be accounted for by the fact that treatment taught patients to reflect on the effect of their behaviour on others and how they may misinterpret the behaviour of others. Effects on self-report data, however, are "suspect" in indi-viduals with psychopathic features. Therefore, effects of treatment were also evaluated using observational data assessed with the Forensic Inpatient Observation Scale (FIOS) (Timmerman, Vasten-burg, & Emmelkamp, 2001). Analyses of these observational data revealed that patients showed more insight into their problems and less oppositional behaviour and distress over time.

Finally, a study of Steels et al. (1998) is of some interest. According to this study, male psychopathic patients were more likely to obtain work and more likely to develop a relationship after discharge from a special hospital than were patients who were classified as mentally ill. The psychopathic group in this study, however, also reoffended more often than did the mentally ill group. This could mean that for psychopaths, psychosocial improvement during treatment is not indicative of abstinence of future reoffending. Presumably, patients who are highly characterized by psychopathic features may be capable of adjusting to what is expected of them in the clinic, but this is not necessarily associated with a structural improvement in their functioning (Timmerman & Emmelkamp, 2005a).

Does psychological treatment make psychopaths worse?

A number of studies found that patients with high levels of psychopathy did not benefit from therapy, but did worse in terms of reoffending after treatment had ended (Heilbrun et al., 1998; Rice et al., 1992; Tengström, Grann, Långström, & Kullgren, 2000). Rice et al. (1992) reported the alarming finding that treatment in the context of a maximum security therapeutic community led to deterioration in terms of reoffences in psychopaths. At follow-up 10½ years after completion of treatment 78% of the treated psychopaths had committed a new violent offence as compared to 55% of untreated psychopaths who went to prison. Since the results of this study were published, there has been some serious concern among clinicians that psychological treatment actually may make psychopaths worse rather than being beneficial. D'Silva, Duggan, and McCarthy (2004), however, reviewed the literature and came to the conclusion that the commonly held belief of an inverse relationship between high scores on the PCL-R and treatment response has not been established in methodologically sound studies. For the sake of clarity, they did not conclude that treatment led to neutral or beneficial effect for psychopaths, but rather concluded that it is too early yet to make any conclusion with respect to worsening of treatment outcome in psychopaths. It still may be that programmes that are beneficial for low- and moderate-risk offenders are not effective or are actually harmful in psychopaths (e.g., Harris & Rice, 2005).

Summary

There is consistent evidence that bad parenting, including lack of discipline, child neglect, and abuse, is associated with children's physical aggression and antisocial behaviour, which may implicate antisocial PD. Other factors involved in the aetiology of antisocial PD are low physiological arousal, early conduct disorders, ADHD, marital disruption, poor language development, and behavioural problems of the mother during her childhood. The effects of environmental factors are presumably mediated by heritability. Bad parenting had relatively little effect on antisocial behaviour in children who were at low genetic risk.

An important distinction was made between antisocial behaviour and the core psychopathic features including lack of remorse, guilt, callousness, and shallow affects. Effects of treatment of antisocial PD are limited and it is doubtful that current interventions have anything to offer to true psychopaths. There is evidence that these core psychopathic features have a strong genetic base, and are highly treatment resistant.

Schizotypal, schizoid, and paranoid personality disorders 9

> Although the current literature demonstrates massive research on the construct of schizotypy ... schizoid PD and paranoid PD have not stimulated a corresponding interest.
>
> (Parnas et al., 2005, p. 2)

Personality disorders from Cluster A have received much less attention from the research community than personality disorders from Cluster B. Most studies on the aetiology and characteristics of the odd/eccentric personality disorders have focused on schizotypal PD. Paranoid PD and schizoid PD have largely been neglected in research studies.

Schizophrenia spectrum disorders

In current views, chronic schizophrenia, which is characterized by severe deterioration across a variety of domains including cognitive and social function, is considered the "end-stage" disease of the schizophrenia continuum, or spectrum. In this view schizotypy, and, to a lesser extent, paranoid and schizoid PDs are construed as a spectrum of vulnerability to psychotic disorder. Individuals with schizotypal and schizoid PDs share common phenomenological, genetic, and biological characteristics with patients with chronic schizophrenia, such as persistent anhedonia and asociality and cognitive impairment, but to a milder degree and more circumscribed (Siever & Davis, 2004). Cognitive disorganization (e.g., odd speech, disturbed thinking patterns) is one of the main characteristics of schizotypal PD and resembles the more severe cognitive disorganization characteristic of patients with schizophrenia. The negative symptoms, which are prominent in schizophrenia, are also present, although to a lesser degree, in patients with schizotypal and schizoid PDs. The cognitive and perceptual distortions of patients with schizotypal PD may represent a less severe variant of positive symptoms (hallucinations and delusions) of schizophrenia. Distrust and paranoid ideation, which are characteristic of schizotypal and paranoid PDs, may reflect a less severe variant of cognitive disorganization, distortions in perception and deficits in thinking processes of patients with schizophrenia. Most available evidence relates to the link between schizotypy and schizophrenia, which will be discussed below.

Schizotypal personality disorder

Schizotypal PD is characterized by peculiar perceptions and strange beliefs (e.g., odd beliefs and magical thinking, unusual perceptual experiences, suspiciousness), interpersonal deficits (e.g., absence of close friends), and disorganized behaviour (e.g., odd speech). These deviations are never as extreme as those found in schizophrenia. In differentiating schizotypal PD from schizophrenia a useful distinguishing characteristic is stress. The disturbances listed above of schizotypal PD are not limited to periods of stress. In ICD-10, schizotypy is not conceptualized as a personality disorder, but as a syndrome.

Some have conceptualized schizotypy, the personality trait underlying schizotypal PD, as consisting of two factors, roughly comparable to the positive and negative symptoms found in schizophrenia. According to this view, *negative schizotypy* reflects a pattern of social withdrawal and anhedonia, the diminished capacity to experience pleasant emotions that may later manifest itself as negative symptoms of schizophrenia. Similarly, *positive schizotypy* reflects idiosyncratic cognitive styles that may later deteriorate into the positive symptoms of schizophrenia, including delusions and hallucinations (Ross, Lutz, & Bailley, 2002).

Generally, individuals with schizotypal PDs are characterized by lower socioeconomic status, lower education, and are often unemployed. Further, they usually do not have a steady relationship and still live with their family of origin, or by themselves (Dickey et al., 2005). In the Dickey et al. (2005) study, half of the schizotypal PD individuals had no close friends. Positive symptoms predominated: unusual perceptual experiences, suspiciousness, and magical thinking/odd beliefs were the three most commonly reported symptoms.

Anxiety symptoms and depression are common in schizotypal individuals. Anxiety and depression appear to be more strongly associated with positive schizotypy than with negative schizotypy (Lewandowski et al., 2006). In a prospective longitudinal study by Johnson, Cohen, et al. (2005), it was found that schizotypal PD traits, identified in adolescence, predicted dysthymic disorder or major depressive disorder in adulthood. It has also been suggested that schizotypal PD is related to the Axis-I obsessive-compulsive disorder (Sobin et al., 2000). Schizotypal PD might represent a risk factor for treatment failure in obsessive-compulsive disorder (Moritz et al., 2004).

Schizotaxia

Meehl (1990) asserted that certain persons, whom he referred to as *schizotypes*, possess a genetic vulnerability for the later development of schizophrenia. Individuals with schizotypy are held to show certain premorbid signs that mark the presence of a diathesis or inherited vulnerability for the development of schizophrenia. In his view, a specific, inherited, neural defect ("schizotaxia") renders some people vulnerable to a latent liability for the development of various forms of schizophrenic illness, measurable along a "schizotypy continuum". Schizotypy is presumed to result from a combination of processes of neural dysmaturation ("schizotaxia") with social learning during development. Meehl suggested that although schizotaxia usually resulted in schizotypal personality, only a minority of such individuals subsequently developed schizophrenia.

In contrast to Meehl (1990), who viewed schizotypy as taxonic in nature, others hold that schizotypy should be considered as a normally distributed personality trait (e.g., Claridge, 1997). In this view, schizotypy is conceptualized as lying on a continuum ranging from causing little psychological distress to being associated with full-blown schizophrenia.

Schizotypy and schizophrenia

Support for a link between schizotypal PD and (chronic) schizophrenia is found in behavioural genetic studies and in experimental studies on cognitive impairment.

Common genetic risk. There are a number of behavioural genetic studies indicating that schizotypal PD is common among first degree relatives of patients with schizophrenia (e.g., Chang et al., 2002; Varma, 1997) and by studies showing that people diagnosed as having a schizotypal PD have an enhanced risk of developing schizophrenia later in life (see Parnas et al., 2005). In addition, neuroimaging studies provide some evidence that patients with schizotypal PD do have the same abnormalities in their brain as patients with schizophrenia, although usually to a lesser extent (see Chapter 4). It has been suggested that especially the disorganized dimension of schizotypal PD may be a vulnerability marker of psychotic disorders (e.g., Cardno, Sham, Murray, & McGuffin, 2001; Parnas et al., 2005). In a recent study, Schürhoff, Laguerre, and Szöke (2005) found that the disorganized dimension of schizotypy was associated with an increased familial risk not only for schizophrenia, but also for psychotic bipolar disorder. The results of this study suggest that schizotypal PD, at least in relatives of psychotic patients, may predispose to psychosis rather than to schizophrenia per se.

Cognitive impairment.   Further support for a common basis for schizotypal PD and schizophrenia is provided by experimental studies, which show that individuals with schizotypal PD and schizophrenia share the same deficits in a number of cognitive domains. Unlike schizophrenia patients, who exhibit severe cognitive impairment across most cognitive functions, patients with schizotypal personality disorder or individuals scoring high on schizotypy exhibit moderate impairment across cognitive domains. Cognitive impairments include:

1   *Attention deficits.*   Studies have shown impairment in schizotypal individuals in both the ability to sustain attention (Lenzenweger, 2001) and ability to inhibit attention (Braunstein-Bercovitz, Rammsayer, Gibbons, & Lubow, 2004; Cadenhead, Swerdlow, Shafer, Diaz, & Braff, 2000; Tsakanikos, 2004).
2   *Memory deficits.*   Deficits in working memory (e.g., Larrison, Ferrante, Briand, & Sereno, 2000; Mitropoulou et al., 2005; Park & McTigue, 1997) and episodic memory (Mitropoulou et al., 2005) have been found to be characteristic of schizotypal individuals.
3   *Impaired executive functioning.*   Studies by Diwadkar et al. (2006) and Laurent et al. (2001) found that executive function is impaired in schizotypal first degree relatives of schizophrenic patients.

These abnormalities foreshadow many of the deficits observed in first-episode schizophrenic patients, and may underlie predisposition to schizophrenia.

Psychometric characteristics

Based on factor analytic studies there is strong evidence that schizotypal PD features are not one-dimensional. Psychometric studies reveal that schizotypy can better be described as a multidimensional construct (e.g., Vollema & van den Bosch, 1995), consisting of positive schizotypy (cognitive-perceptual deficits), negative schizotypy (interpersonal deficits), and a cognitive disorganization factor (Vollema & Hoijtink, 2000). More recently, an additional paranoid factor has been proposed (Stefanis et al., 2004). Raine (1991) developed a self-report questionnaire, the Schizotypal Personality Questionnaire (SPQ), containing subscales for the various schizotypal traits. A three-factor model has repeatedly been found for the SPQ, comprising "cognitive-perceptual deficits" (positive dimension), "interpersonal deficits" (negative dimension), and "disorganization" (disorganized dimension) (e.g., Reynolds, Raine, Mellingen, Venables, & Mednick, 2000). Another measure that is widely used is the Oxford-Liverpool Inventory of Feelings and Experiences (O-LIFE). This measure was introduced in 1995 as a four-scale questionnaire for measuring psychosis-proneness, principally schizotypy. Its items were deliberately chosen to make it suitable for tapping psychotic characteristics in healthy individuals. A series of studies has established its reliability and validity (Mason & Claridge, 2006).

In terms of the Big Five personality dimensions (Five-Factor Model; Costa & McCrae, 1992a), individuals with schizotypal PD are characterized by higher levels of neuroticism and extraversion and lower levels of agreeableness and conscientiousness than persons without schizotypal PD (see Saulsman & Page, 2004).

Emotional processing, reasoning bias, and false perception

Emotional processing. It has been argued that emotions play a significant role in influencing schizotypal personality traits and the peculiar perceptions and beliefs that are characteristic of schizotypal PD. In terms of emotional processes, most of the theorizing and research on peculiar perceptions and beliefs (including delusions) has focused on elevated levels of unpleasant emotions, such as sadness, anger, and anxiety.

Individuals with schizotypal personality traits have been found to pay more attention to their emotions than control participants (Berenbaum et al., 2006; Kerns, 2005). These results raise the possibility that increased attention to emotion may predispose individuals to a wide variety of "errors in thinking", and may be associated with the development of peculiar beliefs and magical thinking. Berenbaum et al. (2006) found that both the cognitive-perceptual disturbances (e.g., "odd beliefs") and suspiciousness of schizotypy were associated with different facets of emotional awareness. Whereas cognitive-perceptual disturbances were associated with attention to emotion and not clarity of emotion, suspiciousness was associated with lower clarity of emotion, and was not associated with attention to emotion. As suggested by the authors: "Individuals who do not understand what they are feeling, and why, are likely to be confused about events that have an emotional impact on them and are thereby more likely to misinterpret other people's behaviors and intentions" (p. 366).

Reasoning bias. Other studies have addressed reasoning bias in schizo-typal individuals. Sellen, Oaksford, and Gray (2005) have presented data that support the notion of a "jumping to conclusions" style of reasoning, presumably mediated via a process of overinclusive thinking. In this study a conditional inference task was used to test logical performance in individuals with high scores on schizotypy. Only one schizotypy factor (impulsive nonconformity, which refers to disinhibited, violent, self-abusive, and reckless behaviours) was related to a failure to take account of the number of counterexamples that characterized the cause–effect conditional statement. Results are inconclusive yet, given that no effects were observed with the remaining schizotypy factors.

False perception. Finally, a study of Tsakanikos and Reed (2005) is of some interest. These investigators found that positive schizotypal symptoms predicted false perceptions in the laboratory. During visual detection of fast-moving words, undergraduate students scoring highly on positive schizotypy reported seeing words that did not exist in the list. On average, each participant saw one to two words that never appeared in the trials; however, participants scoring highly on positive schizotypy were more inclined to see such words. The authors suggest that simultaneous presentation of fast-moving nonwords may have generated past associations or verbal repre-sentations of corresponding words on the basis of some superficial similarity. Presumably, high positive schizotypy scorers were more likely to "translate" their internally generated experiences (i.e., associations and verbal representations of similar-looking/sounding words) into perceptual experiences (i.e., false perceptions of words).

Positive aspects of schizotypy: Creativity

In discussing the negative effects of schizotypal personality, we should not neglect that schizotypy is also associated with creativity (Claridge, 1997; Nette, 2001). It has been suggested that the link with artistic creativity has evolutionary significance, its function being to attract mates, like that of the peacock's tail, and so enhance reproductive success (see Nette & Clegg, 2006). To test this hypothesis Nette and Clegg (2006) examined the relationship between schizotypy and mating success in a large sample of British artistically creative adults (e.g., poets and artists). The results show significant positive relationships between "unusual experiences" (positive schizotypy) and mating success (number of partners). This relationship was mediated by creative activity; those high in unusual experiences produced poetry or art more seriously, and this in turn increased mating success. The anhedonia component of schizotypy (negative schizotypy), however, was found to decrease creative activity, and had a negative effect on mating success. Nette and Clegg see these results as supporting the hypothesis that schizotypal traits are maintained in the human population because the negative effects in terms of psychosis and other psychopathology are countered by increased mating success. Leaving the plausibility of this theory to the reader, the question remains which factors determine when schizotypy may have primarily positive effects in terms of artistic creativity and when it has primarily negative effects in terms of (psychiatric) impairment.

Schizoid personality disorder

There are many accounts in the literature of schizoid personality, but more than 90% of these accounts are psychodynamically oriented theoretical contributions based on case descriptions. Unfortunately, there is a clear lack of empirical studies testing these psychodynamic theoretical propositions. Another problem with this literature is that the psychodynamic position of schizoid personality deviates in important aspects from the current nosology in terms of DSM-IV-TR, being more inferential and phenomenological. Unfortunately, by not using formally agreed upon diagnostic criteria for schizoid PD the prevalence of this personality disorder – estimated at less than 2% in community studies (see Chapter 3) – might be quite distorted as reflected in a statement by McWilliams, a foremost authority in this area: "I have always been more interested in exploring individual differences than in arguing about what is and is not pathology, and I have found that when individuals with schizoid dynamics – whether patients, colleagues, or personal friends – sense that their disclosures will not be disdained …, they are willing to share with me a lot about their inner world. As is true in many other realms, when one becomes open to seeing something, one sees it everywhere" (p. 1). Unfortunately, few empirical studies have investigated characteristics of schizoid PD.

Does the prevalence of schizoid personality disorder increase with age?

Engels et al. (2003) studied the prevalence of personality disorders in five different age groups ranging from 17 to 87 years. Elderly people from the community and older mental health patients reported more schizoid characteristics compared to younger individuals. This may, however, be an artefact related to decrease of interest in sexual activity and decrease of social network, which is common among the elderly. Thus, lack of friends, doing solitary activities and little interest in sexual activities, which are three out of seven criteria of detachment from social relationships of schizoid PD, may be the result of factors related to ageing rather than to a life-long personality disorder. Only four of these criteria are needed in order to fulfil the requirements of detachment in the context of a schizoid PD.

Big Five personality traits

In the study of Ross et al. (2002), both schizoid and schizotypal PD symptoms were negatively associated with extraversion and agreeableness on the NEO-PI-R. However, openness to experiences was the trait that distinguished schizoid from schizotypal individuals. Higher levels of schizotypal symptoms were related to higher levels of openness, whereas higher levels of schizoid symptoms were related to lower levels of openness. When examining lower order traits, hostility and self-consciousness were positively associated with schizoid symptoms, indicating a propensity for self-focus in social situations but also a tendency to externalize blame for current failures. In a recent meta-analysis compiling data from 15 clinical and nonclinical studies (lack of) openness to experience explained more variance in schizoid PD traits than in schizotypal PD traits (Saulsman & Page, 2004). Taken together, there is strong evidence that openness to experience is the distinguishing personality factor differentiating schizoid PD from schizotypal PD.

Neurodevelopment

There is some evidence that nutritional deficiency during early gestation is related to congenital anomalies of the central nervous system which increase the risk of schizoid PD. As discussed in Chapter 3, exposure to severe famine in the Dutch Hunger Winter at the end of the Second World War was associated with the development of schizoid PD. Men exposed prenatally to severe maternal nutritional deficiency during the first trimesters of pregnancy exhibited increased risk for schizoid PD (odds ratio 2:1), which was comparable to the increased risk of schizophrenia (odds ratio 2:0). The results suggest that prenatal nutritional deficiency was associated with a greater risk of schizoid PD (Hoek, Susser, Buck, Lumey, Lin, & Gorman, 1996; Susser et al., 1996). Social class did not confound these results. This finding coincides with a corresponding increase in risk of congenital anomalies of the central nervous system. A neuroimaging study revealed that this nutritional deficiency during the first trimester of gestation was indeed associated with aberrant early brain development in patients (Hulshoff Pol et al., 2000).

Paranoid personality disorder

Paranoid PD refers to individuals whose perceptions are pervaded with mistrust and suspiciousness and who are inclined to interpret motivations of others as being malicious. Paranoid PD should be differentiated from paranoid delusions and hallucinations associated with Axis-I psychotic disorders (Freeman, Garety, Kuipers, Fowler, & Bebbington, 2002). Individuals identified as having a paranoid PD in early adulthood may be at elevated risk for recurrent or chronic unipolar depression later in life (Johnson, Cohen, et al., 2005). Further, an association between paranoid PD and posttraumatic stress disorder has been reported (Gomez-Beneyto et al., 2006).

Big Five personality traits

In terms of the Big Five personality dimensions (Five-Factor Model; Costa & McCrae, 1992a), individuals with paranoid PD are characterized by high levels of neuroticism and low levels of agreeableness.

Several studies examining the relationship between the Five-Factor Model of personality and personality disorders have revealed that the paranoid disorder was positively associated with neuroticism (Brieger, Sommer, Blöink, & Marneros, 2000) and negatively associated with agreeableness (Shopshire & Craik, 1994). Other studies found a negative link with extraversion (see Saulsman & Page, 2004). Research into forgiveness is also of some relevance to paranoid PD. Forgiveness, defined as the disposition to abort one's anger at persons one takes to have wronged one culpably, was found to be inversely linked to paranoid tendencies in a large nonclinical sample (Munoz Sastre, Vinsonneau, Chabrol, & Mullett, 2005). The results revealed a strong positive correlation between enduring resentment and willingness to avenge on the one hand, and paranoid tendencies on the other.

Theoretical contributions

Individuals suffering from paranoid PD are inclined to blame other people for their own misfortunes. In psychodynamic theory paranoid ideas are conceptualized as defence mechanisms which serve to: "ward off the blows stemming from the feelings of shame and humiliation that were caused by the critical, punitive environment such individuals typically experienced during their development" (Salvatore, Nicolò, & Dimaggio, 2005, p. 252). Seen in this context, the distrust and lack of confidence in others associated with paranoid individuals are cognitive defences against the subjects' feelings of low self-esteem and the perception that they will be rejected and fail. Also, Gilbert (2002) maintains that paranoid ideation should be viewed as an overstated defence mechanism. Individuals with paranoid traits are hypervigilant and continuously scanning the environment for warning signals that their self-image is being threatened. In such situations, subcortical information processing systems are activated and take over from cortical information processing (Gilbert, 2002).

Conceptualizations from a cognitive therapy perspective (Beck et al., 2004) emphasize the basic assumption among individuals with paranoid PD that others are malevolent, deceptive, and ready to attack if they get the chance. If one is vigilant for subtle indications that others are not to be trusted, one easily sees many actions on the part of others that might be interpreted as evidence that people are indeed malicious, and deserve retaliation. Individuals with paranoid

PD are assumed to believe that showing any weakness may encourage attack.

Finally, in a thought-provoking paper, Fenigstein and Vanable (1992) suggested that self-consciousness might be associated with paranoid ideation. In a series of studies Fenigstein and colleagues demonstrated that self-consciousness heightened the tendency to engage in seemingly paranoid inferences. Subjects who were high in public self-consciousness (i.e., who tended to focus on the publicly observable aspects of themselves) were more likely to infer that another's behaviour was being intentionally directed towards them than individuals low in self-consciousness.

Attributional bias, reasoning bias, and emotional perception

Attributional bias. What experimental evidence is available to support the contention that paranoid tendencies are linked to attempts to maintain self-esteem by attributing negative events to the actions of other people? There is considerable evidence that subjects with paranoid ideation are inclined to attribute negative events to outside sources. For example, in an experimental study by Kinderman and Bentall (1997) patients with delusions of persecution tended to avoid self-blame, and instead tended to choose external attributions that located blame in other individuals. These patients have a *personalizing* bias rather than a general external attribution for negative events, i.e., they blame other people rather than the situation. Other studies also suggest that paranoid ideation is a mechanism by which individuals protect the self against anxiety, depression, or low self-esteem associated with personal failures by attributing blame to others (Bentall, Kinderman, & Kaney, 1994; Kramer, 1998; Trower & Chadwick, 1995), although not all studies supported this view (McKay, Langdon, & Coltheart (2005).

Reasoning bias. There is also some evidence that individuals with delusions and delusion-prone individuals demonstrate a reasoning bias (Garety & Freeman, 1999), which might be of some relevance to individuals with paranoid PD. These studies reveal that patients with delusions have a so-termed "jump-to-conclusions" reasoning style on a probabilistic reasoning task. Research so far suggests that they require less information before making a decision, thus enhancing the likelihood of inaccurate beliefs being formed too rapidly (e.g., Conway et al., 2002; Fear & Healy, 1997).

Emotional perception. Another line of experimental research has focused on sensitivity to emotional stimuli, particularly negative emotions, in individuals with delusions and paranoid ideation. In a recent study (Combs, Michael, & Penn, 2006) the effect of paranoia, as measured on a continuum, on emotion perception was investigated. A group of patients with persecutory delusions was compared with three sub-clinical groups (high, moderate, and low paranoid ideation). For negative emotions (particularly anger), higher levels of paranoid ideation (patients with persecutory delusions and individuals with high paranoid ideation) were linked to a performance deficit on emotion perception tasks. No differences were found on positive emotion tasks.

Finally, patients with persecutory delusions (e.g., Bentall et al., 1994) and individuals who score high on paranoid ideation (Fenigstein, 1997) have been shown to have improved recall for threatening stimuli. They were able to recall more threatening words on memory recall tasks than non-paranoid controls.

Concluding remarks. The experimental paradigms on reasoning bias, attributional bias, and emotional perception have not yet been tested on patients formally diagnosed with paranoid PD. Although it is tempting to assume that the process demonstrated in nonclinical subjects and patients with persecutory delusions generalizes to individuals with paranoid PD, this still requires further empirical study.

Depression in adolescence

Having had a depressive disorder during adolescence is a major risk factor for schizotypal and schizoid PD. The odds of developing an adult schizotypal PD increased by three times and of developing an adult schizoid PD by ten times given a prior diagnosis of major depression in adolescence (Ramklint, von Knorring, von Knorring, & Ekselius, 2003). However, this association also holds the other way around. In a prospective longitudinal study by Johnson, Cohen, et al. (2005) it was found that Cluster A traits in adolescence predicted the development of unipolar depressive disorders by middle adulthood. Of the Cluster A traits, only schizotypal PD traits, identified between ages 14 and 22, were significantly associated with risk for dysthymic disorder or major depressive disorder by a mean age of 33. However, individuals identified as having any DSM-IV Cluster A (paranoid, schizoid, or schizotypal) PD by a mean age of 22 years were at elevated risk for recurrent or chronic unipolar depression. It has also been suggested that there might be a relationship between Asperger syndrome and the development of schizotypal PD, but there are no firm data yet to confirm this association (Battaglia, 2005).

Inadequate coping style

Finally, individuals with Cluster A personality disorders are characterized by inadequate coping. In a study by Bijttebier and Vertommen (1999), schizotypal, schizoid, and paranoid PD traits were linked to a lack of social support seeking and the tendency to engage in avoidant strategies in a clinical sample. Of course, given the correlational nature of the data, this cannot be taken as evidence that inadequate coping strategies are causal in the development of personality disorders.

Treatment

Patients with Cluster A personality disorders will usually not refer themselves to mental health facilities, despite the impairment associated with this disorder. As noted by Isohani and Tienari (2005), "after the 31-year follow-up of 11017 persons in the register-based Northern Finland 1966 Birth Cohort we have only four hospital-treated cases" (p. 87). If patients are seen in clinical settings this is usually as relatives of a schizophrenic patient or because of treatment of an Axis-I disorder or a comorbid Cluster B or C disorder. Schizoid PD is exceptionally rare in community-based services, but is more common in forensic mental health settings. Given this state of affairs there is little in the way of clinical guidelines about how to treat the Cluster A personality disorders.

According to a diathesis-stress model, persons with type A personality disorders are biologically vulnerable to develop schizophrenia. An inability to cope in the social environment is thought to be a significant source of stress and to contribute to an exacerbation of symptoms eventually leading to psychotic symptoms in some patients (Bijttebier & Vertommen, 1999). If the model is correct, coping skills training (to deal more adequately with stressors) may have something to offer to these patients. Four types of intervention have been developed to teach schizophrenic patients or their family to deal more adequately with stress: social skills training, cognitive rehabilitation, family education, and cognitive-behaviour therapy. Although these types of interventions have been empirically evaluated in a number of controlled studies and found to be effective in schizophrenic patients (see Emmelkamp, 2004), these interventions have not yet been evaluated in patients with Cluster A personality disorders.

In social skills training, patients are trained in basic skills such as conversation skills and assertiveness, in order to respond to stressors more adequately and thus reduce subsequent stress. Social skills training aims to improve the quality of life by increasing the individual's social competence. Brenner et al. (1995) designed a treatment programme (Integrated Psychological Therapy) in which cognitive function training was combined with social skills training. In contrast to social skills training programmes, which focus on improving patients' coping efforts, the behavioural family training programmes are designed to improve the relatives' coping efforts and to reduce negative affect towards the patient. The best-known programmes are those of Falloon, Boyd, and McGill (1984) in the USA, consisting of an educational programme, communication training, and problem-solving training, and of Tarrier and his colleagues (1998) in the UK. This programme also involves an educational component, coping skills training, and problem solving.

Over the last decade behaviour therapy procedures for schizo-phrenia have also included cognitive approaches and there are no a priori reasons why these programmes would also not be beneficial to patients with Cluster A personality disorders. Cognitive-behaviour therapy for schizophrenia has been developed in the United Kingdom. Although there are some differences between various programmes, most aim to reduce the stresses of patients, strengthen adaptive coping skills, and focus on psychotic beliefs. The emphasis is on gently challenging the patient's underlying cognitive assumptions and reality testing. The therapy usually includes a number of behavioural strategies such as relaxation, anxiety management, problem solving, and activity planning. There is a clear need to study all these inter-ventions in patients with Cluster A personality disorders.

Interventions for schizotypal PD

A few studies have investigated interventions in patients at risk for developing psychotic disorders, including patients with schizotypal PD (McGorry et al., 2002; Morrison et al., 2004), but data from these studies have not been analysed for individuals with schizotypal PD only. A recent randomized controlled trial (Nordentoft et al., 2006) investigated whether "integrated treatment" reduced transition to psychosis for first-contact patients diagnosed with schizotypal disorder. Integrated treatment was based on a modified Assertive Community Treatment model provided by a multidisciplinary team; home visits were an integrated part of the treatment model. Treatment focused on reduction of substance abuse and social skills training. Further, psychoeducation was offered to patients and their family members. Although cognitive-behavioural treatment was not offered systematically, social skills training and family involvement were based on cognitive-behavioural principles. In addition, antipsychotic medication was prescribed in a number of cases. The effects of integrated treatment were compared with the effects of care as usual. Integrated treatment reduced the risk of developing a psychotic disorder. At 2-year follow-up, the proportion diagnosed with a psychotic disorder was 25.0% for patients randomized to integrated treatment, compared to 48.3% for patients randomized to standard treatment. No information is provided on whether treatment was also effective in changing personality traits of the patients.

In another randomized controlled trial conducted in Germany (Liberman & Robertson, 2005) the effects of an 8-week social skills training intervention were investigated in high school students who scored high on schizotypal traits. At 1-year follow-up, the treated group showed improvements in schizotypal traits and social competence; the control group did not improve. Finally, there are a few controlled studies into the effects of pharmacotherapy with patients with schizotypal PDs, suggesting that low dosage antipsychotic medication may be of some benefit (Parnas et al., 2005).

Summary

Most studies into the characteristics of individuals with Cluster A personality disorders have investigated schizotypal PD; the research basis of schizoid PD and paranoid PD is rather meagre. Individuals with schizotypal PD share phenomenological, genetic, and biological characteristics with patients with chronic schizophrenia. Relatively few data are available with respect to precursors of Cluster A personality disorders. Laboratory-based assessment of neurocognition and memory systems and paradigms from experimental psychopathology (e.g., emotional information processing) have hardly been used in studying patients *formally diagnosed* with Cluster A personality disorders: most studies involved individuals scoring high on schizotypy or individuals scoring high on paranoid ideation or delusional patients. However, these approaches hold promise in elucidating the neurobehavioural facets, development, and diagnostic boundaries of these personality disorders and may eventually be heuristic with respect to interventions for these disorders and prevention of progress into psychotic disorders. Unfortunately, there are no evidence-based treatments for patients with Cluster A personality disorders, but (elements of) treatments which have been found effective in patients with psychotic disorders may also prove beneficial to patients with Cluster A disorders.

Recommended reading

Bateman, A. W., & Fonagy, P. (2004). *Psychotherapy for borderline PD: Mentalization based treatment*. Oxford, UK: Oxford University Press.

Beck, A. T., Freeman, A., & Davis, D. D. (2003). *Cognitive therapy of personality disorders*. New York: Guilford Press.

Clarkin, J. F., & Lenzenweger, M. F. (Eds.). (1996). *Major theories of personality disorder* (pp. 106–140). New York: Guilford Press.

Hilsenroth, M. J., & Segal, D. L. (Eds.). (2003). *Comprehensive handbook of psychological assessment: Vol. 2. Personality assessment*. New York: Wiley.

Linehan, M. M. (1993). *Cognitive behavioural treatment of borderline personality disorder*. New York: Guilford Press.

Livesley, W. J. (Ed.). (2001). *Handbook of personality disorders: Theory, research and treatment* (pp. 277–306). New York: Guilford Press.

Maj, M., Akiskal, H. S., Mezzich, J. E., & Okasha, A. (Eds.). (2005). *Personality disorders*. Hoboken, NJ: Wiley.

Oldham, J. M., Skodol, A. E., & Bender, D. S. (Eds.). (2005). *Textbook of personality disorders*. Washington, DC: American Psychiatric Publishing.

Paris, J. (2003). *Personality disorders over time: Precursors, course, and outcome*. Washington, DC: American Psychiatric Publishing.

Patrick, C. J. (Ed.). (2005). *Handbook of psychopathy*. New York: Guilford Press.

Sampson, M., McCubbin, R., & Tyrer, P. (2006). *Personality disorders and community mental health teams*. Chichester, UK: Wiley.

Stone, M. H. (2006). *Personality-disordered patients: Treatable and untreatable*. Washington, DC: American Psychiatric Publishing.

Yeomans, F. E., Clarkin, J. F., & Kernberg, O. F. (2004). *A primer for transference focussed psychotherapy for borderline personality disorder*. New York: Aronson.

Young, J. E., Klosko, J. S., & Weishaar, M. E. (2003). *Schema-focused therapy: A practitioner's guide*. New York: Guilford Press.

References

Aaronson, C. J., Bender, D. S., Skodol, A. E., & Gunderson, J. G. (2006). Comparison of attachment styles in borderline personality disorder and obsessive-compulsive personality disorder. *Psychiatric Quarterly, 77,* 69–80.

Akhtar, S., & Thomson, J. A. (1982). Overview: Narcissistic personality disorder. *American Journal of Psychiatry, 139,* 12–20.

Akiskal, H. S. (1981). Subaffective disorders: Dysthymic, cyclothymic and bipolar II disorders in the "borderline" realm. *Psychiatric Clinics of North America, 4,* 25–46.

Alarcon, R. D. (2005). Cross-cultural issues. In J. M. Oldham, A. E. Skodol, & D. S. Bender (Eds.), *Textbook of personality disorders* (pp. 561–578). Washington, DC: American Psychiatric Publishing.

Alden, L. (1989) Short-term structured treatment for avoidant personality disorder. *Journal of Consulting and Clinical Psychology, 57,* 756–764.

Alden, L. E., & Capreol, M. J. (1993). Avoidant personality disorder: Interpersonal problems as predictors of treatment response. *Behaviour Therapy, 24,* 357–376.

Alden, L. E., Laposa, J. M., Taylor, C. T., & Ryder, A. G. (2002). Avoidant personality disorder: Current status and future directions. *Journal of Personality Disorders, 16,* 1–29.

Allen, J. P., Hauser, S. T., & Borman-Spurrell, E. (1996). Attachment theory as a framework for understanding sequelae of severe adolescent psychopathology: An 11-year follow-up study. *Journal of Consulting and Clinical Psychology, 64,* 254–263.

Allen, L. C., Mackenzie, D. L., & Hickman, L. J. (2001). The effectiveness of cognitive behavioral treatment for adult offenders: A methodological, quality-based review. *International Journal of Offender Therapy and Comparative Criminology, 45,* 498–514.

Allport, G. W. (1937). *Personality: A psychological interpretation.* New York: Henry Holt.

Alterman, A. I., Cacciola, J. S., & Rutherford, M. J. (1993). Reliability of the Revised Psychopathy Checklist in substance abuse patients. *Psychological Assessment, 54,* 442–448.

Alterman, A. I., McDermott, P. A., Cacciola, J. S., Rutherford, M. J., Boardman, C. R., McKay, J. R., & Cook, T. G. (1998). A typology of antisociality in methadone patients. *Journal of Abnormal Psychology, 107,* 412–422.

American Psychiatric Association. (1968). *Diagnostic and statistical manual of mental disorders* (2nd ed.) (DSM-II). Washington, DC: APA.

American Psychiatric Association. (1980). *Diagnostic and statistical manual of mental disorders* (3rd ed.) (DSM-III). Washington, DC: APA.

American Psychiatric Association. (1987) *Diagnostic and statistical manual of mental disorders* (rev. 3rd ed.) (DSM-III-R). Washington, DC: APA.

American Psychiatric Association. (1994) *Diagnostic and statistical manual of mental disorders* (4th ed.) (DSM-IV). Washington, DC: APA.

American Psychiatric Association. (2000). *Diagnostic and statistical manual of mental disorders* (4th ed., text revision) (DSM-IV-TR). Washington, DC: APA.

American Psychiatric Association. (2001). *Practice guideline for the treatment of patients with borderline personality disorder*. Washington, DC: APA.

Andersson, P., & Perris, C. (2000). Attachment styles and dysfunctional assumptions in adults. *Clinical Psychology and Psychotherapy, 7*, 47–53.

Ando, J., Suzuki, A., Yamagata, S., Kijima, N., Maekawa, H., Ono, Y., & Jang, K. L. (2004). Genetic and environmental structure of Cloninger's temperament and character dimensions. *Journal of Personality Disorders, 18*, 379–393.

Andrews, D. A., Zinger, I., Hoge, R. D., Bonta, J., Gendrau, P., & Cullen, F. T. (1990). Does correctional treatment work? A clinically relevant and psychologically informed meta-analysis. *Criminology, 28*, 369–403.

Arntz, A. (1999). Do personality disorders exist? On the validity of the concept and its cognitive-behavioural formulation and treatment. *Behaviour Research and Therapy, 37*(Suppl. 1), S97–134.

Arntz, A. (2005a). Introduction to special issue: Cognition and emotion in borderline personality disorder. *Journal of Behaviour Therapy and Experimental Psychiatry, 36*, 167–172.

Arntz, A. (2005b). Pathological dependency: Distinguishing functional from emotional dependency. *Clinical Psychology: Science and Practice, 12*, 411–416.

Arntz, A., Dreessen, L., Schouten, E., & Weertman, A. (2004). Beliefs in personality disorders: A test with the Personality Disorder Belief Questionnaire. *Behaviour Research and Therapy, 42*, 1215–1225.

Arntz, A., Klokman, J., & Sieswerda, S. (2005). An experimental test of the schema mode model of borderline personality disorder. *Journal of Behaviour Therapy and Experimental Psychiatry, 36*, 226–239.

Arntz, A., & Veen, G. (2001). Evaluations of others by borderline patients. *Journal of Nervous and Mental Disease, 189*, 513–521.

Arseneault, L., Moffitt, T. E., Caspi, A., Taylor, A., Rijsdijk, F. V., Jaffee, S. R., et al. (2003). Strong genetic effects on cross-situational antisocial behaviour among 5-year-old children according to mothers, teachers, examiner-observers, and twins' self-reports. *Journal of Child Psychology and Psychiatry, 44*, 832–848.

Baird, A. A., Veague, H. B., & Rabbit, C. E. (2005). Developmental precipitants of borderline personality disorder. *Development and Psychopathology, 17*, 1031–1041.

Bandura, A. (1973). *Aggression: A social learning analysis*. Englewood Cliffs, NJ: Prentice-Hall.

Barber, J. P., Morse, J. Q., Krakauer, I. D., Chittams, J., & Crits-Christoph, K. (1997). Change in obsessive-compulsive and avoidant personality disorders following time-limited supportive-expressive therapy. *Psychotherapy, 34*, 133–143.

Barkataki, I., Kumari, V, Das, M., Taylor, P., & Sharma, T. (2006). Volumetric structural brain abnormalities in men with schizophrenia or antisocial personality disorder. *Behavioural Brain Research, 169*, 239–247.

Baron, M., Gruen, R., & Rainer, J. D. (1985). A family study of schizophrenic and normal control probands: Implications for the spectrum concept of schizophrenia. *American Journal of Psychiatry, 142,* 447–455.

Barry, C. T., Frick, P. J., DeShazo, T. M., McCoy, M. G., Ellis, M., & Loney, B. R. (2000). The importance of callous-unemotional traits for extending the concept of psychopathy to children. *Journal of Abnormal Psychology, 109,* 335–340.

Bartholomew, K., & Horowitz, L. M. (1991). Attachment styles among young adults: A test of a four-category model. *Journal of Personality and Social Psychology, 61,* 226–244.

Bateman, A. W., & Fonagy, P. (1999). The effectiveness of partial hospitalization in the treatment of borderline personality disorder: A randomized controlled trial. *American Journal of Psychiatry, 156,* 1563–1569.

Bateman, A. W., & Fonagy, P. (2001). Treatment of borderline personality disorder with psychoanalytically oriented partial hospitalization: An 18-month follow-up. *American Journal of Psychiatry, 158,* 36–42.

Bateman, A. W., & Fonagy, P. (2003). The development of an attachment-based treatment program for borderline personality disorder. *Bulletin of the Menninger Clinic, 67,* 187–211.

Bateman, A. W., & Fonagy, P. (2004a). Mentalisation-based treatment of borderline PD. *Journal of Personality Disorders, 18,* 36–51.

Bateman, A. W., & Fonagy, P. (2004b). *Psychotherapy for borderline PD: Mentalization based treatment.* Oxford, UK: Oxford University Press.

Battaglia, M. (2005). A developmental genetic look at schizotypal disorder. In M. Maj, H. S. Akiskal, J. E. Mezzich, & A. Okasha (Eds.), *WPA series evidence and experience in psychiatry: Vol. 8. Personality disorders* (pp. 100–103). Hoboken, NJ: Wiley.

Battle, C. L., Shea, M. T., Johnson, D. M., Yen, S., Zlotnick, C., Zanarini, M. C., et al. (2004). Childhood maltreatment associated with adult personality disorders: Findings from the collaborative longitudinal personality disorders study. *Journal of Personality Disorders, 18,* 193–211.

Baumeister, R. F., Smart, L., & Boden, J. (1996). Relation of threatened egotsim to violence and agression: The dark side of high self-esteem. *Psychological Review, 103,* 5–33.

Beck, A. T., Butler, A. C., Brown, G. K., Dahlsgaard, K. K., Newman, C. F., & Beck, J. S. (2001). Dysfunctional beliefs discriminate personality disorders. *Behaviour Research and Therapy, 39*(10), 1213–1225.

Beck, A. T., & Freeman, A. (1990). *Cognitive therapy of personality disorders.* New York: Guilford Press.

Beck, A. T., Freeman, A., & Davis, D. D. (2003). *Cognitive therapy of personality disorders* (2nd ed.). New York: Guilford Press.

Beck, A. T., Freeman, A., & Davis, D. D. (2004). *Cognitive therapy of personality disorders.* New York: Guilford Press.

Beck, A. T., & Young, J. E. (1985). Cognitive therapy of depression. In D. Barlow (Ed.), *Clinical handbook of psychological disorders: A step-by-step treatment manual* (pp. 187–213). New York: Guilford Press.

Becker, D., & Lamb, S. (1994). Sex bias in the diagnosis of borderline personality disorder and posttraumatic stress disorder. *Professional Psychology Research and Practice, 25,* 53–61.

Bender, D. S., Dolan-Sewell, R. T., Skodol, A. E., Sanislow, C. J. G., Dyck, I. R., et al. (2001). Treatment utilization by patients with personality disorders. *American Journal of Psychiatry, 158,* 295–302.

Bender, D. S., Skodol, A. E., Pagano, M. E., Dyck, I. R., Grilo, C. M., Shea, M. T., et al. (2006). Prospective assessment of treatment use by patients with personality disorders. *Psychiatric Services, 57,* 254–257.

Benjamin, L. S. (1996). *Interpersonal diagnosis and treatment of personality disorders* (2nd ed.). New York: Guilford Press.

Benning, S. D., Patrick, C. J., Blonigen, D. M., Hicks, B. M., & Iacono, W. G. (2005). Estimating facets of psychopathy from normal personality traits: A step toward community epidemiological investigations. *Assessment, 12,* 3–18.

Ben-Porath, Y. S., & Waller, N. G. (1992a). "Normal" personality inventories in clinical assessment: General requirements and the potential for using the NEO personality inventory. *Psychological Assessment, 4,* 14–19.

Ben-Porath, Y. S., & Waller. N. G. (1992b). Five big issues in clinical personality assessment: A rejoinder to Costa and McCrae. *Psychological Assessment, 4,* 23–25.

Bentall, R. P., Kinderman, P., & Kaney, S. (1994). The self, attribution processes and abnormal beliefs: Towards a model of persecutory delusions. *Behaviour Research and Therapy, 32,* 331–341.

Berenbaum, H., Boden, M. T., Baker, J. P., Dizen, M., Thompson, R., & Abramowitz, A. (2006). Emotional correlates of the different dimensions of schizotypal personality disorder. *Journal of Abnormal Psychology, 115,* 359–368.

Bernstein, D. P., Cohen, P., Skodol, A., Bezirganian, D., & Brook, J. S. (1996). Childhood antecedents of adolescent personality disorders. *American Journal of Psychiatry, 153*(Suppl.), 907–913.

Bernstein, D. P., Cohen, P., Velez, C. N., Schwab-Stone, M., Siever, L. J., & Shinsato, L. (1993). Prevalence and stability of the DSM-III-R personality disorders in a community-based survey of adolescents. *American Journal of Psychiatry, 150,* 1237–1243.

Bijttebier, P., & Vertommen, H. (1999). Coping strategies in relation to personality disorders. *Personality and Individual Differences, 26,* 847–856.

Black, D. W., Baumgard, C. H., Bell, S. E., & Kao, C. (1996). Death rates in 71 men with antisocial personality disorder. A comparison with general population mortality. *Psychosomatics, 37,* 131–136.

Black, D. W., Monahan, P., Baumgard, C. H., & Bell, S. E. (1997). Predictors of long-term outcome in 45 men with antisocial personality disorder. *Annals of Clinical Psychiatry, 9,* 211–217.

Black, D. W., Noyes, R., Pfohl, B., Goldstein, R. B., & Blum, N. (1993). Personality disorder in obsessive-compulsive volunteers, well comparison subjects, and their first-degree relatives. *American Journal of Psychiatry, 150,* 1226–1232.

Blair, R. J. R., Jones, J., Clark, F., & Smith, M. (1997). The psychopathic individual: A lack of responsiveness to distress cues? *Psychophysiology, 34,* 192–198.

Blair, R. J. R., Mitchell, D. G. V., Peschardt, K. S., Colledge, E., Leonard, R. A., Shine, J. H., et al. (2004). Reduced sensitivity to others' fearful expressions in psychopathic individuals. *Personality and Individual Differences, 37,* 1111–1122.

Blair, R. J. R., Mitchell, D. G. V., Richell, R. A., Kelly, S., Leonard, R. A., Newman, C., & Scott, S. K. (2002). Turning a deaf ear to fear: Impaired recognition of vocal affect in psychopathic individuals. *Journal of Abnormal Psychology, 111,* 682–686.

Blair, R. J. R., Peschardt, K. S., Budhani, S., Mitchell, D. G. V., & Pine, D. S. (2006). The development of psychopathy. *Journal of Child Psychology and Pychiatry, 47,* 262–275.

Blair, R. J. R., Sellars, C., Strickland, I., & Clark, F. (1995). Emotion attributions in the psychopath. *Personality and Individual Differences, 194,* 431–437.

Blais, M. (1997). Clinician ratings of the

five-factor model of personality and the DSM-IV personality disorders. *Journal of Nervous and Mental Disease, 185,* 388–394.

Blais, M. A., Hilsenroth, M. J., & Castlebury, F. D. (1997). Content validity of the DSM-IV borderline and narcissistic personality disorder criteria sets. *Comprehensive Psychiatry, 38,* 31–37.

Blais, M. A., Hilsenroth, M. J., & Fowler, C. J. (1998). Rorschach correlates of the DSM-IV histrionic personality disorder. *Journal of Personality Assessment, 70,* 355–364.

Blais, M. A., McCann, J. T., Benedict, K. B., & Norman, D. K. (1997). Toward an empirical/theoretical grouping of the DSM-III-R personality disorders. *Journal of Personality Disorders, 11,* 191–198.

Blashfield, R. K., & Intoccia, V. (2000). Growth of the literature on the topic of personality disorders. *American Journal of Psychiatry, 57,* 472–473.

Blatt, S. J. (1991). A cognitive morphology of psychopathology. *Journal of Nervous and Mental Disease, 179,* 449–458.

Blatt, S. J. (2004). *Experiences of depression: Theoretical, clinical and research perspectives.* Washington, DC: American Psychological Association.

Block, J. (1995). A contrarian view of the five-factor approach to personality description. *Psychological Bulletin, 117,* 187–215.

Bogaerts, S., Vanheule, S., & deClercq, T. (2005). Recalled parental bonding, adult attachment style, and personality disorders in child molesters: A comparative study. *Journal of Forensic Psychiatry and Psychology, 16,* 445–458.

Bogaerts, S., Vervaeke, G., & Goethals, L. (2004). A comparison of relational attitude and personality disorders in the explanation of child molestation. *Sexual Abuse: Journal of Research and Treatment, 16,* 37–47.

Bohus, M., Haaf, B., Simms, T., Limberger, M. F., Schmahl, C., Unckel, C., et al. (2004). Effectiveness of inpatient dialectical behavioral therapy for borderline PD: A controlled trial. *Behaviour Research and Therapy, 42,* 487–499.

Bor, W., McGee, T. R., & Fagan, A. A. (2004). Early risk factors for adolescent antisocial behaviour: An Australian longitudinal study. *Australian and New Zealand Journal of Psychiatry, 38,* 365–372.

Bouchard, T. J., Lykken, D. T., McGue, M., Segal, N. L., & Tellegen, A. (1990). Sources of human psychological differences: The Minnesota study of twins reared apart. *Science, 250,* 223–228.

Bowden-Jones, O., Iqbal, M. Z., Tyrer, P., Seivewright, N., Cooper, S., & Judd, A. (2004). Prevalence of personality disorder in alcohol and drug services and associated comorbidity. *Addiction, 99,* 1306–1314.

Bowlby, J. (1977). The making and breaking of affectional bonds: I. Aetiology and psychopathology in the light of attachment theory. *British Journal of Psychiatry, 130,* 201–210.

Bradley, R., Jenei, J., & Westen, D. (2005). Etiology of borderline personality disorder: Disentangling the contributions of intercorrelated antecedents. *Journal of Nervous and Mental Disease, 193,* 24–31.

Bradley, R., & Westen, D. (2005). The psychodynamics of borderline personality disorder: A view from developmental psychopathology. *Developmental Psychopathology, 17,* 927–957.

Braunstein-Bercovitz, H., Rammsayer, T., Gibbons, H., & Lubow, R. E. (2004). Latent inhibition deficits in high-schizotypal normals: Symptom-specific or anxiety-related? *Schizophrenia Research, 53,* 109–121.

Brennan, K. A., Clark, C. L., & Shaver, P. R.

(1998). Self-report measurement of adult attachment: An integrative overview. In J. A. Simpson & W. S. Rholes (Eds.), *Attachment theory and close relationships* (pp. 46–76). New York: Guilford Press.

Brennan, K. A., & Shaver, P. R. (1998). Attachment styles and personality disorders: Their connections to each other and to parental divorce, parental death, and perceptions of parental caregiving. *Journal of Personality, 66,* 835–878.

Brennan, P. A., Grekin, E. R., & Mednick, S. A. (1999). Maternal smoking during pregnancy and adult male criminal outcomes. *Archives of General Psychiatry, 56,* 215–219.

Brennan, P. A., Raine, A., Schulsinger, F., Kirkegaard-Sorensen, L., Knop, J., Hutchings, B., et al. (1997). Psychophysiological protective factors for male subjects at high risk for criminal behavior. *American Journal of Psychiatry, 154,* 853–855.

Brenner, H. D., Roder, V., Hodel, B. M., Kienzie, N., Reed, D., & Liberman, R. P. (1995). *Integrated psychological therapy for schizophrenic patients.* Bern, Switzerland: Hogrefe & Huber.

Brieger, P., Sommer, S., Blöink, R., & Marneros, A. (2000). The relationship between five-factor personality measurements and ICD-10 personality disorder dimensions: Results from a sample of 229 subjects. *Journal of Personality Disorders, 14,* 282–290.

Briere, J., & Gil, E. (1998). Self-mutilation in clinical and general population samples: Prevalence, correlates and functions. *American Journal of Orthopsychiatry, 68,* 600–620.

Brinkley, C. A., Newman, J. P., Widiger, T. A., & Lynam, D. R. (2004). Two approaches to parsing the heterogeneity of psychopathy. *Clinical Psychology: Science and Practice, 11,* 69–94.

Brown, G. K., Newman, C. F.,

Charlesworth, S. E., Crits-Christoph, P., & Beck, A. T. (2004). An open clinical trial of cognitive therapy for borderline personality disorder. *Journal of Personality Disorders, 18,* 257–271.

Buffington-Vollum, J., Edens, J. F., Johnson, D. W., & Johnson, J. K. (2002). Psychopathy as a predictor of institutional misbehavior among sex offenders: A prospective replication. *Criminal Justice and Behavior, 29,* 497–511.

Bumby, K. M., & Hansen, D. J. (1997). Intimacy deficits, fear of intimacy, and loneliness among sexual offenders. *Criminal Justice and Behaviour, 24,* 315–331.

Butcher, J. N., Dahlstrom, W. G., Graham, J. R., Tellegen, A., & Kaemmer, B. (1989). *MMPI-2 (Minnesota Multiphasic Personality Inventory-2): Manual for administration and scoring.* Minneapolis, MN: University of Minnesota Press.

Button, T. M., Scourfield, J., Martin, N., Purcell, S., & McGuffin, P. (2005). Family dysfunction interacts with genes in the causation of anti-social symptoms. *Behaviour Genetics, 35,* 115–120.

Cadenhead, K. S., Swerdlow, N. R., Shafer, K. M., Diaz, M., & Braff, D. L. (2000). Modulation of the startle response and startle laterality in relatives of schizophrenic patients and in subjects with schizotypal personality disorder: Evidence of inhibitory deficits. *American Journal of Psychiatry, 157,* 1660–1668.

Cale, E. M., & Lilienfeld, S. O. (2002a). Histrionic personality disorder and antisocial personality disorder: Sex-differentiated manifestations of psychopathy? *Journal of Personality Disorders, 16,* 52–72.

Cale, E. M., & Lilienfeld, S. O. (2002b). Sex differences in psychopathy and antisocial personality disorder: A review and integration. *Clinical Psychology Review, 22,* 1179–1207.

Campbell, S. B., Pierce, E. W., Moore, G., & Marakovitz, S. (1996). Boys' externalizing problems at elementary school age: Pathways from early behavior problems, maternal control, and family stress. *Development and Psychopathology, 8*, 701–719.

Caplan, P. J. (1987). The Psychiatric Association's failure to meet its own standards: The dangers of the self-defeating personality disorder category. *Journal of Personality Disorders, 1*, 178–182.

Cappe, R. F., & Alden, L. E. (1986). A comparison of treatment strategies for clients functionally impaired by extreme shyness and social avoidance. *Journal of Consulting and Clinical Psychology, 54*, 796–801.

Cardno, A. G., Sham, P. C., Murray, M., & McGuffin, P. (2001). Twin study of symptom dimensions in psychosis. *British Journal of Psychiatry, 179*, 39–45.

Caspi, A., McClay, J., Moffitt, T. E., Mill, J., Martin, J., Craig, I. W., et al. (2002). Role of genotype in the cycle of violence in maltreated children. *Science, 297*, 851–854.

Caspi, A., & Silva, P. A. (1995). Temperamental qualities at age three predict personality traits in young adulthood: Longitudinal evidence from a birth cohort. *Child Development, 66*, 486–498.

Chambless, D. L., & Ollendick, T. H. (2001). Empirically supported psychological interventions: Controversies and evidence. *Annual Review of Psychology, 52*, 685–716.

Chang, C. J., Chen, W. J., Liu, S. K., Cheng, J. J., Yang, W. C., Chang, H. J., et al. (2002). Morbidity risk of psychiatric disorders among the first degree relatives of schizophrenia patients in Taiwan. *Schizophrenia Bulletin, 28*, 379–392.

Chavira, D. A., Grilo, C. M., Shea, M. T., Yen, S., Gunderson, J. G., Morey, L. C., et al. (2003). Ethicity and four personality disorders. *Comprehensive Psychiatry, 44*, 483–491.

Chen, H., Cohen, P., Johnson, J. G., Kasen, S., Sneed, J. R., & Crawford, T. N. (2004). Adolescent personality disorders and conflict with romantic partners during the transition to adulthood. *Journal of Personality Disorders, 18*, 507–525.

Chiesa, M., Fonagy, P., Holmes, J., & Drahorad, C. (2004). Residential versus community treatment of personality disorder: A comparative study of three treatment programs. *American Journal of Psychiatry, 161*, 1463–1470.

Christian, R., Frick, P. J., Hill, N., Tyler, L. A., & Frazer, D. (1997). Psychopathy and conduct problems in children: II. Subtyping children with conduct problems based on their interpersonal and affective style. *Journal of the American Academy of Child and Adolescent Psychiatry, 36*, 233–241.

Claridge, C. (Ed.). (1997). *Schizotypy: Implications for illness and health.* Oxford, UK: Oxford University Press.

Clark, L. A. (1993a). *Manual for the Schedule for Nonadaptive and Adaptive Personality.* Minneapolis, MN: University of Minnesota Press.

Clark, L. A. (1993b). Personality disorder diagnosis: Limitations of the Five-Factor model. *Psychological Inquiry, 4*, 100–104.

Clark, L. A., & Harrison, D. (2001). Assessment instruments. In W. J. Livesley (Ed.), *Handbook of personality disorders: Theory, research and treatment* (pp. 277–306). New York: Guilford Press.

Clark, L. A., Livesley, W. J., & Morey, L. (1997). Personality disorder assessment: The challenge of construct validity. *Journal of Personality Disorders, 11*, 205–231.

Clark, L. A., Livesley, W. J., Schroeder, M. L., & Irish, S. (1996). The structure of maladaptive traits: Convergent validity between two systems. *Psychological Assessment, 8,* 294–303.

Clarkin, J. F., Foelsch, P. A., Levy, K. N., Hull, J. W., Delaney, J. C., & Kernberg, O. F. (2001). The development of a psychodynamic treatment for patients with borderline personality disorder: A preliminary study of behavioural change. *Journal of Personality Disorders, 15,* 487–495.

Clarkin, J. F., Hull, J. W., & Hurt, S. W. (1993). Factor structure of borderline personality disorder criteria. *Journal of Personality Disorders, 7,* 137–143.

Clarkin, J. F., & Levy, K. N. (2006). Psychotherapy for patients with borderline personality disorder: Focusing on the mechanisms of change. *Journal of Clinical Psychology, 62,* 405–410.

Clarkin, J. F., Levy, K. N., Lenzenweger, M. F., & Kernberg, O. F. (2004). The Personality Disorders Institute Borderline Personality Disorder Research Foundation randomized control trial for borderline personality disorder: Rationale, methods, and patient characteristics. *Journal of Personality Disorders, 18,* 52–72.

Clarkin, J. F., Widiger, T. A., Frances, A. J., Hurt, S. W., & Gilmore, M. (1983). Prototypic typology and the borderline personality disorder. *Journal of Abnormal Psychology, 92,* 263–275.

Clarkin, J. F., Yeomans, F. E., & Kernberg, O. F. (1999). *Psychotherapy for borderline personality.* New York: Wiley.

Cleckley, H. (1941). *The mask of sanity* (1st ed.). St Louis, MO: Mosby.

Cloninger, C. R. (1987). A systematic method for clinical description and classification of personality variants. *Archives of General Psychiatry, 44,* 573–588.

Cloninger, C. R. (2000). A practical way to diagnose personality disorders: A proposal. *Journal of Personality Disorders, 14,* 99–106.

Cloninger, C. R. (2005). Antisocial personality disorder: A review. In M. Maj, H. S. Akiskal, J. E. Mezzich, & A. Okasha (Eds.), *Personality disorders* (pp. 125–169). Chichester: Wiley.

Cloninger, C. R., Przybeck, T. R., & Svrakic, D. M. (1991). The Tridimensional Personality Questionnaire: US normative data. *Psychological Reports, 69,* 1047–1051.

Cloninger, C. R., Przybeck, T. R., Svrakic, D. M., & Wetzel, R. D. (1994). *The Temperament and Character Inventory (TCI): A guide to its development and use.* St Louis, MO: Center for Psychobiology of Personality, Washington University.

Cloninger, C. R., Svrakic, D. M., & Przybeck, T. R. (1993). A psychobiological model of temperament and character. *Archives of General Psychiatry, 50,* 975–990.

Coccaro, E. F., Bergeman, C. S., & McClearn, G. E. (1993). Heritability of irritable impulsiveness: A study of twins reared together and apart. *Psychiatry Research, 48,* 229–242.

Cogswell, A., & Alloy, L. B. (2006). The relation of neediness and axis-II pathology. *Journal of Personality Disorders, 20,* 16–21.

Coid, J. (2003). Epidemiology, public health and the problem of personality disorder. *British Journal of Psychiatry, 182*(Suppl. 44), S3–S10.

Coid, J. (2005). Correctional populations: Criminal careers and recidism. In J. M. Oldham, A. E. Skodol, & D. S. Bender (Eds.), *Textbook of personality disorders* (pp. 579–606). Washington, DC: American Psychiatric Publishing.

Coid, J., Yang, M., Tyrer, P., Roberts, A., & Ullrich, S. (2006). Prevalence and correlates of personality disorder in Great Britain. *British Journal of Psychiatry, 188,* 423–431.

Collins, J. J., & Bailey, S. L. (1990).

Traumatic stress disorder and violent behavior. *Journal of Traumatic Stress, 3,* 203–220.

Combs, D. R., Michael, C. O., & Penn, D. W. (2006). Paranoia and emotion perception across the continuum. *British Journal of Clinical Psychology, 45,* 19–31.

Compton, W. M., Conway, K. P., Stinson, F. S., Colliver, J. P., & Grant, B. F. (2005). Prevalence, correlates, and comorbidity of DSM-IV antisocial personality syndromes and alcohol and specific drug use disorders in the United States: Results from the National Epidemiologic Survey on Alcohol and Related Conditions. *Journal of Clinical Psychiatry, 66,* 677–685.

Compton, W. M., Cottler, L. B., Jacobs, J. L., Ben-Abdallah, A., & Spitznagel, E. L. (2003). The role of psychiatric disorders in predicting drug dependence treatment outcomes. *American Journal of Psychiatry, 160,* 890–895.

Conway, C. R., Bollini, A. M., Graham, B. G., Keefe, R. S. E., Schiffman, S. S., & McEvoy, J. V. (2002). Sensory acuity and reasoning in delusional disorder. *Comprehensive Psychiatry, 43,* 175–178.

Cooke, D. J., Michie, C., Hart, S. D., & Clark, D. (2005). Assessing psychopathy in the UK: Concerns about cross-cultural generalisability. *British Journal of Psychiatry, 186,* 335–341.

Coolidge, F. L., Thede, L. T., & Jang, K. L. (2001). Heritability of personality disorders in childhood: A preliminary investigation. *Journal of Personality Disorders, 15,* 33–40.

Coolidge, F. L., Thede, L. T., & Jang, K. L. (2004). Are personality disorders psychological manifestations of executive function? Bivariate heritability evidence from a twin study. *Behaviour Genetics, 34,* 75–86.

Cormier, J., LeFauveau, P., & Loas, G. (2006). Personnalité dépendante et risque d'hétéro-agressivité: étude d'une cohorte de 252 sujets consultant en médecine légale [Dependent personality and hetero-agressive risks: Study of group of 252 patients in forensic medicine]. *Annales Medico-Psychologiques, 164,* 230–236.

Costa, P. T., & McCrae, R. R. (1992a). The five-factor model of personality and its relevance to personality disorders. *Journal of Personality Disorders, 6,* 343–359.

Costa, P. T., Jr., & McCrae, R. R. (1992b). *Revised NEO Personality Inventory (NEO-PI-R) and NEO Five-Factor Inventory (NEO-FFI) professional manual.* Odessa, FL: Psychological Assessment Resources.

Costa, P. T., Jr., & McCrae, R. R. (1995). Domains and facets: Hierarchical personality assessment using the revised NEO Personality Inventory. *Journal of Personal Assessment,* **64,** 21–50.

Costa, P., Samuels, J., Bagby, M., Daffin, L., & Norton, H. (2005). Obsessive-compulsive personality disorder: A review. In M. Maj, H. S. Akiskal, J. E. Mezzich, & A. Okasha (Eds.), *Personality disorders* (pp. 405–439). Chichester, UK: Wiley.

Cramer, V., Torgersen, S., & Kringlen, E. (2006). Personality disorders and quality of life: A population study. *Comprehensive Psychiatry, 47,* 178–184.

Crawford, T. N., Cohen, P., & Brook, J. S. (2001). Dramatic-erratic personality disorder symptoms: Continuity from early adolescence into adulthood. *Journal of Personality Disorders, 15,* 319–335.

Crick, N., & Dodge, K. (1994). A review and reformulation of social information-processing mechanisms in children's social adjustment. *Psychological Bulletin, 115,* 74–101.

Cyranowski, J. M., Frank, E., Winter, E., Rucci, P., Novick, D., Pilkonis, P., et al. (2004). Personality pathology and outcome in recurrently depressed women over 2 years of maintenance interpersonal psychotherapy. *Psychological Medicine, 34,* 659–669.

Damasio, H., Grabowski, T., Frank, R., Galaburda, A. M., & Damasio, A. R. (1994). The return of Phineas Gage: Clues about the brain from the skull of a famous patient. *Science, 264,* 1102–1105.

Davidson, K. (2006, February). *Finally—the results of the BOSCOT trial: A randomised controlled trial of cognitive behaviour therapy for borderline personality disorder.* Paper presented at the annual conference of the British and Irish Group for the Study of Personality Disorder, Nothingham, UK.

Davis, R. T., Blashfield, R. K., & McElroy, R. A. (1993). Weighting criteria in the diagnosis of a personality disorder: A demonstration. *Journal of Abnormal Psychology, 102,* 319–322.

Davison, G. C., & Neale, J. M. (1998). *Abnormal psychology* (7th ed.). New York: Wiley.

De Clerq, B., & de Fruyt, F. (2003). Personality disorder symptoms in adolescence: A five-factor model perspective. *Journal of Personality Disorders, 17,* 269–292.

De Cubas, M. M., & Field, T. (1993). Children of methadone-dependent women: Developmental outcomes. *American Journal of Orthopsychiatry, 63,* 266–276.

De Fruyt, F., DeClercq, B. J., van de Wiele, L., & van Heeringen, K. (2006). The validity of Cloninger's psychobiological model versus the five-factor model to predict DSM-IV personality disorders in a heterogeneous psychiatric sample: Domain facet and residualized facet descriptions. *Journal of Personality Disorders, 74,* 479–487.

Depue, R. A., & Lenzenweger, M. F. (2001). A neurobehavioral dimensional model. In W. J. Livesley (Ed.), *Handbook of personality disorders* (pp. 136–176). New York: Guilford Press.

Derks, F. C. H. (1996). A forensic day treatment program for personality-disordered criminal offenders. *International Journal of Offender Therapy and Comparative Criminology, 40,* 123–134.

Dickey, C. C., McCarley, R. W., Niznikiewicz, M. A.,Voglmaier, M. M., Seidman, L. J., Kim, S., & Shenton, M. E. (2005). Clinical, cognitive, and social characteristics of a sample of neuroleptic-naive persons with schizotypal personality disorder. *Schizophrenia Research, 78,* 297–308.

Dickinson, K. A., & Pincus, A. L. (2003). Interpersonal analysis of grandiose and vulnerable narcissism. *Journal of Personality Disorders, 17,* 188–207.

Dimeff, L. A., McDavid, J., & Linehan, M. M. (1999). Pharmacotherapy for borderline personality disorder: A review of the literature and recommendation for treatment. *Journal of Clinical Psychology in Medical Settings, 6,* 113–138.

Diwadkar, V. A., Montrose, D. M., Dworakowski, D., Sweeney, J., & Keshavan, M. S. (2006). Genetically predisposed offspring with schizotypal features: An ultra high-risk group for schizophrenia? *Progress in Neuro-Psychopharmacology and Biological Psychiatry, 30,* 230–238.

Dodge, K. A., Bates, J. E., & Pettit, G. S. (1990). Mechanisms in the cycle of violence. *Science, 250,* 1678–1683.

Dodge, K. A., & Pettit, G. S. (2003). A biopsychosocial model of the development of chronic conduct problems in adolescence. *Developmental Psychology, 39,* 349–371.

Dodge, K. A., Pettit, G. S., Bates, J. E., & Valente, E. (1995). Social information-processing patterns partially mediate the effect of early physical abuse on later conduct problems. *Journal of Abnormal Psychology, 104,* 632–643.

Dolan, M. C., & Anderson, I. M. (2003). The relationship between serotonergic function and the Psychopathy Checklist: Screening version. *Journal of Psychopharmacology, 17,* 216–222.

Drake, R. E., Adler, D. A., & Vaillant, G. E. (1988). Antecedents of personality disorders in a community sample of men. *Journal of Personality Disorders, 2,* 60–68.

Dreessen, L., & Arntz, A. (1998). The impact of personality disorders on treatment outcome of anxiety disorders: Best evidence synthesis. *Behaviour Research and Therapy, 36,* 483–504.

Dreessen, L., Arntz, A., Hendriks, T., Keune, N., & van den Hout, M. (1999). Avoidant personality disorder and implicit schema-congruent information processing bias: A pilot study with a pragmatic inference task. *Behaviour Research and Therapy, 37,* 619–632.

D'Silva, K., Duggan, C., & McCarthy, L. (2004). Does treatment really make psychopaths worse? A review of the evidence. *Journal of Personality Disorders, 18,* 163–177.

Durrett, C., & Westen, D. (2005). The structure of axis II disorders in adolescents: A cluster- and factor-analytic investigation of DSM-IV categories and criteria. *Journal of Personality Disorders, 19,* 440–461.

Dutton, D. G. (2002). *The abusive personality: Violence and control in intimate relationships.* New York: Guilford Press.

Dutton, D. G., & Kerry, G. (1999). Modus operandi and personality disorder in incarcerated spousal killers. *International Journal of Law and Psychiatry, 22,* 287–299.

Dutton, D. G., Saunders, K., Starzomski, A. J., & Bartholomew, K. (1994). Intimacy-anger and insecure attachment as precursors of abuse in intimate relationships. *Journal of Applied Social Psychology, 24,* 1367–1386.

Dyce, J. A., & O'Conor, B. P. (1998). Personality disorders and the five-factor model: A test of facet-level predictions. *Journal of Personality Disorders, 12,* 31–45.

Eaves, L. J., Heath, A. C., Martin, N. G., Maes, H. H., Neale, M. C., Kendler, K. S., et al. (1999). Comparing the biological and cultural inheritance of personality and social attitudes in the Virginia 30,000 study of twins and their relatives. *Twin Research, 2,* 62–80.

Eaves, L. J., Silberg, J. L., Meyer, J. M., Maes, H. H., Simonoff, E., Pickles, A., et al. (1997). Genetics and developmental psychopathology: 2. The main effects of genes and environment on behavioral problems in the Virginia Twin Study of Adolescent Behavioral Development. *Journal of Child Psychology and Psychiatry and Allied Disciplines, 38,* 965–980.

Ebstein, R. P. (2006). The molecular genetic architecture of human personality: Beyond self-report questionnaires. *Molecular Psychiatry, 11,* 427–445.

Edens, J. F., Buffington-Vollum, J. K., Colwell, K. W., Johnson, D. W., & Johnson, J. K. (2002). Psychopathy and institutional misbehavior among incarcerated sex offenders: A comparison of the Psychopathy Checklist–Revised and the Personality Assessment Inventory. *International Journal of Forensic Mental Health, 1,* 49–58.

Edens, J. F., Marcus, D. K., Lilienfeld, S. O., & Poythress, N. (2006). Psychopathic, not psychopath: Taxometric evidence for the dimensional structure of psychopathy. *Journal of Abnormal Psychology, 115,* 131–144.

Edens, J. F., Skeem, J. L., Cruise, K. R., & Cauffman, E. (2001). Assessment of "juvenile psychopathy" and its association with violence: A critical review. *Behavioral Sciences and the Law, 19*, 53–80.

Egeland, B., Weinfield, N., Bosquet, M., & Cheng, V. (2000). Remembering, repeating, and working through: Lessons from attachment-based interventions. In J. D. Osofsky & H. E. Fitzgerald (Eds.), *WAIMH handbook of infant mental health: Vol. 4. Infant mental health in groups at high risk* (pp. 35–89). New York: Wiley.

Ehrensaft, M. K. (2005). Interpersonal relationship and sex differences in the development of conduct problems. *Clinical Child and Family Psychology Review, 8*, 39–63.

Ehrensaft, M. K., Wasserman, G. A., Verdelli, L., Greenwald, S., Miller, L. S., & Davies, M. (2003). Maternal antisocial behavior, parenting practices, and behavior problems in boys at risk for antisocial behavior. *Journal of Child and Family Studies, 12*(1), 27–40.

Ekselius, L., Lindstron, E., von Knorring, L., Bodlund, O., & Kullgren, G. (1994). A principal component analysis of the DSM-III-R axis II personality disorders. *Journal of Personality Disorders, 8*, 140–148.

Ekselius, L., & von Knorrig, L. (1999). Changes in personality status during treatment with sertraline or citalopram. *British Journal of Psychiatry, 174*, 444–448.

Emmelkamp, P. M. G. (1982). *Phobic and obsessive compulsive disorder*. New York: Plenum.

Emmelkamp, P. M. G. (2004). Behavior therapy with adults. In M. Lambert (Ed.), *Bergin and Garfield's handbook of psychotherapy and behavior change* (5th ed., pp. 393–446). New York: Wiley.

Emmelkamp, P. M. G., Benner, A., Kuipers, A., Feiertag, G. A., Koster, H. C., & van Apeldoorn, F. J. (2006). Comparison of brief dynamic and cognitive-behavioural therapies in avoidant personality disorder. *British Journal of Psychiatry, 189*, 60–64.

Emmelkamp, P. M. G., Bouman, T. K., & Scholing, A. (1992). *Anxiety disorders*, Chichester, UK: Wiley.

Emmelkamp, P. M. G., & Scholing, A. (1997). Anxiety disorders in childhood and adolescence. In C. A. Essau & F. Petermann (Eds.), *Developmental psychopathology: Epidemiology, diagnostics and treatment* (pp. 219–264). Reading, UK: Harwood Academic Publishers.

Emmelkamp, P. M. G., & Vedel, E. (2006). *Evidence-based treatment in alcohol and drug abuse*. New York: Brunner-Routledge/Taylor & Francis.

Emmons, R. A. (1984). Factor analysis and construct validity of the Narcissistic Personality Inventory. *Journal of Personality Assessment, 48*, 291–299.

Engels, G. I., Duijsens, I. J., Haringsma, R., & van Putten, C. M. (2003). Personality disorders in the elderly compared to four younger age groups: A cross-sectional study of community residents and mental health patients. *Journal of Personality Disorders, 17*, 447–459.

Eysenck, H. J., & Eysenck, S. B. G. (1975). *Manual of the Eysenck Personality Questionnaire*. London: Hodder & Stoughton.

Fahlen, T. (1995). Personality traits in social phobia: Changes during drug treatment. *Journal of Clinical Psychiatry, 56*, 569–573.

Falloon, I. R. H., Boyd, J. L., & McGill, C. (1984). *Family care of schizophrenia*. New York: Guilford Press.

Farrington, D. P. (2005). Family background and psychopathy. In C. J. Patrick (Ed.), *Handbook of psychopathy* (pp. 229–250). New York: Guilford Press.

Farrington, D. P., Jolliffe, D., Loeber, R., Stouthamer-Loeber, M., & Kalb, L. (2001). The concentration of offenders in families, and family criminality in the prediction of boys' delinquency. *Journal of Adolescence, 24,* 579–596.

Fava, M., Farabaugh, A. H., Sickinger, A. H., Wright, E., Alpert, J. E., Sonawalla, et al. (2002). Personality disorders and depression. *Psychological Medicine, 32,* 1049–1057.

Favazza, A. R., & Conterio, K. (1989). Female habitual self-mutilators. *Acta Psychiatrica Scandinavica, 79,* 283–289.

Fear, C. F., & Healy, D. (1997). Probabilistic reasoning in obsessive-compulsive and delusional disorders. *Psychological Medicine, 27,* 199–208.

Fenichel, O. (1977). *Psychoanalytic theory of neurosis.* New York: Norton.

Fenigstein, A. (1997). Paranoid thought and schematic processing. *Journal of Social and Clinical Psychology, 16,* 77–94.

Fenigstein, A., & Vanable, P. A. (1992). Paranoia and self-consciousness. *Journal of Personality and Social Psychology, 62,* 129–138.

First, M., Gibbon, M., Spitzer, R. L., Williams, J. B. W., & Benjamin, L. S. (1997). *User's guide for the Structured Clinical Interview for the DSM-IV Axis II Personality Disorders.* Washington, DC: American Psychiatric Press.

Flett, G. L., Hewitt, P. L., Endler, N. S., & Bagby, R. L. (1995). Conceptualization and assessment of personality factors in depression. *European Journal of Psychology, 9,* 309–350.

Foley, D. L., Eaves, L. J., Wormley, B., Silberg, J. L., Maes, H. H., Kuhn, J., & Riley, B. (2004). Childhood adversity, monoamine oxidase A genotype, and risk for conduct disorder. *Archives of General Psychiatry, 61,* 738–744.

Fonagy, P., & Bateman, A. W. (2006). Mechanisms of change in mentalisation-based treatment of borderline PD. *Journal of Clinical Psychology, 62,* 411–430.

Fonagy, P., Leigh, T., Steele, M., Steele, H., Kennedy, R., Mattoon, G., et al. (1996). The relation of attachment status, psychiatric classification, and response to psychotherapy. *Journal of Consulting and Clinical Psychology, 64,* 22–31.

Fonagy, P., Roth, A., & Higgitt, A. (2005). The outcome of psychodynamic psychotherapy for psychological disorders. *Clinical Neuroscience Research, 4,* 367–377.

Fontana, A., & Rosenheck, R. (2005). The role of war-zone trauma and PTSD in the etiology of antisocial behavior. *Journal of Nervous and Mental Disease, 193,* 203–209.

Ford, M. R., & Widiger, T. A. (1989). Sex bias in the diagnosis of histrionic and antisocial personality disorders. *Journal of Consulting and Clinical Psychology, 57,* 301–305.

Fossati, A., Beauchaine, T. B., Grazioli, F., Borroni, S., Carretta, I., de Vecchi, C., et al. (2006). Confirmatory factor analyses of DSM-IV cluster C personality disorder criteria. *Journal of Personality Disorders, 20,* 186–203.

Fossati, A., Feeney, J. A., Donnati, D., Donini, M. A., Novella, L., Bagnato, M., et al. (2003). Personality disorders and adult attachment dimensions in a mixed psychiatric sample: A multivariate study. *Journal of Nervous and Mental Disease, 191,* 30–37.

Fossati, A., Madeddu, F., & Maffei, C. (1999). Borderline personality disorder and childhood sexual abuse: A meta-analytic study. *Journal of Personality Disorders, 13,* 268–280.

Fossati, A., Maffei, C., Bagnato, M., Donati, D., Namia C., & L. Novella, L. (1999). Latent structure analysis of DSM-IV borderline personality disorder criteria. *Comprehensive Psychiatry, 40,* 72–79.

Fossati, A., Maffei, C., Battaglia, M., Bagnato, M., Donati, D., Donini, M., et al. (2001). Latent class analysis of DSM-IV schizotypal personality disorder criteria in psychiatric patients. *Schizophrenia Bulletin, 27,* 59–71.

Fraley, R. C., & Shaver, P. R. (2000). Adult

romantic attachment: Theoretical developments, emerging controversies, and unanswered questions. *Review of General Psychology, 4,* 132–154.

Frances, A. (1980). The DSM-III personality disorders section: A commentary. *American Journal of Psychiatry, 137,* 1050–1054.

Frances, A. (1993). Dimensional diagnosis of personality—not whether, but when and which. *Psychological Inquiry, 4,* 110–111.

Freeman, D., Garety, P. A., Kuipers, E., Fowler, D., & Bebbington, P. E. (2002). A cognitive model of persecutory delusions. *British Journal of Clinical Psychology, 41,* 331–347.

Freud, S. (1914). Zur Einführung des Narcissmus [On narcissism: An introduction]. In *Gesammelte werke* (vol. XIV, pp. 197–241). Frankfurt, Germany: Fisher Verlag.

Freud, S. (1959). Character and anal eroticism. In S. Freud, *Collected papers* (Vol. 2, pp. 45–48). New York: Basic Books.

Gabbard, G. O. (1989). Two subtypes of narcissistic personality disorder. *Bulletin of the Menninger Clinic, 53,* 527–532.

Gabbard, G. O. (2005). Antisocial personality disorder: A review. In J. M. Oldham, A. E. Skodol, & D. S. Bender (Eds.), *Textbook of personality disorders* (pp. 257–273). Washington, DC: American Psychiatric Publishing.

Galen, L. W., Brower, K. J., Gillespie, B. W., & Zucker, R. A. (2000). Sociopathy, gender, and treatment outcome among outpatient substance abusers. *Drug and Alcohol Dependence, 61,* 23–33.

Garb, H. N. (1997). Race bias, social class bias, and gender bias in clinical judgment. *Clinical Psychology Science and Practice, 4,* 99–120.

Garety, P. A., & Freeman, D. (1999). Cognitive approaches to delusions: A critical review of theories and evidence.

British Journal of Clinical Psychology, 38, 113–155.

Giesen-Bloo, J., & Arntz, A. (2003). World assumptions and the role of trauma in borderline personality disorder. *Journal of Behavior Therapy and Experimental Psychiatry, 36,* 197–208.

Giesen-Bloo, J., van Dyck, R., Spinhoven, P., van Tilburg, W., Dirksen, C., van Asselt, T., et al. (2006). Outpatient psychotherapy for borderline personality disorder: Randomized trial of schema-focused therapy vs transference-focused psychotherapy. *Archives of General Psychiatry, 63,* 649–658.

Gilbert, P. (2002). Evolutionary approaches to psychopathology and cognitive therapy. *Journal of Cognitive Psychotherapy, 16,* 263–294.

Gilmore, M. (1994). *Shot in the heart.* New York: Doubleday.

Glaser, D. (2000). Child abuse and neglect and the brain: A review. *Journal of Child Psychology and Psychiatry and Allied Disciplines, 41,* 97–116.

Goldberg, L. R. (1993). The structure of phenotypic personality traits. *The American Psychologist, 48,* 26–34.

Goldschmidt, L., Day, N. L., & Richardson, G. A. (2000). Effects of prenatal marijuana exposure on child behavior problems at age 10. *Neurotoxicology and Teratology, 22,* 325–336.

Gomez-Beneyto, M., Salazar-Fraile, J., Marti-Sanjuan, V., & Gonzalez-Luan, L. (2006). Posttraumatic stress disorder in primary care with special reference to personality disorder comorbidity. *British Journal of General Practice, 56,* 349–354.

Graham, S., & Hudley, C. (1994). Attributions of aggressive and nonaggressive African American male early adolescents: A study of construct accessibility. *Developmental Psychology, 30,* 365–373.

Grant, B. F., Hasin, D. S., Stinson, F. S.,

Dawson, D. A., Chou, S. P., Ruan, W. J., & Huang, B. (2005). Co-occurrence of 12-month mood and anxiety disorders and personality disorders in the US: Results from the national epidemiologic survey on alcohol and related conditions. *Journal of Psychiatric Research, 39,* 1–9.

Grant, B. F., Hasin, D. S., Stinson, F. S., Dawson, D. A., Chou, S. P., Ruan, W. J., & Pickering, R. P. (2004). Prevalence, correlates, and disability of personality disorders in the United States: Results from the national epidemiologic survey on alcohol and related conditions. *Journal of Clinical Psychiatry, 65,* 948–958.

Grilo, C. M., McGlashan, T. H., Quinlan, D. M., Walker, M. L., Greenfield, D., & Edell, W. S. (1998). Frequency of personality disorders in two age cohorts of psychiatric inpatients. *American Journal of Psychiatry, 155,* 140–142.

Grilo, C. M., Shea, M. T., Sanislow, C. A., Skodol, A. E., Gunderson, J. G., Stout, R. L., et al. (2004). Two-year stability and change of schizotypal, borderline, avoidant, and obsessive-compulsive personality disorders. *Journal of Consulting and Clinical Psychology, 72,* 767–775.

Gude, T., Hoffart, A., Hedley, A., & Rø, Ø. (2004). The dimensionality of dependent personality disorder. *Journal of Personality Disorders, 18,* 604–610.

Gunderson, J. G. (1984). *Borderline personality disorder.* Washington, DC: American Psychiatric Press.

Gunderson, J. G., Bender, D., Sanislow, C., Yen, S., Bame Rettew, J., Dolan-Sewell R., et al. (2003). Plausibility and possible determinants of sudden "remissions" in borderline patients. *Psychiatry, 66,* 111–119.

Gunderson, J. G., & Kolb, J. E. (1984). Discriminating features of borderline personality disorder. *American Journal of Psychiatry, 135,* 792–796.

Gunderson, J. G., Morey, L. C., Stout, R. L., Skodol, A. E., Shea, M. T., McGlashan, T. H., et al. (2004). Major depressive disorder and borderline personality disorder revisited: Longitudinal interactions. *Journal of Clinical Psychiatry, 65,* 1049–1056.

Gunderson, J. G., & Ronningstam, E. (2001). Differentiating narcissistic and antisocial personality disorders. *Journal of Personality Disorders, 15,* 103–109.

Gunderson, J. G., Ronningstam, E., & Bodkin, A. (1990). The Diagnostic Interview for Narcissistic Patients. *Archives of General Psychiatry, 47,* 676–680.

Gunderson, J. G., Ronningstam, E., & Smith, L. E. (1995). Narcissistic personality disorder. In W. J. Livesley (Ed.), *The DSM-IV personality disorders* (pp. 201–212). New York: Guilford Press.

Han, K., Weed, N. C., & Butcher, J. N. (2003). Dyadic agreement on the MMPI-2. *Personality and Individual Differences, 35,* 603–615.

Hansenne, M., Delhez, M., & Cloninger, C. R. (2005). Psychometric properties of the Temperament and Character Inventory–Revised (TCI–R) in a Belgian sample. *Journal of Personality Assessment, 85,* 40–49.

Hare, R. D. (1980). A research scale for the assessment of psychopathy in criminal populations. *Personality and Individual Differences, 12,* 111–119.

Hare, R. D. (1991). *Manual for the Hare Psychopathy Checklist–Revised.* Toronto, Canada: Multi-Health Systems.

Hare, R. D. (2003). *Manual for the Hare Psychopathy Checklist–Revised* (2nd ed.). Toronto, Canada: Multi-Health Systems.

Hare, R. D., Cooke, D. J., & Hart, S. D. (1999). Psychopathy and sadistic personality disorder. In T. Millon, P. H.

Blaney, & R. D. Davis (Eds.), *Oxford textbook of psychopathology* (pp. 555–584). New York: Oxford University Press.

Hare, R. D., & Jutai, J. W. (1988). Psychopathy and cerebral asymmetry in semantic processing. *Personality and Individual Differences, 9,* 329–337.

Harkness, A. R. (1992). Fundamental topics in the personality disorders: Candidate trait dimensions from lower regions of the hierarchy. *Psychological Assessment, 4,* 251–259.

Harkness, A. R., & Lilienfeld, S. O. (1997). Individual differences science for treatment planning: Personality traits. *Psychological Assessment, 9,* 349–360.

Harris, G. T., & Rice, M. E. (2005). Treatment of psychopathy: A review of empirical findings. In C. J. Patrick (Ed.), *Handbook of psychopathy* (pp. 555–572). New York: Guilford Press.

Harris, G. T., Skilling, T. A., & Rice, M. E. (2001). The construct of psychopathy. In M. Tonry & N. Morris (Eds.), *Crime and justice: A review of research* (pp. 197–264). Chicago: University of Chicago Press.

Hart, S. D., & Hare, R. D. (1997). Psychopathy: Assessment and association with criminal conduct. In D. M. Stoff & J. Breiling (Eds.), *Handbook of antisocial behaviour*. New York: Wiley.

Hart, S. D., Kropp, P. R., & Hare, R. D. (1988). Performance of male psychopaths following conditional release from prison. *Journal of Consulting and Clinical Psychology, 56,* 227–232.

Haslam, N. (2003). The dimensional view of personality disorders: A review of the taxometric evidence. *Clinical Psychology Review, 23,* 75–93.

Havens, J. R., & Strathdee, S. A. (2005). Antisocial personality disorder and opioid treatment outcomes: A review. *Addiction Disorders and Their Treatment, 4,* 85–97.

Heilbrun, K., Hart, S. D., Hare, R. D.,

Gustafson, D., Nunez, C., & White, A. J. (1998). Inpatient and postdischarge aggression in mentally disordered offenders: The role of psychopathy. *Journal of Interpersonal Violence, 13,* 514–527.

Heim, C., & Nemeroff, C. B. (2002). Neurobiology of early life stress: Clinical studies. *Seminars in Clinical Neuropsychiatry, 7,* 147–159.

Helfgott, J. B. (2004). Primitive defenses in the language of the psychopath: Considerations for forensic practice. *Journal of Forensic Psychology Practice, 4,* 1–29.

Hemphill, J. F., Hare, R. D., & Wong, S. (1998). Psychopathy and recidivism: A review. *Legal and Criminological Psychology, 3,* 139–170.

Hendin, H. M., & Cheek, J. M. (1997). Assessing hypersensitive narcissism: A reexamination of Murray's narcism scale. *Journal of Research in Personality, 31,* 588–599.

Herbst, J. H., Zonderman, A. B., McCrae, R. R., & Costa, P. T. (2000). Do the dimensions of the temperament and character inventory map a simple genetic architecture? Evidence from molecular genetics and factor analysis. *American Journal of Psychiatry, 157,* 1285–1290.

Herman, J. L., Perry, J. C., & van der Kolk, B. A. (1989). Childhood trauma in borderline personality disorder. *American Journal of Psychiatry, 147,* 490–499.

Hicks, B. M., Krueger, R. F., Iacono, W. G., McGue, M., & Patrick, C. J. (2004). Family transmission and heritability of externalizing disorders: A twin-family study. *Archives of General Psychiatry, 61,* 922–928.

Hildebrand, M. (2004). *Psychopathy in the treatment of forensic patients.* Unpublished dissertation, University of Amsterdam.

Hildebrand, M., de Ruiter, C., & Nijman,

H. (2004). PCL-R psychopathy predicts disruptive behavior among male offenders in a dutch forensic psychiatric hospital. *Journal of Interpersonal Violence, 19,* 13–29.

Hilsenroth, M. J., Handler, L., & Blais, M. A. (1996). Assessment of narcissistic personality disorder: A multi-method review. *Clinical Psychology Review, 16,* 655–683.

Hirschfeld, R. M. A. (1993). Personality disorders: Definition and diagnosis. *Journal of Personality Disorders,* 7(Suppl.), 9–17.

Hodgins, S., Kratzer, L., & McNeil, T. F. (2001). Obstetric complications, parenting, and risk of criminal behavior. *Archives of General Psychiatry, 58,* 746–752.

Hoek, H. W., Susser, E., Buck, K. A., Lumey, L. H., Lin, S. P., & Gorman, J. M. (1998). Schizoid personality disorder after prenatal exposure to famine. *American Journal of Psychiatry, 153,* 1637–1639.

Holdwick, D. J., Hilsenroth, M. J., Castlebury, F. D., & Blais, M. A. (1998). Identifying the unique and common characteristics of the DSM-IV antisocial, borderline, and narcisistic personality diosrders. *Comprehensive Psychiatry, 39,* 277–286.

Hollin, C. R. (1999). Treatment programs for offenders: Meta-analysis, "what works", and beyond. *International Journal of Law and Psychiatry, 22,* 361–372.

Hong, J. P., Samuels, J., Bienvenu, O. J., Hsu, F.-C., Eaton, W. W., Costa, P. T., Jr., & Nestadt, G. (2004). The longitudinal relationship between personality disorder dimensions and global functioning in a community-residing population. *Psychological Medicine, 35,* 891–895.

Huang, B., Grant, B. F., Dawson, D. A., Stinson, F. S., Chou, S. P., Saha, T. D., et al. (2006). Race-ethnicity and the prevalence and co-occurrence of Diagnostic and Statistical Manual of Mental Disorders, Fourth Edition, alcohol and drug use disorders and Axis I and II disorders: United States, 2001 to 2002. *Comprehensive Psychiatry, 47,* 252–257.

Hughes, G., Hogue, T., Hollin, C., & Champion, H. (1997). First-stage evaluation of a treatment programme for personality disordered offenders. *Journal of Forensic Psychiatry, 8,* 515–527.

Hulshoff Pol, H. E., Hoek, H. W., Susser, E., Brown, A. S., Dingemans, A., Schnack, H. G., et al. (2000). Prenatal exposure to famine and brain morphology in schizophrenia. *American Journal of Psychiatry, 157,* 1170–1172.

Humber, E., & Snow, P. C. (2001). The oral language skills of young offenders: A pilot investigation. *Psychiatry, Psychology and the Law, 8,* 1–11.

Ilardi, S. S., & Craighead, W. E. (1995). Personality disorders and response to somatic treatments to major depression: A critical review. *Depression, 2,* 200–217.

Isohani, M., & Tienari, P. (2005). Cluster A personality disorders. In M. Maj, H. S. Akiskal, J. E. Mezzich, & A. Okasha (Eds.), *WPA series evidence and experience in psychiatry: Vol. 8. Personality disorders* (pp. 87–89). Hoboken, NJ: Wiley.

Jacob, C. P., Muller, J., Schmidt, M., Hohenberger, K., Gutknecht, L., Reiff, A., et al. (2005). Cluster B personality disorders are associated with allelic variation of monoamine oxidase A activity. *Neuropsychopharmacology, 30,* 1711–1718.

Jacob, C. P., Strobel, A., Hohenberger, K., Ringel, T., Gutknecht, L., Reif, A., et al. (2004). Association between allelic variation of serotonin transporter function and neuroticism in anxious cluster C personality disorders. *American Journal of Psychiatry, 161,* 569–572.

Jaffee, S. R., Caspi, A., Moffitt, T. E.,

REFERENCES 219

Dodge, K., Rutter, M., Taylor, A., & Tully, L. (2005). Nature–nurture: Genetic vulnerabilities interact with physical maltreatment to promote conduct problems. *Development and Psychopathology, 17,* 67–84.

Jamieson, S., & Marshall, W. L. (2000). Attachment styles and violence in child molesters. *Journal of Sexual Aggression, 5,* 88–98.

Johnson, J. G., Chen, H., & Cohen, P. (2004). Personality disorder traits during adolescence and relationships with family members during the transition to adulthood. *Journal of Consulting and Clinical Psychology, 72,* 923–932.

Johnson, J. G., Cohen, P., Brown, J., Smailes, E. M., & Bernstein, D. P. (1999). Childhood maltreatment increases risk for personality disorders during early adulthood. *Archives of General Psychiatry, 56,* 600–606.

Johnson, J. G., Cohen, P., Chen, H., Kasen, S., Brown, J., & Brook, J. S. (2006). Parenting behaviors associated with risk for offspring personality disorder during adulthood. *Archives of General Psychiatry, 63,* 579–587.

Johnson, J. G., Cohen, P., Gould, M. S., Kasen, S., Brown, J., & Brook, J. S. (2002). Childhood adversities, interpersonal difficulties, and risk for suicide attempts during late adolescence and early adulthood. *Archives of General Psychiatry, 59,* 741–749.

Johnson, J. G., Cohen, P., Kasen, S., & Brook, J. S. (2005). Personality disorder traits associated with risk for unipolar depression during middle adulthood. *Psychiatry Research, 136,* 113–121.

Johnson, J. G., Cohen, P., Kasen, S., & Brook, J. S. (2006a). Personality disorders evident by early adulthood and risk for anxiety disorders during middle adulthood. *Anxiety Disorders, 20,* 408–426.

Johnson, J. G., Cohen, P., Kasen, S., & Brook, J. S. (2006b). Personality disorder traits evident by early adulthood and risk for eating and weight problems during middle adulthood. *International Journal of Eating Disorders, 39,* 184–192.

Johnson, J. G., Cohen, P., Kasen, S., Skodol, A. E., Hamagami, F., & Brook, J. S. (2000). Age-related change in personality disorder trait levels between early adolescence and adulthood: A community-based longitudinal investigation. *Acta Psychiatrica Scandinavica, 102,* 265–275.

Johnson, J. G., Cohen, P., Smailes, E., Kasen, S., Oldham, J. M., Skodol, A. E., & Brook, J. S. (2000). Adolescent personality disorders associated with violence and criminal behaviour during adolescence and adulthood. *American Journal of Psychiatry, 157,* 1406–1412.

Johnson, J. G., Cohen, P., Smailes, E. M., Skodol, A. E., Brown, J., & Oldham, J. M. (2001). Childhood verbal abuse and risk for personality disorders during adolescence and early adulthood. *Comprehensive Psychiatry, 42,* 16–23.

Johnson, J. G., First, M. B., Cohen, P., Skodol, A. E., Kasen, S., & Brook, J. S. (2005). Adverse outcomes associated with personality disorder not otherwise specified in a community sample. *American Journal of Psychiatry, 162,* 1926–1932.

Johnson, J. G., Smailes, E. M., Cohen, P., Brown, J., & Bernstein, D. P. (2000). Associations between four types of childhood neglect and personality disorder symptoms during adolescence and early adulthood: Findings of a community-based longitudinal study. *Journal of Personality Disorders, 14,* 171–187.

Jones, S., Cauffman, E., Miller, J., & Mulvey, E. (2006). Investigating different factor structures of the psychopathy checklist: Youth version:

Confirmatory factor analytic findings. *Psychological Assessment*, 18, 33–48.

Joyce, P. R., McKenzie, J. M., Luty, S. E., Mudler, R. T., Carter, J. D., Sullivan, P. F., & Cloninger, C. R. (2003). Temperament, childhood environment and pyschopathology as risk factors for avoidant and borderline personality disorders. *Australian and New Zealand Journal of Psychiatry*, 37, 756–764.

Joyce, P. R., Rogers, G. R., Miller, A. L., Mulder, R. T., Luty, S. E., & Kennedy, M. A. (2003). Polymorphisms of DRD4 and DRD3 and risk of avoidant and obsessive personality traits and disorders. *Psychiatry Research*, 119, 1–10.

Kalman, D., Longabaugh, R., Clifford, P. R., Beattie, M., & Maisto, S. A. (2000). Matching alcoholics to treatment: Failure to replicate finding of an earlier study. *Journal of Substance Abuse Treatment*, 19, 183–187.

Kalus, O., Bernstein, D. P., & Siever, L. J. (1995). Schizoid personality disorder. In W. J. Livesley (Ed.), *The DSM-IV personality disorders* (pp. 58–71). New York: Guilford Press.

Kamphuis, J. H., de Ruiter, C., Janssen, B., & Spiering, M. (2005). Preliminary evidence for an automated link between sex and power among men who molest children. *Journal of Interpersonal Violence*, 20, 1351–1365.

Kamphuis, J. H., & Emmelkamp, P. M. G. (2000). Stalking: A contemporary challenge for forensic and clinical psychiatry. *British Journal of Psychiatry*, 176, 206–209.

Kamphuis, J. H., Emmelkamp, P. M. G. & de Vries, V. (2004). Informant assessment of the five factor psychological profile of the male post-intimate stalker. *Journal of Personality Assessment*, 82, 169–178.

Kantojärvi, L., Veijola, J., Lalksy, K., Jokelainen, J., Herva, A., Karvonen, J. T., et al. (2004). Comparison of hospital-treated personality disorders and personality disorders in a general population sample. *Nordic Journal of Psychiatry*, 58, 357–362.

Kaplan, M. (1983). A woman's view of DSM-III. *The American Psychologist*, 38, 786–792.

Kasen, S., Cohen, P., Skodol, A. E., Johnson, J. G., & Brook, J. S. (1999). Influence of child and adolescent psychiatric disorders on young adult personality disorder. *American Journal of Psychiatry*, 156, 1529–1535.

Kasen, S., Cohen, P., Skodol, A. E., Johnson, J. G., Smailes, E., & Brook, J. S. (2001). Childhood depression and adult personality disorder: Alternative pathways of continuity. *Archives of General Psychiatry*, 58, 231–236.

Kass, F., Skodol, A. E., Charles, E., Spitzer, R. L., & Williams, J. B. (1985). Scaled ratings of DSM-III personality disorders. *American Journal of Psychiatry*, 142, 627–630.

Keller, M. C., Coventry, W. L., Heath, A. C., & Martin, N. G. (2005). Widespread evidence for non-additive genetic variation in Cloninger's and Eysenck's personality dimensions using a Twin Plus Sibling design. *Behavioral Genetics*, 35, 707–721.

Kellerman, J. (1989). *Silent partner*. New York: Bantam Books.

Kellogg, S. H., & Young, J. E. (2006). Schema therapy for borderline personality disorder. *Journal of Clinical Psychology*, 62, 445–458.

Kemperman, I., Russ, M. J., & Shearin, E. (1997). Self-injurious behaviour and mood regulation in borderline patients. *Journal of Personality Disorder*, 11, 146–157.

Kendler, K. S., Prescott, C. A., Myers, J., & Neale, M. C. (2003). The structure of genetic and environmental risk factors for common psychiatric and substance use disorders in men and women. *Archives of General Psychiatry*, 60, 929–937.

Kernberg, O. F. (1984). *Severe personality disorders*. New Haven, CT: Yale University Press.

Kernberg, O. F. (1996). A psychoanalytic theory of personality disorders. In J. F. Clarkin & M. F. Lenzenweger (Eds.), *Major theories of personality disorder* (pp. 106–140). New York: Guilford Press.

Kerns, J. G. (2005). Positive schizotypy and emotion processing. *Journal of Abnormal Psychology, 114*, 392–401.

Kessler, R. C., McGonacle, K. A., Zhao, S., Nelson, C. B., Hughes, M., Eshelman, S., et al. (1994). Lifetime and 12-month prevalence of DSM-III-R psychiatric disorders in the United States. *Archives of General Psychiatry, 50*, 991–999.

Kiehl, K. A. (2006). A cognitive neuroscience perspective on psychopathy: Evidence for paralimbic system dysfunction. *Psychiatry Research, 142*, 107–128.

Kinderman, P., & Bentall, R. P. (1997). Causal attributions in paranoia and depression: Internal, personal and situational attributions for negative events. *Journal of Abnormal Psychology, 106*, 341–345.

Klonsky, E. D., Oltmanns, T. F., & Turkheimer, E. (2002). Informant-reports of personality disorder: Relation to self-reports and future research directions. *Clinical Psychology: Science and Practice, 9*, 300–311.

Knight, R. A., & Guay, J. P. (2005). The role of psychopathy in sexual coercion against women. In C. J. Patrick (Ed.), *Handbook of psychopathy* (pp. 512–532). New York: Guilford Press.

Kohut, H. (1971). *The analysis of the self*. New York: International Universities Press.

Kohut, H. (1974). *The restoration of the self*. New York: International Universities Press.

Kohut, H. (1982). Introspection, empathy, and the semi-circle of mental health.

International Journal of Psychoanalysis, 63, 395–407.

Kool, S., Schoevers, R., de Maat, S., Van, R., Molenaar, P., Vink, A., & Dekker, J. (2005). Efficacy of pharmacotherapy in depressed patients with and without personality disorders: A systematic review and meta-analysis. *Journal of Affective Disorders, 88*, 269–278.

Koons, R., Robins, C. J., Tweed, J. L., Lynch, T. R., Gonzalez, A. M., Morse, J. Q., et al. (2001). Efficacy of DBT in women veterans with borderline PD. *Behavior Therapy*, 371–390.

Kosson, D. S., Suchy, Y., Mayer, A. R., & Libby, J. (2002). Facial affect recognition in criminal psychopaths. *Emotion, 24*, 398–411.

Kramer, R. M. (1998). Paranoid cognition in social systems: Thinking and acting in the shadow of doubt. *Personality and Social Psychology Review, 2*, 251–275.

Kroll, J. (1988). *The challenge of the borderline patient: Competency in diagnosis and treatment*. New York: W. W. Norton.

Kroner, D. G., & Mills, J. F. (2001). The accuracy of five risk appraisal instruments in predicting institutional misconduct and new convictions. *Criminal Justice and Behavior, 28*, 471–489.

Krueger, R. F. (1999). The structure of common mental disorders. *Archives of General Psychiatry, 56*, 921–926.

Krueger, R. F. (2005). Continuity of axes I and II: Toward a unified model of personality, personality disorders, and clinical disorders. *Journal of Personality Disorders, 19*, 233–261.

Kusumi, I., Masui, T., Kakiuchi, C., Suzuki, K., Akimoto, T., Hashimoto, R., et al. (2005). Relationship between XBP1 genotype and personality traits assessed by TCI and NEO-FFI. *Neuroscience Letters, 391*, 7–10.

Laakso, M. P., Gunning-Dixon, F., Vaurio, O., Repo-Tiihonen, E., Soininen, H., & Tiihonen, J. (2002). Prefrontal volumes in habitually violent subjects with antisocial personality disorder and type 2 alcoholism. *Psychiatry Research–Neuroimaging, 114*, 95–102.

Lahey, B., Moffitt, T. E., & Caspi, A. (Eds.). (2003). *Causes of conduct disorder and juvenile delinquency*. New York: Guilford Press.

Lansford, J. E., Deater-Deckard, K., Dodge, K. A., Bates, J. E., & Pettit, G. S. (2004). Ethnic differences in the link between physical discipline and later adolescent externalizing behaviors. *Journal of Child Psychology and Psychiatry and Allied Disciplines, 45*, 801–812.

Lansford, J. E., Dodge, K. A., Pettit, G. S., Bates, J. E., Crozier, J., & Kaplow, J. (2002). Long-term effects of early child physical maltreatment on psychological, behavioral, and academic problems in adolescence: A 12-year prospective study. *Archives of Pediatrics and Adolescent Medicine, 156*, 824–830.

Larrison, A. L., Ferrante, C. F., Briand, K. A., & Sereno, A. B. (2000). Schizotypal traits, attention and eye-movements. *Progress in Neuropsychopharmacology and Biological Psychiatry, 24*, 357–372.

Laurent, A., Duly, D., Murry, P., Foussard, N., Boccara, S., Mingat, F., et al. (2001). WCST performance and schizotypal features in the first-degree relatives of patients with schizophrenia. *Psychiatry Research, 104*, 133–144.

Leal, J., Ziedonis, D., & Kosten, T. (1994). Antisocial personality disorder as a prognostic factor for pharmacotherapy of cocaine dependence. *Drug and Alcohol Dependence, 35*, 31–35.

Lejuez, C. W., Daughters, S. B., Rosenthal, M. Z., & Lynch, T. R. (2005). Impulsivity as a common process across borderline personality and substance use disorders. *Clinical Psychology Review, 25*, 790–812.

Lenzenweger, M. F. (2001). Reaction time slowing during high-load, sustained attention task performance in relation to psychometrically identified schizotypy. *Journal of Abnormal Psychology, 110*, 290–296.

Lenzenweger, M. F., Loranger, A. W., Korfine, L., & Neff, C. (1997). Detecting personality disorders in a nonclinical population. *Archives of General Psychiatry, 54*, 345–351.

Levenston, G. K., Patrick, C. J., Bradley, M. M., & Lang, P. J. (2000). The psychopath as observer: Emotion and attention in picture processing. *Journal of Abnormal Psychology, 100*, 373–385.

Levy, K. N. (2005). The implications of attachment theory and research for understanding borderline personality disorder. *Development and Psychopathology, 17*, 959–986.

Levy, K. N., Becker, D. F., Grilo, C. M., Mattanah, J. J. F., Garnet, K. E., Quinlan, D. M., et al. (1999). Concurrent and predictive validity of the personality disorder diagnosis in adolescent inpatients. *American Journal of Psychiatry, 156*, 1522–1528.

Levy, K. N., Clarkin, J. F., Yeomans, F. E., Scott, L. N., Wasserman, R. H., & Kernberg, O. F. (2006). The mechanisms of change in the treatment of borderline personality disorder with transference focused psychotherapy. *Journal of Clinical Psychology, 62*, 481–501.

Lewandowski, K. E., Barrantes-Vidal, N., Nelson-Gray, R., Clancy, C., Kepley, H. O., & Kwapil, T. R. (2006). Anxiety and depression symptoms in psychometrically identified schizotypy. *Schizophrenia Research, 8*, 225–235.

Lewis, G., & Appleby, L. (1988). Personality disorders: The patients psychiatrists dislike. *British Journal of Psychiatry, 153*, 44–49.

Liberman, R. P., & Robertson, M. J. (2005). A pilot, controlled skills training study of schizotypal high school students. *Verhaltenstherapie, 15*, 176–180.

Lieb, K., Zanarini, M. C., Schmahl, C., & Linehan, M. M. (2004). Borderline personality disorder. *Lancet, 364*, 453–461.

Lilenfeld, L. R. R., Wonderlich, S., Riso, L. P., Crosby, R., & Mitchel, J. (2006). Eating disorders and personality: A methodological and empirical review. *Clinical Psychology Review, 26*, 299–320.

Lilienfeld, S. O. (2005). Longitudinal studies of personality disorders: Four lessons from personality psychology. *Journal of Personality Disorders, 19*, 547–556.

Lilienfeld, S. O., van Valkenburg, C., Larntz, K., & Akiskal, H. S. (1986). The relationship of histrionic personality disorder to antisocial personality and somatization disorders. *American Journal of Psychiatry, 143*, 718–722.

Linehan, M. M. (1993a). *Cognitive behavioural treatment of borderline personality disorder*. New York: Guilford Press.

Linehan, M. M. (1993b). *Skills training manual for treating borderline personality disorder*. New York: Guilford Press.

Linehan, M. M., Armstrong, H. E., Suarez, A., Allmon, D., & Heard, H. L. (1991). Cognitive-behavioural treatment of chronically parasuicidal borderline patients. *Archives of General Psychiatry, 48*, 1060–1064.

Linehan, M. M., Heard, H. L., & Armstrong, H. E. (1993). Naturalistic follow-up of a behavioural treatment for chronically parasuicidal borderline patients. *Archives of General Psychiatry, 50*, 971–974.

Linehan, M. M., & Kehrer, C. A. (1993). Borderline personality disorder. In D. H. Barlow (Ed.), *Clinical handbook of psychological disorders* (pp. 396–441). New York: Guilford Press.

Linehan, M. M., Schmidt, H., Dimeff, L. A., Craft, J. C., Kanter, J., & Comtois, K. A. (1999). DBT for patients with borderline PD and drug dependence. *American Journal of Addictions, 8*, 279–292.

Links, P. S., Heslegrave, R. J., Mitton, J. E., van Reekum, R., & Patric, J. (1995). Borderline psychopathology and recurrences of clinical disorders. *Journal of Nervous and Mental Disease, 183*(9), 582–586.

Livesley, W. J. (2001). Conceptual and taxonimoc issues. In W. J. Livesley (Ed.), *Handbook of personality disorders: Theory, research and treatment* (pp. 3–38). New York: Guilford Press.

Livesley, W. J. (2003). *Practical management of personality disorder*. New York, NY: Guilford Press.

Livesley, W. J. (2005). The structure and etiology of borderline pathology. In J. Reich (Ed.), *Personality disorders: Current research and treatment* (pp. 21–73). New York: Routledge/Taylor & Francis.

Livesley, W. J., & Jackson, D. N. (in press). *Manual for the dimensional assessment of personality pathology—Basic questionnaire*. Port Huron, MI: Sigma Press.

Livesley, W. J., Jackson, D., & Schroeder, M. L. (1989). A study of the factorial structure of personality pathology. *Journal of Personality Disorders, 3*, 292–306.

Livesley, W. J., Schroeder, M. L., & Jackson, D. N. (1990). Dependent personality disorder and attachment problems. *Journal of Personality Disorders, 4*, 131–140.

Londerville, S., & Main, M. (1981). Security of attachment, compliance, and maternal training methods in the second year of life. *Developmental Psychology, 17*, 289–299.

Loney, B. R., Frick, P. J., Clements, C. B., Ellis, M., & Kerlin, K. (2003). Callous-unemotional traits, impulsivity, and emotional processing in adolescents with antisocial behavior problems, *Journal of Clinical Child and Adolescent Psychology, 32*, 66–80.

Loney, B. R., Frick, P. J., Ellis, M., & McCoy, M. G. (1998). Intelligence, callous-unemotional traits, and antisocial behaviour. *Journal of Psychopathology and Behavioural Assessment 20*, 231–247.

Loranger, A. W. (1999). *International personality disorder examination manual: DSM-IV module*. Washington, DC: American Psychiatric Press.

Lorber, M. F. (2004). Psychophysiology of aggression, psychopathy, and conduct problems: A meta-analysis. *Psychological Bulletin, 130*, 531–552.

Luborsky, L., & Mark, D. (1991). Short term supportive-expressive psychoanalytic psychotherapy. In P. Crits-Cristoph & J. P. Barber (Eds.), *Handbook of short-term dynamic psychotherapy* (pp. 110–136). New York: Basic Books.

Luntz, B. K., & Widom, C. S. (1994). Antisocial personality disorder in abused and neglected children grown up. *American Journal of Psychiatry, 151*, 670–674.

Lykken, D. T. (1995). *The antisocial personalities*. Hillsdale, NJ: Lawrence Erlbaum Associates, Inc.

Lykken, D. T. (2006). The mechanism of emergenesis. *Genes, Brain and Behaviour, 5*, 306–310.

Lynam, D. R., & Widiger, T. A. (2001). Using the five-factor model to represent the DSM-IV personality disorders: An expert consensus approach. *Journal of Abnormal Psychology, 110*, 401–412.

Lyons, M. J., True, W. R., Eisen, S. A., Goldberg, J., Meyer, J. M., Faraone, S. V., et al. (1995). Differential heritability of adult and juvenile antisocial traits. *Archives of General Psychiatry, 52*, 906–915.

Lyons-Ruth, K. (1996). Attachment relationships among children with aggressive behaviour problems: The role of disorganized early attachment patterns. *Journal of Consulting and Clinical Psychology, 64*, 64–73.

Main, M., & Goldwyn, R. (1991) *Adult Attachment Classification System (version 5)*. Berkeley, CA: University of California, Berkeley.

Main, M., & Goldwyn, R. (1994). *Adult Attachment Scoring and Classification Systems (version 6.0)*. Unpublished manuscript, University of California, Berkeley.

Malan, D. H. (1979). *Individual psychotherapy and the science of psychodynamics*. London: Butterworth.

Markon, K. E., Krueger, R. F., & Watson, D. (2005). Delineating the structure of normal and abnormal personality: An integrative hierarchical approach. *Journal of Personality and Social Psychology, 88*, 139–157.

Markovitz, P. J. (2001). Pharmacotherapy. In W. J. Livesley (Ed.), *Handbook of personality disorders* (pp. 475–493). New York: Guilford Press.

Mason, O., & Claridge, G. (2006). The Oxford-Liverpool Inventory of Feelings and Experiences (O-LIFE): Further description and extended norms. *Schizophrenia Research, 82*, 203–211.

Masterson, J. F. (1993). *The emerging self: A developmental, self, and object relations approach to the treatment of the closet narcissistic disorder of the self*. New York: Brunner & Mazel.

Mattia, J. L., & Zimmerman, M. (2001). Epidemiology. In W. J. Livesley (Ed.), *Handbook of personality disorders* (pp. 107–123). New York: Guilford Press.

McCrae, R. R., & Costa, P. T. (1997). Personality trait structure as a human universal. *The American Psychologist, 52*, 509–516.

McFall, M., Fontana, A., Raskind, M., & Rosenheck, R. (1999). Analysis of violent behavior in Vietnam combat veteran psychiatric inpatients with posttraumatic stress disorder. *Journal of Traumatic Stress, 12*, 501–517.

McGlashan, T. H. (2002). The borderline personality disorder practice guidelines: The good, the bad, and the realistic. *Journal of Personality Disorders, 16,* 119–121.

McGlashan, T. H., Grilo, C. M., Skodol, A. E., Gunderson, J. G., Shea, M. T., Morey, L. C., et al. (2000). The Collaborative Longitudinal Personality Disorders Study: Baseline Axis I/II and II/II diagnostic co-occurrence. *Acta Psychiatrica Scandinavica, 102,* 256–264.

McGorry, P. D., Yung, A. R., Phillips, L. J., Yuen, H. P., Francey, S., Cosgrave, E. M., et al. (2002). Randomized controlled trial of interventions designed to reduce the risk of progression to first-episode psychosis in a clinical sample with subthreshold symptoms. *Archives of General Psychiatry, 59,* 921–928.

McKay, J. R., Alterman, A. I., Cacciola, J. S., Mulvaney, F. D., & O'Brien, C. P. (2000). Prognostic significance of antisocial personality disorder in cocaine-dependent patients entering continuing care. *Journal of Nervous and Mental Diseases, 188,* 287–296.

McKay, R., Langdon, R., & Coltheart, M. (2005). Paranoia, persecutory delusions and attributional biases. *Psychiatry Research, 136,* 233–245.

McWilliams, N. (2006). Some thoughts about schizoid dynamics. *Psychoanalytic Review, 93,* 1–24.

Meehl, P. E. (1990). Toward an integrated theory of schizotaxia, schizotypy, and schizophrenia. *Journal of Personality Disorders, 4,* 1–99.

Meehl, P. E. (1992). Factors and taxa, traits and types, differences of degree and differences in kind. *Journal of Personality, 60,* 117–174.

Meehl, P. E. (1995). Bootstraps taxometrics: Solving the classification problem in psychopathology. *The American Psychologist, 50,* 266–275.

Meloy, J. R. (1998). *The psychology of stalking: Clinical and forensic perspectives.* San Diego, CA: Academic Press.

Meloy, J. R. (2004). Indirect personality assessment of the violent true believer. *Journal of Personality Assessment, 82,* 138–146.

Meloy, J. R., & Gothard, S. (1995). Demographic and clinical comparison of obsessional followers and offenders with mental disorders. *American Journal of Psychiatry, 152,* 258–263.

Mennin, D. S., & Heimberg, R. G. (2000). The impact of comorbid mood and personality disorders in the cognitive-behavioral treatment of panic disorder. *Clinical Psychology Review, 20,* 339–357.

Merskey, H. (1995). Commentary on histrionic personality disorder: Where should we go with hysteria? In W. J. Livesley (Ed.), *The DSM-IV personality disorders* (pp. 193–200). New York: Guilford Press.

Messina, N. P., Wish, E. D., & Nemes, S. (1999). Therapeutic community treatment for substance abusers with antisocial PD. *Journal of Substance Abuse Treatment, 17,* 121–128.

Meyer, B., Ajchenbrenner, M., & Bowles, D. P. (2005). Sensory sensitivity, attachment experiences, and rejection responses among adults with borderline and avoidant features. *Journal of Personality Disorders, 19,* 641–658.

Miettunen, J., Kantojärvi, L., Ekelund, J., Veijola, J., Karvonen, J. T., Peltonen, L., et al. (2004). A large population cohort provides normative data for investigation of temperament. *Acta Psychiatrica Scandinavica, 110,* 150–157.

Mikulincer, M., Shaver, P. R., & Pereg, P. (2003). Attachment theory of affect regulation. *Motivation and Emotion, 27,* 77–102.

Miller, J. D., Lynam, D. R., Widiger, T. A., & Leukefeld, C. (2001). Personality disorders as extreme variants of common personality dimensions: Can the five-factor model adequately represent psychopathy? *Journal of Personality, 69,* 253–276.

Miller, W. R., & Rollnick, S. (2002). *Motivational interviewing: Preparing people for change* (2nd ed.). New York: Guilford Press.

Millon, T. (1981). *Disorders of personality.* New York: Wiley.

Millon, T. (1986). A theoretical derivation of pathological personalities. In T. Millon & G. L. Klerman (Eds.), *Contemporary directions in psychopathology: Toward the DSM-IV* (pp. 639–669). New York: Guilford Press.

Millon, T. (1990). *Toward a new personology: An evolutionary model.* New York: Wiley.

Millon, T., & Davis, R. (1995). Conceptions of personality disorders: Historical perspectives, the DSMs, and future directions. In W. J. Livesley (Ed.), *The DSM-IV personality disorders* (pp. 3–28). New York: Guilford Press.

Millon, T., & Grossman, S. D. (2005). Sociocultural factors. In J. M. Oldham, A. E. Skodolk, & D. S. Bender (Eds.), *Textbook of personality disorders* (pp. 223–235). Washington, DC: American Psychiatric Publishing.

Milton, J., McCartney, M., Duggan, C., Evans, C., Collins, M., McCarthy, L., & Larkin, E. (2005). Beauty in the eye of the beholder? How high security hospital psychopathically-disordered patients rate their own interpersonal behaviour. *Journal of Forensic Psychiatry and Psychology, 16,* 552–565.

Minzenberg, M. J., Poole, J. H., & Vinogradov, S. (2006). Adult social attachment disturbance is related to childhood maltreatment and current symptoms in borderline personality disorder. *Journal of Nervous and Mental Disease, 194,* 341–348.

Mitropoulou, V., Harvey, P. D., Zegarelli, G., New, A. S., Silverman, J. M. and Siever, L. J. (2005). Neuropsychological performance in schizotypal personality disorder: Importance of working memory. *American Journal of Psychiatry, 162,* 1896–1903.

Moffitt, T. E. (2005). The new look of behavioral genetics in developmental psychopathology: Gene–environment interplay in antisocial behaviors. *Psychological Bulletin, 131,* 533–554.

Moffitt, T. E., & Farrington, H. L. (1996). Delinquency: The natural history of antisocial behaviour. In: P. A. Silva & W. R. Stanton (Eds.), *From child to adult: The Dunedin Multidisciplinary Health and Development Study* (pp. 163–185). Auckland, New Zealand: Oxford University Press.

Montagne, B., van Honk, J., Kessels, R. P. C., Frigerio, E., Burt, M., van Zandvoort, M. J. E., et al. (2005). Reduced efficiency in recognising fear in subjects scoring high on psychopathic personality characteristics. *Personality and Individual Differences, 38,* 5–11.

Moran, P. (1999). The epidemiology of antisocial personality disorder. *Social Psychiatry and Psychiatric Epidemiology, 34,* 231–242.

Morey, L. C. (1988). Personality disorders in DSM-III and DSM-III-R: Convergence, coverage, and internal consistency. *American Journal of Psychiatry, 145,* 573–577.

Morey, L. C., Gunderson, J. G., Quigly, B. D., Shea, M. T., Skodol, A. E., McGlashan, T. H., et al. (2002). The representation of borderline, avoidant, obsessive-compulsive, and schizotypal personality disorders by the five-factor model. *Journal of Personality Disorders, 16,* 215–234.

Morey, L. C., & Zanarini, M. C. (2000). Borderline personality: Traits and disorder. *Journal of Abnormal Psychology, 109,* 733–737.

Morf, C. C., & Rhodewalt, F. (2001). Unravelling the paradoxes of narcissism: A dynamic self-regulatory processing model of narcissism. *Psychological Inquiry, 12,* 177–196.

Morgan, A. B., & Lilienfeld, S. O. (2000). A meta-analytic review of the relation between antisocial behaviour and neuropsychological measures of executive function. *Clinical Psychology Review, 20,* 113–156.

Moritz, S., Fricke, S., Jacobsen, D., Kloss, M., Wein, C., Rufer, M., et al. (2004). Positive schizotypal symptoms predict treatment outcome in obsessive–compulsive disorder. *Behaviour Research and Therapy, 42,* 217–227.

Morrison, A. P., French, P., Walford, L., Lewis, S. W., Kilcommons, A., Green, J., et al. (2004). Cognitive therapy for the prevention of psychosis in people at ultra-high risk: randomised controlled trial. *British Journal of Psychiatry, 185,* 291–297.

Mulder, R. T. (2002). Personality pathology and treatment outcome in major depression: A review. *American Journal of Psychiatry, 159,* 359–371.

Mulder, R. T. (2004). Depression and personality disorder. *Current Psychiatric Reports, 6,* 51–57.

Munoz Sastre, M. T., Vinsonneau, G., Chabrol, H., & Mullett, E. (2005). Forgivingness and the paranoid personality style. *Personality and Individual Differences, 38,* 765–772.

Nakamura, M., McCarley, R. W., Kubicki, M., Dickey, C. C., Niznikiewicz, M. A., Voglmaier, M. M., et al. (2005). Fronto-temporal disconnectivity in schizotypal personality disorder: A diffusion tensor imaging study. *Biological Psychiatry, 58,* 468–478.

Nestadt, G., Hsu, F., Samuels, J., Bienvenu, O. S., Reti, I., Costa, P. T., & Eaton, W. W. (2006). Latent structure of the DSM-IV personality disorder criteria. *Comprehensive Psychiatry, 47,* 54–62.

Nette, D. (2001). *Strong imagination: Madness, creativity and human nature.* Oxford, UK: Oxford University Press.

Nette, D., & Cregg, H. (2006). Schizotypy, creativity and mating success in humans. *Proceedings of the Royal Society, Series B: Biological Sciences, 273,* 611–615.

Neugebauer, R., Hoek, H. W., & Susser, E. (1999). Prenatal exposure to wartime famine and development of antisocial personality disorder in early adulthood. *Journal of the American Medical Association, 282,* 455–462.

Newton-Howes, G., Tyrer, P., & Johnson, J. (2006). Personality disorder and the outcome of depression: Meta-analysis of published studies. *British Journal of Psychiatry, 188,* 13–20.

Ng, H. M., & Bornstein, R. F. (2005). Comorbidity of dependent personality disorder and anxiety disorders: A meta-analytic review. *Clinical Psychology: Science and Practice, 12,* 395–406.

Nichols, T. L., Ogloff, J. R., Brink, J., & Spidel, A. (2005). Psychopathy in women: A review of its clinical usefulness for assessing risk for aggression and criminality. *Behavioral Science and the Law, 23,* 779–802.

Noftle, E. E., & Shaver, P. R. (2006). Attachment dimensions and the big five personality traits: Associations and comparative ability to predict relationship quality. *Journal of Research in Personality, 40,* 179–208.

Nordahl, H. M., & Nysæter, T. E. (2005). Schema therapy for patients with borderline PD: A single case series. *Journal of Behavior Therapy and Experimental Psychiatry, 36,* 254–264.

Nordahl, H. M., & Stiles, T. C. (2000). The specificity of cognitive personality dimensions in cluster C personality disorders. *Behavioural and Cognitive Psychotherapy, 28,* 235–246.

Norden, K. A., Klein, D. N., Donaldson, S. K., Pepper, C. M., & Klein, L. M. (1995). Reports of the early home environment in DSM-III-R personality disorders. *Journal of Personality Disorders, 9,* 213–223.

Nordentoft, M., Thorup, A., Petersen, L., Øhlenschlæger, J., Melau, M., Christensen, T., et al. (2006). Transition rates from schizotypal disorder to psychotic disorder for first-contact patients included in the OPUS trial. A randomized clinical trial of integrated treatment and standard treatment. *Schizophrenia Research, 83,* 29–40.

O'Connor, B. P., & Dyce, J. A. (1998). A test of models of personality disorder conditions. *Journal of Abnormal Psychology, 107,* 3–16.

Odger, C. L., Reppucci, N. D., & Moretti, M. M. (2005). Nipping psychopathy in the bud: An examination of the convergent, predictive, and theoretical utility of the PCL-YV among adolescent girls. *Behavioral Science and the Law, 23,* 743–763.

Ogloff, J., Wong, S., & Grennwood, A. (1990). Treating criminal psychopaths in a therapeutic community. *Behavioral Sciences and the Law, 8,* 181–190.

Okasha, A., Saad, A., Khalil, A. H., Seif El Dawla, A., & Yehia, N. (2004). Phenomenology of obsessive-compulsive disorder: A transcultural study. *Comprehensive Psychiatry, 35,* 191–197.

Oldham, J. M. (2002). A 44-year-old woman with borderline personality disorder. *Journal of the American Medical Association, 287,* 1029–1037.

Oldham, J. M., & Skodol, A. E. (1991). Personality disorders in the public sector. *Hospital Community Psychiatry, 42,* 481–487.

Oldham, J. M., Skodol, A. E., & Bender, D. S. (2005). *Textbook of personality disorders.* Arlington, VA: American Psychiatric Publishing.

Oldham, J. M., Skodol, A. E., Kellman, H. D., Hyler, S. D., Rosnick, L., & Davies, M. (1992). Diagnosis of DSM-III-R personality disorders by two structured interviews: Patterns of comorbidity. *American Journal of Psychiatry, 149,* 213–220.

Olson, S., Bookstein, F. L., & Theide, K. (1997). Association of prenatal alcohol exposure with behavioral and learning problems in early adolescence. *Journal of the American Academy of Child and Adolescent Psychiatry, 36,* 1187–1194.

Oshima, T. (2001). Borderline personality traits in hysterical neurosis. *Psychiatry Clinical Neuroscience, 55,* 131–136.

Palmer, S. (2006, February). *Cost effectiveness of the BOSCOT trial.* Paper presented at the Annual Conference of the British and Irish Group for the Study of Personality Disorder, Nottingham, UK.

Paris, J. (1995). Commentary on narcissistic personality disorder. In W. J. Livesley (Ed.), *The DSM-IV personality disorders* (pp. 213–217). New York: Guilford Press.

Paris, J. (1996). Antisocial personality disorder: A biopsychosocial model. *Canadian Journal of Psychiatry, 41,* 71–80.

Paris, J. (2002). Commentary on the American Psychiatric Association guidelines for the treatment of borderline personality disorder: Evidence-based psychiatry and the quality of evidence. *Journal of Personality Disorders, 16,* 130–134.

Paris, J. (2005a). Borderline personality disorder. *Canadian Medical Association Journal, 172,* 1579–1583.

Paris, J. (2005b). Neurobiological dimensional models of personality: A review of the models of Cloninger, Depue, and Siever. *Journal of Personality Disorders, 19,* 156–170.

Paris, J., & Zweig-Fank, H. (2001). A 27-year follow-up of patients with borderline personality disorder. *Comprehensive Psychiatry, 42,* 482–487.

Park, S., & McTigue, K. (1997). Working memory and the syndromes of schizotypal personality. *Schizophrenia Research, 26,* 213–220.

Parker, G., Both, L., Olley, A., Hadzi-Pavlovic, D., Irvine, P., & Jacobs, G. (2002). Defining disordered personality functioning. *Journal of Personality Disorders, 16,* 503–522.

Parnas, J., Licht, D., & Bovet, P. (2005). Cluster A personality disorders: A review. In M. Maj, H. S. Akiskal, J. E. Mezzich, & A. Okasha (Eds.), *Personality disorders* (pp. 1–74). Chichester, UK: Wiley.

Passamonti, L., Fera, F., Magariello, A., Cerasa, A, Gioia, M. C., Muglia, M., et al. (2006). Monoamine oxidase-A genetic variations influence brain activity associated with inhibitory control: New insight into the neural correlates of impulsivity. *Biological Psychiatry, 59,* 334–340.

Pelissolo, A., Mallet, L., Baleyte, J. M., Michel, G., Cloninger, C. R., Allilaire, J. F., & Jouvent, R. (2005). The Temperament and Character Inventory–Revised (TCI-R): Psychometric characteristics of the French version. *Acta Psychiatrica Scandinavica, 112,* 126–133.

Perry, J. C. (1992). Problems and considerations in the valid assessment of personality disorders. *American Journal of Psychiatry, 149,* 1645–1653.

Perry, J. C., & Klerman, G. L. (1980). Clinical features of the borderline personality disorder. *American Journal of Psychiatry, 137,* 165–173.

Pfohl, B. (1995). Histronic personality disorder. In W. J. Livesley (Ed.), *The DSM-IV personality disorders* (pp. 173–192). New York: Guilford Press.

Pfohl, B., Blum, N., & Zimmerman, M. (1997). *Structured interview for DSM-IV personality (SIDP-IV).* Washington, DC: American Psychiatric Press.

Pilkonis, P. A., Kim, Y., Proietti, J. M., & Barkham, M. (1996). Scales for personality disorders developed from the Inventory of Interpersonal Problems. *Journal of Personality Disorders, 10,* 355–369.

Plomin, R., McClearn, G. E., Pederson, N. L., Nesselroade, J. R., & Bergeman, C. S. (1989). Genetic influence on adults' ratings of their current family environment. *Journal of Marriage and the Family, 51,* 791–803.

Pretzer, J. (1990). Borderline personality disorder. In A. T. Beck & A. Freeman, (Eds.), *Cognitive therapy of personality disorders.* New York: Guilford Press.

Priel, B., & Besser, A. (2000). Dependency and self-criticism among first-time mothers: The roles of global and specific support. *Journal of Social and Clinical Psychology, 19,* 437–450.

Pritchard, J. C. (1835). *A treatise on insanity.* London: Sherwood, Gilbert & Piper.

Putnam, K. M., & Silk, K. R. (2005). Emotion dysregulation and the development of borderline personality disorder. *Development and Psychopathology, 17,* 899–925.

Quay, H. C. (1965). Psychopathic personality as pathological stimulation-seeking. *American Journal of Psychiatry, 122,* 180–183.

Raine, A. (1991). The SPQ: A scale for the assessment of schizotypal personality based on DSM-III-R criteria. *Schizophrenia Bulletin, 17,* 555–564.

Raine, A. (2002). Biosocial studies of antisocial and violent behavior in children and adults: A review. *Journal of Abnormal Child Psychology, 30,* 311–326.

Raine, A., Brennan, P., & Mednick, S. A. (1994). Birth complications combined with early maternal rejection at age 1 year predispose to violent crime at age 18 years. *Archives of General Psychiatry, 51,* 984–988.

Raine, A., Brennan, P., & Mednick, S. A. (1997). Interaction between birth complications and early maternal rejection in pre-disposing individuals to adult violence: Specificity to serious, early-onset violence. *American Journal of Psychiatry, 154*, 1265–1271.

Raine, A., Reynolds, C., Venables, P. H., Mednick, S. A., & Farrington, D. P. (1998). Fearlessness, stimulation-seeking, and large body size at age 3 years as early predispositions to childhood aggression at age 11 years. *Archives of General Psychiatry, 55*, 745–751.

Raine, A., Venables, P. H., & Williams, M. (1996). Better autonomic conditioning and faster electrodermal half-recovery time at age 15 years as possible protective factors against crime at age 29 years. *Developmental Psychology, 32*, 624–630.

Ramklint, M., von Knorring, A.-L., von Knorring, L., & Ekselius, L. (2003). Child and adolescent psychiatric disorders predicting adult personality disorder: A follow-up study. *Nordic Journal of Psychiatry, 57*, 23–28.

Rasanen, P., Hakko, H., Isohanni, M., Hodgins, S., Jarvelin, M. R., & Tiihonen, J. (1999). Maternal smoking during pregnancy and risk of criminal behavior among adult male offspring in the northern Finland 1996 birth cohort. *American Journal of Psychiatry, 156*, 857–862.

Raskin, R. N., & Hall, C. S. (1981). The Narcissistic Personality Inventory: Alternate form reliability and further evidence of construct validity. *Journal of Personality Assessment, 45*, 159–162.

Raskin, R. N., & Terry, H. (1988). A principal components analysis of the Narcissistic Personality Inventory and further evidence of its construct validity. *Journal of Personality and Social Psychology, 54*, 890–902.

Reich, J. H. (1991). Avoidant and dependent personality traits in relatives of patients with panic disorder, patients with dependent personality disorder and normal controls. *Psychiatry Research, 39*, 89–98.

Reich, J. H., & Green, A. I. (1991). Effect of personality disorders on outcome of treatment. *Journal of Nervous and Mental Disease, 179*, 74–82.

Reid, W. H., & Gacono, C. (2000). Treatment of antisocial personality, psychopathy, and other characterologic antisocial syndromes. *Behavioral Sciences and the Law, 18*, 647–662.

Renneberg, B., Goldstein, A. J., & Phillips, D. (1990). Intensive behavioral group treatment of avoidant personality disorder. *Behavior Therapy, 21*, 363–377.

Resnick, H. S., Foy, D. W., Donahoe, C. P., & Miller, E. N. (1989). Antisocial behavior and post-traumatic stress disorder in Vietnam veterans. *Journal of Clinical Psychology, 5*, 860–866.

Resnick, S., Goodman, M., New, A., & Siever, L. (2005). The biology of borderline personality disorder. In J. Reich (Ed.), *Personality disorders. Current research and treatment* (pp. 43–73). New York: Routledge/Taylor & Francis.

Rettew, D. C. (2000). Avoidant personality disorder, generalized social phobia, and shyness: Putting the personality back into personality disorders. *Harvard Review of Psychiatry, 8*, 283–297.

Reynolds, C. A., Raine, A., Mellingen, K., Venables, P. H., & Mednick, S. A. (2000). Three-factor model of schizotypal personality: Invariance across culture, gender, religious affiliation, family adversity, and psychopathology. *Schizophrenia Bulletin, 26*, 603–618.

Rhee, S. H., & Waldman, I. D. (2002). Genetic and environmental influences on antisocial behavior: A meta-analysis of twin and adoption studies. *Psychological Bulletin, 128*, 490–529.

Rice, M. E., Harris, G., & Cormier, C. (1992). An evaluation of a maximum security therapeutic community for psychopaths and other mental disordered offenders. *Law and Human Behavior, 116*, 399–412.

Rijkeboer, M. M., van den Bergh, H., & van den Bout, J. (2005). Stability and discriminative power of the Young Schema-Questionnaire in a Dutch clinical versus non-clinical population. *Journal of Behavior Therapy and Experimental Psychiatry, 36*, 129–144.

Rinne, T., de Kloet, E. R., Wouters, L., Goekoop, J. G., de Rijk, R. H., & van den Brink W. (2002). Hyperresponsiveness of hypothalamic-pituitary-adrenal axis to combined dexamethasone/corticotropin-releasing hormone challenge in female borderline personality disorder subjects with a history of sustained childhood abuse. *Biological Psychiatry, 52*, 1102–1112.

Robins, C. J., & Chapman, A. L. (2004). Dialectical behaviour therapy: Current status, recent developments, and future directions. *Journal of Personality Disorders, 18*, 73–89.

Robins, L. N., & Regier, D. A. (1991). *Psychiatric disorders in America: The epidemiological cattchment area*. New York: Free Press.

Rogosch, F. A., & Cicchetti, D. (2005). Child maltreatment, attention networks, and potential precursors to borderline personality disorder. *Development and Psychopathology, 17*, 1071–1089.

Ronningstam, E., & Gunderson, J. G. (1990). Identifying criteria for narcissistic personality disorder. *American Journal of Psychiatry, 147*, 918–922.

Ronningstam, E., Gunderson, J. G., & Lyons, M. (1995). Changes in pathological narcissism. *American Journal of Psychiatry, 152*, 253–257.

Rosenberg, P. H., & Miller, G. A. (1989). Comparing borderline definitions: DSM-III borderline and schizotypal personality disorders. *Journal of Abnormal Psychology, 98*, 161–169.

Rosenstein, D. S., & Horowitz, H. A. (1996). Adolescent attachment and psychopathology. *Journal of Consulting and Clinical Psychology, 64*, 244–253.

Ross, S. R., Lutz, C. J., & Bailly, S. E. (2002). Positive and negative symptoms of schizotypy and the five-factor model: A domain and facet level analysis. *Journal of Personality Assessment, 79*, 53–72.

Rutter, M. (1987). Temperament, personality and personality disorder. *British Journal of Psychiatry, 150*, 443–458.

Rydelius, P. A. (1988). The development of antisocial behaviour and sudden violent death. *Acta Psychiatrica Scandinavica, 77*, 398–403.

Sack, A., Sperling, M. B., Fagen, G., & Foelsch, P. (1996). Attachment style, history, and behavioral contrasts for a borderline and normal sample. *Journal of Personality Disorders, 10*, 88–102.

Salekin, R. T. (2002). Psychopathy and therapeutic pessimism: Clinical lore or clinical reality? *Clinical Psychology Review, 22*, 97–112.

Salvatore, G., Nicolò, G., & Dimaggio, G. (2005). Impoverished dialogical relationship patterns in paranoid personality disorder. *American Journal of Psychotherapy, 59*, 247–265.

Sampson, R. J., & Laub, J. H. (1993). *Crime in the making: Pathways and turning points through life*. Cambridge, MA: Harvard University Press.

Sanislow, C. A., Grilo, C. M., & McGlashan, T. H. (2000). Factor analysis of the DSM-III-R borderline criteria in psychiatric inpatients. *American Journal of Psychiatry, 157*, 1629–1633.

Sanislow, C. A., Grilo, C. M., Morey, L. C., Bender, D. S., Skodol, A. E., Gunderson, J. G., et al. (2002). Confirmatory factor analysis of DSM-IV criteria for borderline personality disorder: Findings from the collaborative longitudinal personality disorders study. *American Journal of Psychiatry, 159*(2), 284–290.

Sanislow, C. A., Morey, L. C., Grilo, C. M.,

Gunderson, J. G., Shea, M. T., Skodol, A. E., et al. (2002). Confirmatory factor analysis of DSM-IV criteria for borderline, schizotypal, avoidant and obsessive-compulsive personality disorders: Findings from the Collaborative Longitudinal Personality Disorder Study. *Acta Psychiatrica Scandinavica, 105,* 28–36.

Saulsman, L. M., & Page, A. C. (2004). The five-factor model and personality disorder empirical literature: A meta-analytic review. *Clinical Psychology Review, 23,* 1055–1085.

Savard, C., Sabourin, S., & Lussier, Y. (2006). Male sub-threshold psychopathic traits and couple distress. *Personality and Individual Differences, 40,* 931–942.

Savitz, J. B., & Ramesar, R. S. (2004). Genetic variants implicated in personality: A review of the more promising candidates. *American Journal of Medical Genetics–Neuropsychiatric Genetics, 131B,* 20–32.

Scheel, K. R. (2000). The empirical basis of dialectical behaviour therapy: Summary, critique, and implications. *Clinical Psychology: Science and Practice, 7,* 68–86.

Schmahl, C., & Bremner, J. D. (2005). Neuroimaging in borderline personality disorder. *Psychiatry Research, 40,* 419–427.

Schotte, C., de Doncker, D., Maes, M., Cluydts, R., & Cosyns, P. (1993). MMPI assessment of the DSM-III-R histrionic personality disorder. *Journal of Personality Assessment, 60,* 500–510.

Schürhoff, F., Laguerre, A., & Szöke, A. (2005). Schizotypal dimensions: Continuity between schizophrenia and bipolar disorders. *Schizophrenia Research, 80,* 235–242.

Scott, S. (1998). Fortnightly review: Aggressive behaviour in childhood. *British Medical Journal, 316,* 202–206.

Seagrave, D., & Grisso, T. (2002). Adolescent development and the measurement of psychopathy. *Law and Human Behavior, 26,* 219–239.

Seivewright, H., Tyrer, P., & Johnson, T. (2002). Change in personality status in neurotic disorders. *Lancet, 359,* 2253–2254.

Seivewright, H., Tyrer, P., & Johnson, T. (2004). Persistent social dysfunction in anxious and depressed patients with personality disorder. *Acta Psychiatrica Scandinavica, 109,* 104–109.

Sellen, J. L., Oaksford, M., & Gray, N. S. (2005). Schizotypy and conditional reasoning. *Schizophrenia Bulletin, 3,* 105–116.

Shaw, D. S., Ingoldsby, E., Gilliom, M., & Nagin, D. (2003). Trajectories leading to school-age conduct problems. *Developmental Psychology, 38,* 480–491.

Shaw, D. S., & Vondra, J. I. (1995). Infant attachment security and maternal predictors of early behaviour problems: A longitudinal study of low income families. *Journal of Abnormal Child Psychology, 23,* 335–357.

Shaw, D., Winslow, E., Owens, E., Vondra, J., Cohn, J., & Bell, R. (1998). The development of early externalizing problems among children from low-income families: A transformational perspective. *Journal of Abnormal Child Psychology, 26,* 95–107.

Shea, M. T., Pilkonis, P. A., Beckham, E., Collins, J. F., Elkin, I., Sotsky, S. M., & Docherty, J. P. (1990). Personality disorders and treatment outcome in the NIMH Treatment of Depression Collaborative Research Program. *American Journal of Psychiatry, 147,* 711–718.

Shea, M. T., Stout, R., Gunderson, J., Morey, L. C., Grilo, C. M., McGlashan, T., et al. (2002). Short-term diagnostic stability of schizotypal, borderline, avoidant, and obsessive-compulsive personality disorders. *American Journal of Psychiatry, 159,* 2036–2041.

Shea, M. T., Widiger, T. A., & Klein, M. H. (1992). Comorbidity of personality disorders and depression: Implications for treatment. *Journal of Consulting and Clinical Psychology, 60*, 857–868.

Shea, M. T., Zlotnick, C., Dolan, R., Warshaw, M. G., Phillips, K. A., Brown, P., & Keller, M. B. (2000). Personality disorders, history of trauma, and posttraumatic stress disorder in subjects with anxiety disorders. *Comprehensive Psychiatry, 41*, 315–325.

Shedler, J., & Westen, D. (2004a). Dimensions of personality pathology: An alternative to the five-factor model. *American Journal of Psychiatry, 161*, 1743–1754.

Shedler, J., & Westen, D. (2004b). Refining personality disorder diagnosis: Integrating science and practice. *American Journal of Psychiatry, 161*, 1350–1365.

Shih, R. A., Belmonte, P. L., & Zandi, P. P. (2004). A review of the evidence from family, twin and adoption studies for a genetic contribution to adult psychiatric disorders. *International Review of Psychiatry, 16*, 260–283.

Shopshire, M. S., & Craik, K. H. (1994). The five-factor model of personality and the DSM-III-R personality disorders: Correspondence and differentiation. *Journal of Personality Disorders, 8*, 41–52.

Siever, L., & Davis, K. L. (1991). A psychobiological perspective on the personality disorders. *American Journal of Psychiatry, 148*, 1647–1658.

Siever, L. J., & Davis, K. L. (2004). The pathophysiology of schizophrenia disorders: Perspectives from the spectrum. *American Journal of Psychiatry, 161*, 398–413.

Siever, L. J., Torgersen, S., Gunderson, J. G., Livesley, W. J., & Kendler, K. S. (2002). The borderline diagnosis III: Identifying endophenotypes for genetic studies. *Biological Psychiatry, 51*, 964–968.

Silverman, A. B., Reinherz, H. Z., & Giaconia, R. M. (1996). The long-term sequelae of child and adolescent abuse: A longitudinal community study. *Child Abuse and Neglect, 20*, 709–723.

Simeon, D., & Favazza, A. R. (2001). Self-injurious behaviors: Phenomenology and assessment. In D. Simeon & E. Hollander (Eds.), *Self-injurious behaviors: Assessment and treatment* (pp. 1–28). Washington, DC/London: American Psychiatric Publishing.

Simonoff, E., Elander, J., Holmshaw, J. M., Pickles, A., Murray, R., & Rutter, M. (2004). Predictors of antisocial personality: Continuities from childhood to adult life. *British Journal of Psychiatry, 184*, 118–127.

Simpson, E. B., Yen, S., Costello, E., Rosen, K., Begin, A., Pistorello, J., & Pearlstein, T. (2004). Combined DBT and fluoxetine in the treatment of borderline PD. *Journal of Clinical Psychiatry, 65*, 379–385.

Singleton, N., Bumpstead, R., & O'Brien, M. (2001). *Psychiatric morbidity among adults living in private households, 2000.* London: Her Majesty's Stationery Office.

Skeem, J. L., & Mulvey, E. P. (2001). Psychopathy and community violence among civil psychiatric patients: Results from the MacArthur Violence Risk Assessment Study. *Journal of Consulting and Clinical Psychology, 69*, 358–374.

Skodol, A. E., Grilo, C. M., Pagano, M. E., Bender, D. S., Gunderson, J. G., Shea, M. T., et al. (2005). Effects of personality disorders on functioning and well-being in major depressive disorder. *Journal of Psychiatric Practice, 11*, 363–368.

Skodol, A. E., Gunderson, J. G., McGlashan, T. H., Dyck, I. R., Stout, R. L., Bender, D. S., et al. (2002). Functional impairment in patients with schizotypal, borderline, avoidant, or obsessive-compulsive personality disorder. *American Journal of Psychiatry, 159,* 276–283.

Slavney, P. R., & McHugh, P. R. (1973). The hysterical personality: A controlled study. *Archives of General Psychiatry, 30,* 325–329.

Slutske, W. S., Heath, A. C., Dinwiddie, S. H., Madden, P. A. F., Bucholz, K. K., Dunne, M. P., et al. (1998). Common genetic risk factors for conduct disorder and alcohol dependence. *Journal of Abnormal Psychology, 107,* 363–374.

Smallbone, S. W., & Dadds, M. R. (1998). Childhood attachment and adult attachment in incarcerated adult male sex offenders. *Journal of Interpersonal Violence, 13,* 555–572.

Snowling, M. J., Adams, J. W., Bowyer-Crane, C., & Tobin, V. (2000). Levels of literacy among juvenile offenders: The incidence of specific reading difficulties. *Criminal Behaviour and Mental Health, 10,* 229–241.

Sobin, C., Blundell, M. L., Weiller, F., Gavigan, C., Haiman, C., & Karayiorgou, M. (2000). Evidence of a schizotypy subtype in OCD. *Journal of Psychiatric Research, 34,* 15–24.

Soderstrom, H., Blennow, K., Sjodin, A. K., & Forsman, A. (2003). New evidence for an association between the CSF HVA:5-HIAA ratio and psychopathic traits. *Journal of Neurology, Neurosurgery and Psychiatry, 74,* 918–921.

Soderstrom, H., Nilsson, T., Sjodin, A. K., Carlstedt, A., & Forsman, A. (2005) The childhood-onset neuropsychiatric background to adulthood psychopathic traits and personality disorders. *Comprehensive Psychiatry, 46,* 111–116.

Soler, J., Carlos Pascual, J. C., Campins, J., Barrachina, J., Puigdemont, D., Alvarez, E., & Perez, V. (2005). Double-blind, placebo-controlled study of DBT plus olanzapine for borderline PD. *American Journal of Psychiatry, 162,* 1221–1224.

Sperling, M. B., & Berman, W. H. (1991). An attachment classification of desperate love. *Journal of Personality Assessment, 56,* 45–55.

Sperry, L. (2006). *Cognitive behavior therapy of DSM-IV-TR personality disorders: Highly effective interventions for the most common personality disorders* (2nd ed.). New York: Routledge.

Sprock, J. (2000). Gender-typed behavioral examples of histrionic personality disorder. *Journal of Psychopathology and Behavioral Assessment, 22,* 107–122.

Steels, M., Roney, G., Larkin, E., Jones, P., Croudace, T., & Duggan, C. (1998). Discharged from special hospital under restrictions: A comparison of the fates of psychopaths and the mentally ill. *Criminal Behaviour and Mental Health, 8,* 39–55.

Stefanis, N. C., Smyrnis, N., Avramopoulos, D., Evdokimidis, I., Ntzoufras, I., & Stefanis, C. N. (2004). Factorial composition of self-rated schizotypal traits among young males undergoing military training. *Schizophrenia Bulletin, 30,* 335–350.

Stein, M. B., Yehuda, R., Koverola, C., & Hanna, C. (1997). Enhanced dexamethasone suppression of plasma cortisol in adult women traumatized by childhood sexual abuse. *Biological Psychiatry, 42,* 680–686.

Stevens, D., Charman, T., & Blair, R. J. R. (2001). Recognition of emotion in facial expressions and vocal tones in children with psychopathic tendencies. *Journal of Genetic Psychology, 162,* 201–211.

Stone, M. (2003). Borderline and histrionic personallity disorders: A review. In M. Maj, H. S. Akiskal, J. E. Mezzich, & A. Okasha (Eds.), *Personality disorders* (pp. 173–192). New York: Wiley.

Stone, M. H. (1990). *Long-term follow-up study of borderlines: The fate of borderlines.* New York: Guilford Press.

Stone, M. H. (2005). Borderline and histrionic personality disorder: A review. In M. Maj, H. S. Akiskal, J. E. Mezzich, & A. Okasha (Eds.),

Personality disorders (pp. 201–231). Chichester, UK: Wiley.

Stone, M. H. (2006). *Personality-disordered patients: Treatable and untreatable.* Washington, DC: American Psychiatric Press.

Strack, S. (1987). Development and validation of an adjective check list to assess the Millon personality types in a normal population. *Journal of Personality Assessment, 51,* 572–587.

Strack, S., & Lorr, M. (1997). Invited essay: The challenge of differentiating normal and disordered personality. *Journal of Personal Disorders, 11,* 105–122.

Stromquist, V. J., & Strauman, T. J. (1992). Children's social constructs: II. Nature, assessment, and association with adaptive and maladaptive behavior. *Social Cognition, 9,* 330–358.

Stuart, S., Pfohl, B., Battaglia, M., Bellodi, L., Grove, W., & Cadoret, R. (1998). The co-occurrence of DSM-III-R personality disorder. *Journal of Personality Disorders, 12,* 302–315.

Susser, E., Neugebauer, R., Hoek, H. W., Brown, A. S., Lin, S., Labovib, S., & Gorman, M. (1996). Schizophrenia after prenatal famine: Further evidence. *Archives of General Psychiatry, 53,* 25–31.

Sutton, S. K., Vitale, J. E., & Newman, J. P. (2002). Emotion among women with psychopathy during picture perception. *Journal of Abnormal Psychology, 102,* 610–619.

Svartberg, M., Stiles, T. C., & Seltzer, M. H. (2004). Randomized, controlled trial of the effectiveness of short-term dynamic psychotherapy and cognitive therapy for cluster C personality disorders. *American Journal of Psychiatry, 161,* 810–817.

Svrakic, D. M., Whitehead, C., Przybeck, T. R., & Cloninger, C. R. (1993). Differential diagnosis of personality disorders by the seven-factor model of temperament and character. *Archives of General Psychiatry, 50,* 991–999.

Swenson, C. R., Sanderson, C., Dulit, R. A., & Linehan, M. M. (2001). The application of DBT for patients with borderline PD on inpatient units. *Psychiatric Quarterly, 72,* 307–324.

Takahashi, T., Suzuki, M., Zhou, S.-Y., Tanino, R., Hagino, H., Kawasaki, Y., et al. (2006). Morphologic alterations of the parcellated superior temporal gyrus in schizophrenia spectrum. *Schizophrenia Research, 83,* 131–143.

Tarrier, N., Yusupoff, L., Kinney, C., McCarthy, E., Gledhill, A., Haddock, G., & Morris, J. (1998). Randomised controlled trial of intensive cognitive behaviour therapy for patients with chronic schizophrenia. *British Medical Journal, 317,* 303–307.

Taylor, J., Iacono, W. G., & McGue, M. (2000). Evidence for a genetic etiology of early-onset delinquency. *Journal of Abnormal Psychology, 109,* 634–643.

Taylor, J., & Lang, A. R. (2005). Psychopathy and substance use disorders. In C. J. Patrick (Ed.), *Handbook of psychopathy* (pp. 495–511). New York: Guilford Press.

Taylor, C. T., Laposa, J. M., & Alden, L. E. (2004). Is avoidant personality disorder more than just social avoidance? *Journal of Personality Disorders, 18,* 571–594.

Taylor, S. (1995). Commentary on borderline personality disorder. In W. J. Livesley (Ed.), *The DSM-IV personality disorders* (pp. 165–172). New York: Guilford Press.

Tellegen, A. (1982). *Brief manual for the Multidimensional Personality Questionnaire.* Unpublished manuscript, Department of Psychology, University of Minnesota, Minneapolis.

Tellegen, A. (1985). Structures of mood and personality and their relevance to assessing anxiety, with an emphasis on self-report. In A. H. Tuma & J. Maser (Eds.), *Anxiety and the anxiety disorders* (pp. 681–706). Hillsdale, NJ: Lawrence Erlbaum Associates.

Tellegen, A. (1993). Folk concepts and psychological concepts of personality and personality disorder. *Psychologial Inquiry, 4,* 122–130.

Tengström, A., Grann, M., Längström, N., & Kullgren, G. (2000). Psychopathy (PCL-R) as a predictor of violent recidivism among criminal offenders with schizophrenia. *Law and Human Behavior, 24,* 45–58.

Tienari, P., Wynne, L. C., Läksy, K., Moring, J., Nieminen, P., Sorri, A., et al. (2003). Genetic boundaries of the schizophrenia spectrum: Evidence from the Finnish Adoptive Family Study of Schizophrenia. *American Journal of Psychiatry, 160,* 1587–1594.

Timmerman, I. G. H., & Emmelkamp, P. M. G. (2004). Relationship between attachment styles and cluster B personality disorders in prisoners and forensic inpatients. *International Journal of Law and Psychiatry, 29,* 48–56.

Timmerman, I. G. H., & Emmelkamp, P. M. G. (2005a). The effects of cognitive-behavioral treatment for forensic inpatients. *International Journal of Offender Therapy and Comparative Criminology, 49,* 590–606.

Timmerman, I. G. H., & Emmelkamp, P. M. G. (2005b). Parental rearing style and personality disorders in prisoners and forensic patients. *Clinical Psychology and Psychotherapy, 12,* 191–200.

Timmerman, I. G. H., & Emmelkamp, P. M. G. (2006). Attachment, personality disorders and criminal behaviour. *International Journal of Law and Psychiatry, 29,* 48–56.

Timmerman, I. G. H., Vastenburg, N. C., & Emmelkamp, P. M. G. (2001). The Forensic Inpatient Observation Scale (FIOS): Development, reliability and validity. *Criminal Behaviour and Mental Health, 11,* 144–162.

Todorov, A., & Bargh, J. A. (2002). Automatic sources of aggression. *Aggression and Violent Behavior, 7,* 53–68.

Torgersen, S. (2005). Epidemiology. In J. M. Oldham, A. E. Skodol, & D. S. Bender (Eds.), *Textbook of personality disorders* (pp. 129–142). Washington, DC: American Psychiatric Publishing.

Torgersen, S., Edvardsen, J., Oien, P. A., Onstad, S., Skre, S., Lygren, S., & Kringlen, E. (2002). Schizotypal personality disorder inside and outside the schizophrenic spectrum. *Schizophrenia Research, 54,* 33–38.

Torgersen, S., Kringlen, E., & Cramer, V. (2001). The prevalence of personality disorders in a community sample. *Archives of General Psychiatry, 58,* 590–596.

Torgersen, S., Lygren, S., Oien, P. A., Skre, I., Onstad, S., Edvardsen, J., et al. (2000). A twin study of personality disorders. *Comprehensive Psychiatry, 41,* 416–425.

Trapnell, P. D., & Wiggins, J. S. (1990). Extension of the Interpersonal Adjective Scales to include the Big Five dimensions of personality. *Journal of Personality and Social Psychology, 59,* 781–790.

Trompenaars, F. J., Masthoff, E. D., van Heck, G. L., Hodiamont, P. P., & de Vries, J. (2006). Relationship between mood related disorders and quality of life in a population of Dutch adult psychiatric outpatients. *Depression and Anxiety, 23,* 353–363.

Trower, P., & Chadwick, P. (1995). Pathways to defense of self: A theory of two types of paranoia. *Clinical Psychology: Science and Practice, 2,* 263–278.

Trull, T. J., & Durrett, C. A. (2005). Categorical and dimensional models of personality disorder. *Annual Review of Clinical Psychology, 1,* 355–380.

Trull, T. J., Sher, K. J., Minks-Brown, C., Durbin, J., & Burr, R. (2000). Borderline personality disorder and substance use disorders: A review and integration. *Clinical Psychology Review, 20,* 235–253.

Trull, T. J., & Widiger, T. A. (1997).

Structured Interview for the Five-Factor Model. Odessa, FL: Psychological Assessment Resources.

Trull, T. J., Widiger, T. A., & Burr, T. (2001). A structured interview for the assessment of the five-factor model of personality: Facet-level relations to the axis II personality disorders. *Journal of Personality, 69,* 175–198.

Trull, T. J., Widiger, T. A., Lynam, D. R., & Costa, P. T. (2003). Borderline personality disorder from the perspective of general personality functioning. *Journal of Abnormal Psychology, 112,* 192–202.

Tsakanikos, E. (2004). Latent inhibition, visual pop-out and schizotypy: Is disruption of latent inhibition due to enhanced stimulus salience? *Personality and Individual Differences, 37,* 1347–1358.

Tsakanikos, E., & Reed, P. (2005). Positive schizotypal symptoms predict false perceptual experiences in nonclinical populations? *Journal of Nervous and Mental Disease, 193,* 809–812.

Turner, R. M. (2000). Naturalistic evaluation of DBT-oriented treatment for borderline PD. *Cognitive and Behavioral Practice, 7,* 413–419.

Tyler, K. A., Whitbeck, L. B., Hoyt, D. R., & Johnson, K. D. (2003). Self-mutilation and homeless youth: The role of family abuse, street experiences, and mental disorders. *Journal of Research on Adolescence, 13,* 457–474.

Tyrer, P. (1988). *Personality disorders: Diagnosis, management and course.* London: Wright.

Tyrer, P. (1992). Flamboyant, erratic, dramatic, borderline, antisocial, sadistic, narcissistic, histrionic and impulsive personality disorders: Who cares which? *Criminal Behaviour and Mental Health, 2,* 95–104.

Tyrer, P. (1995). Are personality disorders well classified in DSM-IV? In W. J. Livesley (Ed.), *The DSM-IV personality disorders* (pp. 29–42). New York: Guilford Press.

Tyrer, P. (1999). Borderline personality disorder: A motley diagnosis in need of reform. *Lancet, 354*(9196), 2095–2096.

Tyrer, P. (2001). Personality disorder: A new respect for an old acquaintance. *British Journal of Psychiatry, 179,* 81–84.

Tyrer, P. (2002). Practice guideline for the treatment of borderline personality disorder: A bridge too far. *Journal of Personality Disorders, 16,* 113–118.

Tyrer, P. (2005). The anxious cluster of personality disorders: A review. In M. Maj, H. S. Akiskal, J. E. Mezzich, & A. Okasha (Eds.), *Personality disorders* (pp. 349–375). Chichester, UK: Wiley.

Tyrer, P., & Johnson, T. (1996). Establishing the severity of personality disorder. *American Journal of Psychiatry, 153,* 1593–1597.

Tyrer, P., Mitchard, S., Methuen, C., & Ranger, M. (2003). Treatment rejecting and treatment seeking personality disorders: Type R and Type S. *Journal of Personality Disorders, 17,* 263–268.

Tyrer, P., & Mulder, R. (2006). Management of complex and severe personality disorders in community mental health services. *Current Opinion in Psychiatry, 19,* 400–404.

Tyrer, P., Seivewright, N., Ferguson, B., Murphy, S., & Johnson, A. L. (1993). The Nottingham study of neurotic disorder. *British Journal of Psychiatry, 16,* 219–226.

Ullman, L. P., & Krasner, L. (1969). *A psychological approach to abnormal behavior.* New York: Prentice Hall.

Vaillant, G. E., & Perry, J. C. (1980). Personality disorders. In H. I. Kaplan, A. M. Freedman, & B. J. Sadock (Eds.), *Comprehensive textbook of psychiatry* (3rd ed., Vol. 2, pp. 1562–1590). Baltimore: Williams & Wilkins.

Van Bakel, H. J. A., & Riksen-Walraven, J. M. (2004). Stress reactivity in 15-month-old infants: Links with infant temperament, cognitive competence, and attachment security. *Developmental Psychobiology, 44*, 157–167.

Van den Bosch, L. M. C., Verheul, R., Schippers, G. M., & van den Brink, W. (2002). Dialectical behavior therapy of borderline patients with and without substance use problems, implementation and long term effects, *Addictive Behaviors, 27*, 911–923.

Van den Oord, E. J. C. G., Verhulst, F. C., & Boomsma, D. I. (1996). A genetic study of maternal and paternal ratings of problem behaviors in 3-year-old twins. *Journal of Abnormal Psychology, 105*, 349–357.

Van der Kolk, B. A. (1996). The complexity of adaptation to trauma: Self-regulation, stimulus discrimination, and characterological development. In B. A. van der Kolk, A. C. McFarlane, & L. Weisaeth (Eds.), *Traumatic stress: The effects of overwhelming experience on mind, body, and society* (pp. 182–213). New York: Guilford Press.

Van Ecke, Y., Chope, R. C., & Emmelkamp, P. M. G. (2005). Immigrants and attachment status: Research findings with Dutch and Belgian immigrants in California. *Social Behaviour and Personality, 33*, 657–674.

Van IJzendoorn, M. J., & Bakermans-Kranenburg, M. J. (1996). Attachment representations in mothers, fathers, adolescents, and clinical groups: A meta-analytic search for normative data. *Journal of Consulting and Clinical Psychology, 64*, 8–21.

Van IJzendoorn, M. J., Feldbrugge, J. T. T. M., Derks, F. C. H., de Ruiter, C., Verhagen, F. M. C., Philipse, M. W. G. et al. (1997). Attachment representations of personality-disordered criminal offenders. *American Journal of Orthopsychiatry, 67*, 449–459.

Van Velzen, C. J. M., & Emmelkamp, P. M. G. (1996). The assessment of personality disorders: Implications for cognitive and behavior therapy. *Behaviour Research and Therapy, 34*, 655–668.

Van Velzen, C. J. M., & Emmelkamp, P. M. G. (1999). The relationship between anxiety disorders and personality disorders: Prevalence rates and comorbidity models. In J. Derksen, H. Groen, & C. Maffei (Eds.), *Treatment of personality disorders* (pp. 129–153). New York: Plenum.

Van Velzen, C. J. M., Emmelkamp, P. M. G., & Scholing, A. (1997). The impact of personality disorders on behavioral treatment outcome for social phobia. *Behaviour Research and Therapy, 35*, 889–900.

Van Velzen, C. J. M., Emmelkamp, P. M. G., & Scholing, A. (2000). Generalized social phobia versus avoidant personality disorder: Differences in psychopathology, personality traits, and social and occupational functioning. *Journal of Anxiety Disorders, 14*, 395–411.

Varma, S. L. (1997). Psychiatric morbidity in the first-degree relatives of schizophrenic patients. *American Journal of Medical Genetics–Neuropsychiatric Genetics, 74*, 7–11.

Veen, G., & Arntz, A. (2000). Multidimensional dichotomous thinking characterizes borderline personality disorder. *Cognitive Therapy and Research, 24*, 23–45.

Verheul, R. (2005). Clinical utility of dimensional models for personality pathology. *Journal of Personality Disorders, 19*, 283–302.

Verheul, R., van den Bosch, L. M. C., & Ball, S. A. (2005). Substance abuse. In J. M. Oldham, A. E. Skodol, & D. S. Bender (Eds.), *Textbook of personality disorders* (pp. 463–475). Arlington, VA: American Psychiatric Publishing.

Verheul, R., van den Bosch, L. M. C., Koeter, M. W. J. de Ridder, M. A. J., Stijnen, T., & van den Brink, W. (2003).

DBT for women with borderline PD. *British Journal of Psychiatry, 182,* 135–140.

Verheul, R., & Widiger, T. A. (2004). A meta-analysis of the prevalence and usage of the personality disorder not otherwise specified (PD-NOS) diagnosis. *Journal of Personal Disorders, 18,* 309–319.

Viding, E., Blair, R. J., Moffitt, T. E., & Plomin, R. (2005). Evidence for substantial genetic risk for psychopathy in 7-year-olds. *Journal of Child Psychology and Psychiatry, 46,* 592–597.

Vollebergh, W. A. M., Iedema, J., Bijl, R. V., de Graaf, R., Smit, F., & Ormel, J. (2001). The structure and stability of common mental disorders: The NEMESIS study. *Archives of General Psychiatry, 58,* 597–603.

Vollema, M. G., & Hoijtink, H. (2000). The multidimensionality of self-report schizotypy in psychiatric populations: An analysis using multidimensional Rasch models. *Schizophrenia Bulletin, 26,* 565–575.

Vollema, M. G., & van den Bosch, R. J. (1995). The multidimensionality of schizotypy. *Schizophrenia Bulletin, 21,* 19–32.

Wakschlag, L. S., & Hans, S. L. (1999). Relation of maternal responsiveness during infancy to the development of behavior problems in high-risk youths. *Developmental Psychology, 35,* 569–579.

Waldman, I. D., & Hyun Rhee, S. (2005). Genetic and environmental influences on psychopathy and antisocial behavior. In C. J. Patrick (Ed.), *Handbook of psychopathy* (pp. 205–228). New York: Guilford Press.

Warren, J. I., Burnette, M. L., South, S. C., Chauhan, P., Bale, R., Friend, R., & van Patten, I. (2003). Psychopathy in women: Structural modeling and comorbidity. *International Journal of Law and Psychiatry, 26,* 223–242.

Watson, C. G., Barnett, M., Nikunen, L.,

Schultz, C., Randolph-Elgin, T., & Mendez, C. M. (1997). Lifetime prevalences of nine common psychiatric/personality disorders in female domestic abuse survivors. *Journal of Nervous and Mental Disease, 185,* 645–647.

Weertman, A., Arntz, A., Schouten, E., & Dreessen, L. (2005). Influences of beliefs and personality disorders on treatment outcome in anxiety patients. *Journal of Consulting and Clinical Psychology, 73,* 936–944.

West, M., Rose, M. S., McDonald, S., & Hashman, K. (1996). Attachment problems in borderline forensic patients, *American Journal of Forensic Psychiatry, 17,* 43–53.

West, M., Sheldon, A., & Reiffer, L. (1987). An approach to the delineation of adult attachment: Scale development and reliability. *Journal of Nervous and Mental Disorders, 175,* 738–741.

Westen, D., & Arkowitz-Westen, L. (1998). Limitations of axis-II in diagnosing personality pathology in clinical practice. *American Journal of Psychiatry, 155,* 1767–1771.

Westen, D., & Chang, C. (2000). Personality pathology in adolescence: A review. *Adolescent Psychiatry, 25,* 61–100.

Westen, D., & Shedler, J. (1999a). Revising and assessing axis II, Part I: Developing a clinically and empirically valid assessment method. *American Journal of Psychiatry, 156,* 258–272.

Westen, D., & Shedler, J. (1999b). Revising and assessing axis II, Part II: Toward an empirically based and clinically useful classification of personality disorders. *American Journal of Psychiatry, 156,* 273–285.

Westen, D., Shedler, J., Durrett, C., Glass, S., & Martens, A. (2003). Personality diagnoses in adolescence: DSM-IV axis II diagnoses and an empirically derived alternative. *American Journal of Psychiatry, 160,* 952–966.

Westermeyer, J., & Thuras, P. (2005). Association of antisocial personality disorder and substance disorder morbidity in a clinical sample. *American Journal of Drug and Alcohol Abuse, 31,* 93–110.

White, C. N., Gunderson, J. G., & Zanarini, M. C. (2003). Family studies of borderline personality disorder: A review. *Harvard Review of Psychiatry, 11,* 8–19.

Widiger, T. A. (1992). Categorical versus dimensional classification: Implications from and for research. *Journal of Personality Disorders, 6,* 287–300.

Widiger, T. A. (1993). The DSM-III-R categorical personality disorder diagnoses: A critique and an alternative. *Psychological Inquiry, 4,* 75–90.

Widiger, T. A. (1993). Reply to commentators: From B to Z. *Psychological Inquiry, 4,* 135–141.

Widiger, T. A. (1998). Four out of five ain't bad. *American Journal of Psychiatry, 55,* 865–866.

Widiger, T. A. (2000). Gender bias in the diagnosis of personality disorders. *Harvard Mental Health Letter, 16,* 5–7.

Widiger, T. A. (2002). Personality disorders. In M. M. Anthony & D. H. Barlow (Eds.), *Handbook of assessment and treatment planning for psychological disorders* (pp. 453–480). New York: Guilford Press.

Widiger, T. A., & Coker, L. A. (2002). Assessing personality disorders. In J. N. Butcher (Ed.), *Clinical personality assessment: Practical approaches* (2nd ed., pp. 407–434). New York: Oxford University Press.

Widiger, T. A., & Costa, P. T. (1994). Personality and personality disorders. *Journal of Abnormal Psychology, 103,* 78–91.

Widiger, T. A., & Frances, A. (1985). The DSM-III personality disorders. *Archives of General Psychiatry, 42,* 615–623.

Widiger, T. A., Frances, A. J., Pincus, H. A., Davis, W. W., & First, M. B. (1991). Toward an empirical classification for the DSM-IV. *Journal of Abnormal Psychology, 100,* 280–288.

Widiger, T. A., Frances, A., Spitzer, R. L., & Williams, J. B. (1988). The DSM-III-R personality disorders: An overview. *American Journal of Psychiatry, 145,* 786–795.

Widiger, T. A., & Lynam, D. R. (1998). Psychopathy and the five-factor model of personality. In T. Millon, E. Simonsen, M. Birket-Smith, & R. D. Davis (Eds.), *Psychopathy: Antisocial, criminal, and violent behavior* (pp. 171–187). New York: Guilford Press.

Widiger, T. A., Mangine, S., Corbitt, E. M., Ellis, C. G., & Thomas, G. V. (1995). *Personality Disorder Interview–IV: A semistructured interview for the assessment of personality disorders.* Odessa, FL: Psychological Assessment Resources.

Widiger, T. A, & Samuel, D. B. (2005). Evidence-based assessment of personality disorders. *Assessment, 17,* 278–287.

Widiger, T. A., & Simonsen, E. (2005). Alternative dimensional models of personality disorder: Finding a common ground. *Journal of Personality Disorders, 19,* 315–338.

Widiger, T. A., Simonsen, E., Krueger, R., Livesley, W. J., & Verheul, R. (2005). Personality disorder research agenda for the DSM-V. *Journal of Personality Disorders, 19,* 110–130.

Widiger, T. A., Trull, T. J., Hurt, S. W., Clarkin, J., & Frances, A. (1987). A multidimensional scaling of the DSM-III personality disorders. *Archives of General Psychiatry, 44,* 557–563.

Wink, P. (1991). Two faces of narcissism. *Journal of Personality and Social Psychology, 61,* 590–597.

Winston, A., Laikin, M., Pollack, J.,

Samstag, L. W., McCullough, L., & Muran, J. C. (1994). Short-term psychotherapy of personality disorders. *American Journal of Psychiatry, 151,* 190–194.

Wolff, S. (1991). "Schizoid" personality in childhood and adult life I: The vagaries of diagnostic labelling. *British Journal of Psychiatry, 159,* 615–620.

Wolfgang, M. E., Figlio, R. M., & Sellin, T. (1972). *Delinquency in a birth cohort.* Chicago: University of Chicago Press.

Woodworth, M., & Porter, S. (2002). In cold blood: Characteristics of criminal homicides as a function of psychopathy. *Journal of Abnormal Psychology, 111,* 436–445.

Wooton, J. N., Frick, P. J., Shelton, K. K., & Silverthorn, P. (1997). Ineffective parenting and childhood conduct problems: The moderating role of callous-unemotional traits. *Journal of Consulting and Clinical Psychology, 65,* 301–308.

World Health Organization. (1992). *The ICD-10 classification of mental and behavioural disorders.* Geneva, Switzerland: WHO.

World Health Organization. (2002). *World report on violence and health.* Geneva, Switzerland: WHO.

Yates, T. M. (2004). The developmental psychopathology of self-injurious behaviour: Compensatory regulation in posttraumatic adaptation. *Clinical Psychology Review, 24,* 35–74.

Yen, S., Shea, M. T., Battle, C. L., Johnson, D. M., Zlotnick, C., Dolan-Sewell, R., et al. (2002). Traumatic exposure and posttraumatic stress disorder in borderline, schizotypal, avoidant, and obsessive-compulsive personality disorders: Findings from the Collaborative Longitudinal Personality Disorders Study. *Journal of Nervous and Mental Disease, 190,* 510–518.

Yoon, J., Hughes, J., Gaur, A., & Thompson, B. (1999). Social cognition in aggressive children: A meta-analytic view. *Cognitive and Behavioral Practice, 6,* 320–331.

Young, J. E., Klosko, J. S., & Weishaar, M. E. (2003). *Schema-focused therapy: A practitioner's guide.* New York: Guilford Press.

Younge, S. L., Oetting, E. R., & Deffenbacher, J. L. (1996). Correlations among maternal rejection, dropping out of school, and drug use in adolescents. *Journal of Clinical Psychology, 52,* 96–102.

Zanarini, M. C., & Frankenburg, F. R. (1997). Pathways to the development of borderline personality disorder. *Journal of Personality Disorders, 11,* 93–104.

Zanarini, M., Frankenburg, F. R., Chauncey, D. L., & Gunderson, J. G. (1987). The Diagnostic Interview for Borderlines: Interrater and test–retest reliability. *Comprehensive Psychiatry, 28,* 467–480.

Zanarini, M. C., Frankenburg, F. R., Hennen, J., Reich, B., & Silk, K. R. (2005). Psychosocial functioning of borderline patients and axis II comparisons subjects followed prospectively for six years. *Journal of Personality Disorders, 19,* 19–29.

Zanarini, M. C., Frankenburg, F. R., Hennen, J., & Silk, K. R. (2003). The longitudinal course of borderline psychopathology: 6-year prospective follow-up of the phenomenology of borderline personality disorder. *American Journal of Psychiatry, 147,* 274–283.

Zanarini, M. C., Frankenburg, F. R., Hennen, J., & Silk, K. R. (2004). Mental health service utilisation by borderline personality disorder patients and axis II comparison subjects followed prospectively for 6 years. *Journal of Clinical Psychiatry, 65,* 28–36.

Zanarini, M., Gunderson, J. G., Frankenburg, F. R., & Chauncey, D. L. (1989). The Revised Diagnostic Interview for Borderlines: Discriminating borderline personality disorder from other axis II disorders. *Journal of Personality Disorders, 3,* 10–18.

Zanarini, M. C., Gunderson, J. G., Frankenburg, F. R., & Chauncey, D. L. (1990). Discriminating borderline personality disorder from other axis II disorders. *American Journal of Psychiatry, 147,* 161–176.

Zelli, A., Huesmann, L. R., & Cervone, D. (1995). Social inference and individual differences in aggression: Evidence for spontaneous judgments of hostility. *Aggressive Behavior, 21,* 405–417.

Zimmerman, M. (1994). Diagnosing personality disorders. *Archives of General Psychiatry, 51,* 225–245.

Zimmerman, M., & Coryell, W. (1990). Diagnosing personality disorders in the community. *Archives of General Psychiatry, 47,* 527–531.

Zimmerman, M., Pfohl, B., Coryell, W., Stangl, D., & Corenthal, C. (1988). Diagnosing personality disorders in depressed inaptients: A comparison of patient and informant interviews. *Archives of General Psychiatry, 45,* 733–737.

Zimmerman, M., Rothschild, L., & Chelminski, I. (2005). Prevalence of DSM-IV personality disorders in psychiatric outpatients. *American Journal of Psychiatry, 162,* 1911–1918.

Author index

Aaronson, C. J. 94
Ablow, J. C. 76
Abramowitz, A. 189, 190
Adams, J. W. 176
Adler, D. A. 88
Ajchenbrenner, M. 104, 105, 106, 110
Akhtar, S. 155
Akimoto, T. 75
Akiskal, H. S. 121, 157
Alarcon, R. D. 57
Alden, L. E. 61, 109, 112
Allen, J. P. 95
Allen, L. C. 180
Allilaire, J. F. 82
Allmon, D. 139, 140, 142, 144
Alloy, L. B. 104
Allport, G. W. 23
Alpert, J. E. 69
Alterman, A. I. 63, 70, 166
Alvarez, E. 142
American Psychiatric Association (APA) 2, 4, 22, 25, 26, 27, 43, 51, 116, 120, 127, 147, 149, 156
Anderson, I. M. 84, 171
Andersson, P. 90
Ando, J. 82
Andrews, D. A. 180
Appleby, L. 2
Arkowitz-Westen, L. 19, 20

Armstrong, H. E. 139, 140, 142, 144
Arntz, A. 27, 32, 68, 101, 102, 103, 104, 106, 124, 126
Arsenault, L. 76

Bagby, M. 108
Bagby, R. L. 103
Bagnato, M. 59, 61, 121
Bailey, S. E. 186
Bailey, S. L. 177
Baird, A. A. 84, 96
Baker, J. P. 189, 190
Bakermans-Kranenburg, M. J. 93
Bale, R. 169
Baleyte, J. M. 82
Ball, S. A. 69, 71
Bame Rettew, J. 52
Bandura, A. 172
Barber, J. P. 108
Bargh, J. A. 164
Barkham, M. 42
Barnett, M. 102
Baron, M. 78
Barrachina, J. 142
Barrantes-Vidal, N. 187
Barry, C. T. 170, 173
Bartholomew, K. 91, 92, 160
Bateman, A. W. 124, 125, 127, 136, 138, 145
Bates, J. E. 88, 165, 175

Battaglia, M. 61, 197
Battle, C. L. 64, 87
Baumeister, R. F. 153
Baumgard, C. H. 52, 53
Beattie, M. 69
Beauchaine, T. B. 100
Bebbington, P. E. 193
Beck, A. T. 100, 101, 106, 111, 138, 149, 150, 153, 158, 194
Beck, J. S. 101
Becker, D. F. 21
Beckham, E. 68, 70
Begin, A. 141
Bell, R. 175
Bell, S. E. 52, 53
Belmonte, P. L. 78
Ben-Abdallah, A. 69
Bender, D. S. 4, 51, 52, 55, 56, 59, 94, 112, 116, 121, 122, 132
Benedict, K. B. 27
Benjamin, L. S. 33, 40, 42
Benner, A. 111, 112
Benning, S. D. 170
Ben-Porath, Y. S. 36
Bentall, R. P. 195, 196
Berenbaum, H. 189, 190
Bergeman, C. S. 74, 75
Berman, W. H. 94
Bernstein, D. P. 21, 29, 87, 88
Besser, A. 103
Bezirganian, D. 21

Subject index

Extraversion, 33–34, 75, 92–93, 107, 154, 189, 192, 194

Family education, 197–198
Forensic issues, 53, 56, 57, 102, 169–172, 174–175, 177, 180–182

Gender difference, 45, 50, 58–60, 174

Histrionic personality disorder
  assessment, 157–158
  clinical picture, 11–12, 156
  gender bias, 156–157
  prevalence, 48–50
  treatment, 158

ICD-10, 49, 150, 186
Impairment, 2–4, 20–22, 24, 54–56, 108, 112, 191, 197
  cognitive impairment, 85, 185, 187–188
Information processing, 106, 124–127, 163–165, 173, 189–190, 195–196

"Lumping and splitting", 26, 31

Medical student's syndrome, 20
Medication, see Pharmacotherapy
Memory deficits, 188
Mentalization Based Treatment, 127, 136–138, 144–145
Minnesota Multiphasic Personality Inventory – Revised (MMPI-2), 41, 157
Motivational enhancement, 178–179
Multiaxial system of diagnosis, 4, 32
Murder, 53, 102, 171, 174

Narcissistic personality disorder
  assessment, 41, 154–155
  clinical picture, 12–13, 149–151
  closet narcissist, 155
  covert narcissist, 155
  hypersensitive narcissist, 155
  prevalence, 48–50
  theories and models of, 152–154
  treatment, 150
NEO-PI, NEO-PI-R, 33–36, 42
Neurobiology, 83–86, 188, 193

Neuroticism, 33–34, 75, 92–93, 100, 107, 120, 189, 193–194

Obsessive-compulsive personality disorder, 107–108
  clinical picture, 16–17
  impairment, 55, 108
  overlap with obsessive-compulsive disorder, 107–108
  prevalence, 48–50, 108
  toilet training, 107
  treatment, 108–109
Odd cluster, see Cluster A
Openness to experience, 33–35, 92–93, 192

Paranoid personality disorder, 193–196
  clinical picture, 6–7, 193
  prevalence, 48–50
  treatment, 197–199
Personality Disorder
  atypical personality disorder, 31
  DSM-IV-TR definition, 2
  effects on treatment of anxiety disorders, 66
  effects on treatment of depression, 66–67
  effects on treatment of substance abuse, 69–70
  general definition, 1–3
  heterogeneity within diagnosis, 28, 121
  ICD-10 definition, 3
  mixed personality disorder, 19
  other personality disorder, 19
  severe, 62, 156
  type R, treatment resistant, 20
  type S, treatment seeking, 20
Personality Disorder Not Otherwise Specified (NOS), 17, 19, 22, 25
Personality traits, 75–76
Pharmacotherapy, 20, 68–70, 108, 127, 129, 141–142, 146–148
Physiological arousal, 165, 172
Polythetic diagnostic criteria, 28
Post-traumatic stress, 64, 84, 120, 177, 194
Pre-/perinatal precursors, 86, 175–176, 193
Provisional diagnoses, 5, 26
Psychodynamic therapy, 108–113, 127, 135–138, 144–145, 180